Police Reform

Forces for Change

Police Reform

Forces for Change

Stephen P. Savage

OXFORD

UNIVERSITY PRESS

Great Clarendon Street, Oxford OX2 6DP

Oxford University Press is a department of the University of Oxford.
It furthers the University's objective of excellence in research, scholarship,
and education by publishing worldwide in

Oxford New York

Auckland Cape Town Dar es Salaam Hong Kong Karachi
Kuala Lumpur Madrid Melbourne Mexico City Nairobi
New Delhi Shanghai Taipei Toronto

With offices in

Argentina Austria Brazil Chile Czech Republic France Greece
Guatemala Hungary Italy Japan Poland Portugal Singapore
South Korea Switzerland Thailand Turkey Ukraine Vietnam

Oxford is a registered trademark of Oxford University Press
in the UK and in certain other countries

Published in the United States
by Oxford University Press Inc., New York

British Library Cataloguing in Publication Data

Data available

Library of Congress Cataloging in Publication Data

Data available

Typeset by Laserwords Private Limited, Chennai, India
Printed in Great Britain
on acid-free paper by
Biddles Ltd, King's Lynn, Norfolk

ISBN 978–0–19–921864–6 (Hbk.)
ISBN 978–0–19–921863–9 (Pbk.)

10 9 8 7 6 5 4 3 2 1

To the memory of **Tom Williamson,**
Police Reformer (1947–2007)

Foreword

Police reform has become a constant of modern policing. After decades of relative stability, the police in England and Wales—'the last unreconstructed' public service—have been through more than ten years and several overlapping phases of change. There have been very few books that have attempted to view the whole period from the election of Margaret Thatcher to the present as a continuous period of change.

For those of us whose careers map onto that same period, the author has chosen wisely. The era of Sir Edmund Davies' proposals to settle pay and conditions for policing in 1978 felt like a cliff edge to those of us who entered the service at that point. The 1970s had seen poor pay and a bleeding of experience and morale, with low numbers and little investment. Suddenly, from 1979–1981, the service had an enormous influx of new officers, with accompanying public and political expectations. Yet, the 1980s, for all their promise, saw the police embroiled in the miners' strike with a lasting impact on their public support and ended with a Royal Commission as a result of the sins of the past. The Police Service responded with a far-sighted 'quality of service' initiative built on review jointly run by all three staff associations. However, as Professor Savage shows, this brief self-improvement era was superseded by wave after wave of government-led reform. Policing, as he suggests, had become too politically important to be left to the police or their local governance. The story is still rolling. April 2007 saw the creation of the National Policing Improvement Agency, designed to put the leadership of policing improvement back with the profession.

I have been waiting for this book for some time and I have been waiting for Professor Savage to write it. He is uniquely well qualified to do so, having researched key aspects of each phase of the reform programme—public consultation in the 1980s, quasi-markets in the 1990s, and the Association of Chief Police Officers most recently. He has also, at Portsmouth University, created one of the key institutions that have taught police officers and other criminal justice professionals to understand what is happening to them and equip them to shape it. I know that this book is a product not just of the author's own learning but also of the interaction with so many of us—myself included—who have been challenged by him over the years.

Peter Neyroud QPM
Chief Constable and Chief Executive of the
National Policing Improvement Agency

Acknowledgements

I would like to thank the editorial team at Oxford University Press for their assistance throughout this project, with an approach that was 'firm but fair'. I would also like to thank those who have offered advice and assistance on the initial book proposal and on specific subjects covered in the book, including Sarah Charman, John Grieve, Les Johnston, and Tim Newburn. Tom Willamson also offered invaluable help—Tom passed away just before work on this book was completed, but he advised on its progress until the very end. I am indebted to my management colleagues at the Institute of Criminal Justice Studies, Mark Button, Stephen Cope, Jane Creaton, and Mike Nash, for tolerating my less than totally focused approach to teamwork over the period in question. Other colleagues at the Institute have helped shape my thinking—usually by means of a flip-chart—including Phil Clements, Nathan Hall, John Jones, Becky Milne, and Mike Nash. Thanks to Nick and Jon for their encouragement to keep going, and to Liz Charman, for her help with the little ones at critical times. Finally, I owe a great personal debt to Sarah, for her huge support before and during work on this book—without which it might never have seen the light of day—and to Daniel and Jacob, who paid the price of my head being steeped for far too long in the past rather than the present.

Steve Savage
April 2007

Contents

Abbreviations

ACC	Association of County Councils
ACF	Advocacy Coalition Framework
ACJS	Academy of Criminal Justice Sciences
ACPO	Association of Chief Police Officers
AMA	Association of Metropolitan Authorities
ASBO	Anti-Social Behaviour Orders
BCU	Basic Command Unit
BV	Best Value
BVPI	Best Value Performance Indicators
CCRC	Criminal Cases Review Commission
CID	Criminal Investigation Department
COP	Community Oriented Policing
CPOSA	Chief Police Officers' Staff Association
CSO	Community Support Officer
DFID	Department for International Affairs
DPPB	District Policing Partnership Boards
FMI	Financial Management Initiative
HMIC	Her Majesty's Inspectors of Constabulary
ILP	Intelligence-Led Policing
IPCC	Independent Police Complaints Commission
MBO	Management by Objectives
MPS	Metropolitan Police Service
NCIS	National Criminal Intelligence Service
NCPE	National Centre for Policing Excellence
NCS	National Crime Squad
NIM	National Intelligence Model
NPIA	National Policing Improvement Agency
NPM	New Public Management
NPT	Neighbourhood Policing Teams
NUM	National Union of Mineworkers
PACE	Police and Criminal Evidence Act 1984
PBO	Policing by Objectives
PCA	Police Complaints Authority
PCB	Police Complaints Board
PCSO	Police Community Support Officer
POP	Problem-Oriented Policing

Abbreviations

RCCJ	Royal Commission on Criminal Justice
RCCP	Royal Commission on Criminal Procedure
SOCA	Serious Organised Crime Agency
VFM	Value for Money
ZTP	Zero Tolerance Policing

Introduction

The television drama *Life on Mars* appeared on our screens in 2006 to expose in stark terms the extent of *change* in British policing in the recent past. It involved a police detective, CI Sam Tyler who, after going into a coma following a collision with a car, wakes up in 1973. He soon discovers an alien world of policing far removed from his own. The station he worked in is in seeming chaos; files are piled high on every available surface and officers lounge around (all of them smoking) with apparently little to do. Interactions are full of sexist banter and language and Tyler's query about the whereabouts of his 'PC terminal' are met with the question 'is he a police officer?' An officer then comes in to announce that a woman has been found strangled and takes out of his pocket a necklace and make-up that were taken from the body of the dead woman; the 'exhibits' are tossed on to a desk and then littered with the crumbs from the sandwich he is eating. Tyler then asks if officers have 'preserved the crime scene' only to be told that her body 'is already on the slab'. Although officers knew the woman had been with two men in a car not long before she disappeared they had not interviewed them because they had already decided they were not responsible for her disappearance.

Later, because Tyler was thought to be unwell, he was given medical care by a WPC Cartright who told Tyler that was one of the things she did because she was in the 'Women's Department' in the station. She had taken a degree—clearly the only one other than Tyler in the station who had—and when Tyler asked her for her ideas about the murder in front of her male colleagues (her degree was in psychology), her colleagues laughed and made sexist comments about what she might be better at. Then the real hero appears on the scene: DCI Gene Hunt. Clearly the 'sheriff' in town, Hunt demonstrates his own particular investigative skills. A friend of the victim is to be 'interviewed' for further information; Gene prefers to interview her in the room set aside for 'lost and found' because it has 'thick walls'. Tyler decides to start the interview with a gentle and sensitive line of questioning which seemed to be failing; at that point Tyler is replaced by Hunt who sees the interviewee on her own. He was clearly going to stand no 'nonsense' and soon comes back with valuable 'information' which the sensitive questioning had not. Tyler's response to Hunt was 'where I come from you'd be looking at suspension'. Other facets of police conduct circa 1973 are on display: a heavy drinking culture (Tyler's preference for a diet coke did not go down well), destruction of important evidence, a total disinterest in gathering evidence—'hunches' will do—and police brutality. DCI Hunt's policing philosophy was summed up by the statement 'the law is putting bad people away'.

On all accounts *Life on Mars* was an accurate reflection of policing in the 1970s, and possibly for some time after that. However, what was also revealing about the series was how *different* policing then seemed to be in comparison with twenty-first century British policing, with its interview suites, psychologically-informed interview methods, rule-bound treatment of suspects and witnesses, anti-sexist and diversity policies, sophisticated scenes of crime and forensic techniques and 'open' and 'ethical' investigations. Clearly policing had come a long way in those three decades or so. This begs the question which is the central concern of this study: how and why did we get from 'then' to 'now', from DCI Gene Hunt to DC Sam Tyler.

This book is an attempt to identify the 'forces for change' in British policing and in particular how change in policing is articulated with *police reform*. It will identify what can be called *policy drivers* for police reform and how they have worked to initiate, force, support, or shape police reform in Britain. The focus will be on the period from the late 1970s until the present, some three decades of change and reform. The choice of time frame, although always open to challenge and inevitably to a degree arbitrary, can be justified in the following ways. First, as Downes and Morgan (1997; 2007) and Garland (2001: 96–8) have argued, 1979, with the election of Margaret Thatcher's Conservative government, was a watershed in British history on law and order because it was the point at which the politicization of law and order along political party lines, which had been building up in the years before, came to the fore; Thatcher had played a key part in the politicization of law and order (Savage, 1990) and her election victory was to prove very much a turning point for law and order policy. Activity on the criminal justice policy front, from that point onwards, was to become hectic and even, under Labour, frantic. Policing policy was to be part of that. Secondly, as Reiner (2000: 50–80) has argued, the more specific politicization of British *policing* began to take hold in the mid–1970s and accelerated at pace through the 1980s. As a consequence, debate over and controversy about policing has been rife, and with the politicization of policing have come a wide range of changes to policing *policy* and the positioning of the police sector within the public sector as a whole. This has served to make the period since 1979 by far the most active in terms of change and reform in British policing.

In drawing out the 'policy drivers' for police reform across this time frame the study will engage with concepts, frameworks and models which have been developed within public policy analysis, some of which have already been worked into the analysis of criminal justice and policing policy to good effect by Jones and Newburn (Jones and Newburn, 2007; Newburn, 2002). Central amongst those concepts and frameworks will be:

- *Policy disasters theory* (Dunleavy, 1995), used to account for the relationship between policy 'failures' and policy change and reform;
- *Policy transfer* (Evans and Davies, 1999), a model developed to explain how policies in one country or system can be 'imported' into other countries and systems;
- *New public management* (Ranson and Stewart, 1994), a framework for explaining the trajectories of management reforms and organisational change in the public sector;
- *Policy networks* theory (Marsh, 1998), a framework for understanding the interconnectedness of policy actors, interests and resources, and the policy process;
- *Policy entrepreneurs* (Mintrom, 1997), a concept used to identify key policy actors responsible for activating or facilitating policy change.

In these respects this study will be an analysis of *policy change* in the policing context, how change 'happens' and what forces have underpinned the reforms of and within British policing witnessed since the late 1970s. 'Reforms' in this context operate at three main levels. First, there are specific and discrete policy changes, which might be 'one offs', focused on particular policing methods, models, institutions and techniques. An example of this would be 'problem-oriented policing' (discussed in Chapter 2), a specific model of policing which emerged in Britain in the 1990s (under American influence). Secondly, there are *reform programmes*, attempts (usually by government) to engage the police service in, or force the police into, a range of linked and overlapping reforms. There have been two significant examples of reform programmes, discussed at various points in this study; the reform agenda launched by the Conservative government in the early-to-mid 1990s, and the 'radical' programme of police reform which the Labour government set out in the early years of the new century. Thirdly, linked to reform 'programmes' in some respects, there are *policy paradigms*, which are more to do with 'ways of thinking' about policing and which can involve shifts in the mindset within or about policing. Policy *paradigms* can entail fundamental changes in the 'philosophy' or 'mission' of policing and can in turn generate their own packages of specific reforms. An example of this is 'community-oriented policing', discussed at various points in this study, which was a policing paradigm which began to take hold in the 1980s, and which subsequently spawned a range of more specific policy forms, such as 'neighbourhood policing', a model which was to be a key component of police reform in the early parts of the twenty-first century. Either in terms of specific policies, reform programmes or 'policy paradigms' this study will explore the forces for change across such areas as: *police governance and accountability*; the *police organization* and *police management; policing styles* and *policing models*;

policing structures and *policing agencies*; the *police role* and *police community relations; police training* and *conditions of employment.*

Although the focus for this study will be on the policy dynamics which operate largely at the 'meso-level' of the policy process (Daugbjerg and Marsh, 1998), operating between the level of the state and decision-making on the ground, it is important at this stage to reflect on the more 'structural' forces which have underpinned change and reform in British policing. As well as the policy drivers which will be the focus of this study, there are various 'contextual drivers' for change in policing which warrant consideration.

Police Reform: Contextual Drivers

The contextual drivers for police reform operate at a variety of levels; some of them are specific to the British situation, some of them are more global developments and impact on police organizations across nation states. Specific to the British situation would be *legislative* changes which have broad impact across British institutions which, in turn, are reflected in the workings of the police organization. There are two major examples of this. Firstly, there is the field of *human rights* legislation, of significance for all institutions but particularly for the police, given the nature of the police role and its proximity to human rights issues. The *Human Rights Act 1998* gave direct effect in the United Kingdom to the European Convention on Human Rights and had wide reaching consequences for law enforcement agencies (Neyroud and Beckley, 2001; Crawshaw, Cullen and Williamson, 2007). Although legislation in Britain such as the *Police and Criminal Evidence Act 1984* (PACE) effectively covered key areas which were the subject of the Act, the Act places continuing pressures on the police organization to be complaint with the principles embodied in the European Convention; as such a range of potential developments in policing, for example around 'covert policing', will be restrained by the provisions of the Human Rights Act (Patten, 1999: 18). Neyroud and Beckley (2001: 68–70) argue that the implications of the human rights agenda for policing are 'profound' and list some of the areas of policing activity and policies relating to them which can potentially come under scrutiny as a result of the Act including: the use of police powers; the use of force; police decision-making; the duty of care (sensitive in the context of the use of custody of arrested persons) and accountability. In the context of the latter, for example, the human rights agenda points to *independent oversight* (Neyroud and Beckley, 2001: 70) which, in the context of police reform, has been a critical issue, as shall be seen in later chapters.

The second area field of legislation, created as general provision and subsequently mirrored within the police organization, relates to *equal opportunities* and *diversity*. There have been significant reforms within policing along the lines of equal opportunities and diversity, some of which were driven by matters 'internal' to the police organization, the most obvious of which was the fallout from the police response to the murder of Stephen Lawrence and the subsequent Macpherson Inquiry (Macpherson Inquiry) discussed in Chapter 1. Macpherson in fact took what was initially identified as a 'policing problem', in this case 'institutionalised racism', and made it an issue for the whole public sector; some of Macpherson's recommendations were to lead to the Race Relations (Amendments) Act 2000 (Rowe, 2004: 34), which was to apply to all public services. However, many changes within the police organization have worked in the opposite direction—general legislation impacting on equal opportunities and diversity policies within the police service. Brown (1997) examined how 'equalities' legislation in the form of the Sex Discrimination Act 1975, have helped to forge changes in the status and treatment of women officers within the police service, such as the pay and conditions of employment of women officers. For example, 'women's departments' within British police forces, as mentioned earlier in the context of *Life on Mars*, which effectively prohibited women from the mainstream of policing and placed a ceiling on the promotion of women officers as a consequence, could not survive the Act, even if other more elusive forms of discrimination along gender lines could (Heidensohn, 1996; Coffey, Brown and Savage, 1992). Rowe (2004) has documented how equalities legislation to challenge racial discrimination has impacted on the recruitment, retention, and career prospects of minority ethnic officer within the police organization. Parallel developments have taken place in relation to sexual orientation, age, and religious belief (Clements, 2006: 65–8). In these ways, general frameworks of legislation, introduced as cross-sector initiatives across Britain, will always act as drivers for reform within the police organization.

However, other 'contextual drivers' for police reform operate on a *global*, rather than a national, stage. These globalized developments constitute what some scholars refer to as characteristic features of 'post-modern' or 'late modern' societies (Kumar, 1995; Giddens, 1998; Bauman, 2001), features which place pressures on institutions and organizations within those societies to operate in certain ways and take particular forms—including, of course, the police organization. They involve fundamental changes in the constitution of societies along a range of dimensions. The basis of globalization lies in fundamental economic change in terms of the internationalization of capitalist production and the international movement of financial resources. In the globalized economy traditional organizational forms and practices are challenged and undermined; in order to stay competitive in the global economy economic units and processes are pressured to move in the 'post-Fordist' (Piore and Sabel, 1984) directions of flexibility, decentralization, and customer-orientation (Giddens, 1998). The economic changes associated with globalization have been accompanied by forms of social, cultural, and political restructuring.

Amongst others, Garland (2001: 76–89) and Johnston (1998 and 2000: 19–28) have identified the social and political changes which have been associated with globalization as a means of drawing out their significance for the shaping of crime, justice, and law enforcement organizations in 'late modernity'; that framework will be adapted briefly here, in terms of two dimensions of 'restructuring'.

Socio-cultural restructuring

Policing is largely about the settling of 'social conflict' (Fielding, 2005), either by formal law enforcement or by means of 'order maintenance' (Reiner, 2000: 112–13). If that is the case then policing and the police organization will be shaped by the configurations of social structures and cultures within which the police are located. Under 'late modernity' social and cultural restructuring has fundamentally shifted the social basis within which policing works. This has taken a number of forms. First, *social stratification* has been recast in terms of the increasing pluralization of social divisions. For much of the past two centuries social stratification in the developed societies has been based largely on social class, forged around economic relations and cultural and political divisions reflected the class-based nature of social structures. Post-modern societies however are based increasingly on the fragmentation of social stratification; societies are now differentiated along lines of religion, ethnicity, age, consumption patterns, region, and gender, as well as economic relations. 'Order maintenance' in the context of social pluralism becomes increasingly complex and presents a range of new challenges for policing and creates demands on the police organization, demands which the organization has not always been able to accommodate, such as those relating to police relations with minority ethnic communities (Holdaway, 1996). Furthermore, of course, social divisions along the lines of ethnicity also relate to one major contemporary challenge for the police and security sector: countering terrorism. Responding to the terrorist threat whilst delivering on the other core functions of the police is one of the most testing dilemmas for police organizations, in Britain in particular (McLaughlin, 2007: 197–217; Matassa and Newburn, 2003).

Secondly, late modernity is characterized by *mass consumption*. Consumption patterns have shifted in the direction of mass access to consumer goods and lifestyles previously enjoyed only by the better off—reflected initially in the spread of ownership of television sets and cars, mass consumption has since embraced other consumer goods such as foreign travel and communications technologies. Garland (2001: 86) identifies one consequence of mass consumption which it could be argued is particularly significant in relation to crime (and as such policing). 'Consumption patterns and lifestyles that were once confined to the rich and famous were now held out to everyone, with disturbing consequences for the expectations of masses of would-be consumers.' Those deprived of the opportunities to partake in this mass consumption nevertheless *expect* to be able to; crime may be one way in which those excluded from legitimate access to the lifestyles enjoyed by the many live seek to realize those expectations. Mass consumption also creates mass opportunities for crime, such as the impact of the spread of mobile phones on street robberies (Briscoe, 2001).

A third feature of late modernity are shifts in mass *culture* which have undermined the old bases of social order. One consequence of mass consumption is access to the mass media and the images and messages it disseminates about the relationship between citizens and the authorities. Exposure to such things as TV consumer shows serves to create expectations of fair treatment and social rights and increase cynicism and scepticism about those in authority, and the images of those in authority coming from political satire shows help undermine respect for 'superiors' and further a decline in automatic deference to authority. The power of the church and the state to set down moral frameworks for the community has diminished along with that, leading to the fragmentation of moralities and moral relativism. In the crime context this has meant that some parts of the former machineries of social control and order have broken down, weakening the forces which 'control out crime' (Braithwaite, 1989; Garland, 2001: 90). In the policing context these cultural shifts have created new forms of challenge, not only in terms of crime but also in terms of rising levels of expectations from citizens about the standards of treatment they should receive from the police on the one hand, and the decline in levels of respect from some parts of the community for the authority which the police represent. If the 'clip round the ear' was ever a way by which the police officer maintained order in the community, that would not work in the new cultural climate.

Political restructuring involves the restructuring of the state and government and relates to two main sets of process. First, driven primarily by the consequences of the oil crisis following the Arab/Israeli War in 1973/4 (Gamble, 1981) and the economic recessions which followed, governments, faced with a burgeoning 'fiscal crisis' (O'Connor, 1973) across the developed world were forced to re-examine the role of the state and the relationship between the public and private sectors. By the late 1970s and early 1980s this had started to take the form of attempts to 'roll back the state' and reconfigure the role and ethos of the public sector. 'Rolling back the state' in practice meant the reigning in of welfare expenditure and the privatization of public corporations. The reconfiguration of the role and ethos of the public sector meant variously the introduction of 'quasi-markets' into the public services (Bartlett and Le Grand, 1993), the separation of 'purchasers' from 'providers' of public services, and the application of private sector management techniques to public sector organizations, all designed to produce economies and efficiencies in an ever-tightening economic environment. Eventually these modes were to be consolidated in the emergence of what became known as 'New Public Management' (Ranson and Stewart, 1994), a framework of managing the public sector organization based on business process models drawn from the private sector. As will be seen in subsequent chapters, this framework and the techniques associated with it have had a significant impact on the police organization. Secondly, government and the state have been forced to operate within an increasingly 'internationalized' context. The flow of business operations on a globalized basis has meant that governments have lost a degree of control over their own destiny, reducing the 'sovereignty' once enjoyed by the individual state over its domain. For policing, the process of internationalization is mirrored in the internationalization of crime in the form of organized crime in areas such as drugs and people trafficking (Levi, 2003), and organizationally is most evident in the formation of 'transnational' police organizations, such as Interpol and Europol (Walker, 2003) and in the formation of national police agencies, such as the Serious Organised Crime Agency (as discussed later in this volume), whose remit in part, is to operate on the international level in responding to the challenges of international organized crime.

The political restructuring associated with late modernity involved one particular dimension which is of special significance to police reform: the rise of the 'regulatory state'. One of the ideological themes to emerge from the economic recession of the mid- to late 1970s was that governments were 'doing too much'. Not only had governments tended to have committed to extremely high levels of public expenditure on social welfare programmes, they had also intervened extensively on the economic front with public investment in and in some cases state ownership of major corporations. In terms of the movement to 'roll back the state'—along the lines of 'the business of government is not the government of business'—pulling back from direct engagement in the economic management of private markets became the norm across many developed societies, and particularly Britain (Gamble, 1988). 'Rolling back the state', however, also had an equivalent relating to the *public* sector. New Public Management would extol the virtues of devolving public service *delivery* from state institutions, particularly state institutions, to a range of agencies and bodies, public, private and voluntary, leaving the state/government with responsibility for policy and oversight of delivery. This was a form of 'rolling back the state' which, in the words of Osborne and Gaebler (1992) was about separating 'steering' from 'rowing': governments should as far as possible have responsibility for 'steering' public policy (make policy) but leave the 'rowing' side—service delivery—to other agencies and bodies operating closer to the point of delivery. One dimension of the 'steering' function would be *regulation* and oversight of delivery. For this reason what emerged were forms of *regulatory state* which involve 'governing at a distance' (Shearing 1993). The regulatory state has been defined as 'a shift in the style of governance away from direct provision of public services . . . and towards the oversight of provision of public services by others' (Scott, 2000). One consequence of this model of public sector management is that there are (seemingly contradictory) processes of both *centralization* and *decentralization* in the restructuring of the public services. *Centralization* takes place because in relinquishing aspects of delivery of services, central government tend to establish new forms of regulatory bodies, for audit and inspection for example (Cope and Goodship, 2002), which can monitor standards of service delivery. Central governments also in this scenario endeavour to set out national *plans* and the like which the delivery agents are to work to; governments under this framework tend to become increasingly *directive* in policy terms. *Decentralization* takes place because of the *dispersal* of the service function across a range of bodies which tend to be locally based. As shall be seen in subsequent discussions in this study, the model of 'regulatory governance' and the 'push and pull' between centralization and decentralization associated with it, were to become significant drivers of police reform in a range of ways.

These contextual drivers for change in policing provide the backcloth against which the study of policy drivers for British policing reform can now proceed. 'British' in this context refers essentially to policing in England and Wales. Scottish policing, although subject to some of the reforms and changes documented in the chapters that follow, is a different policing system in many key respects, making it difficult to generalize across with policing in England and Wales. Policing in the Northern Ireland, although relevant to some parts of this study, is not included in the term 'British policing', because of the very different conditions under which policing in that part of Britain has developed and operates (Mulcahy, 2006).

Chapter 1 will examine the relationship between 'system failure' and police reform. It will be argued that system failure, or 'scandal', have been major drivers of change and reform of policing, not least because of the vulnerability of policing to 'go wrong'. Chapter 2 will consider the extent to which policing in Britain has been under the influence of policing and ideas about policing from abroad. It will identify in particular the extent to which American influences have played a role in shaping British policing; it will also reflect on overseas influences in the opposite direction—how British policing has been 'exported'. Chapter 3 will discuss the development and impact of 'new public management' within British policing and the ways in which the pursuit of 'value for money' has changed the organization and workings of the police. Chapter 4 will examine the role of 'forces from within' the British police in shaping policing and the police organization. This will involve considering the part played by 'police visionaries', key police 'thinkers', in leading policing in particular directions. It will also involve examining the role of 'police pressure groups' in the police reform process—both as sources of resistance to reform and sources of influence over the shape of police reform. Chapter 5 will study police reform from the perspective of the 'politics' and 'politicization' of policing. It will be argued that the public police occupy a pivotal role in the politics of crime and law and order, and that this has contradictory consequences for the police, both 'protecting' the police from reform on the one hand, and making the police very much a target for reform on the other. The book will then conclude with reflections on the likely shape of police reform in the future.

This study will not be an attempt to cover each and every police reform over the period under review—and no doubt some readers will wonder why other areas of reform are missing—nor will it be concerned with the very different although clearly important task of evaluating reforms, or assessing the impact of reforms on the quality of policing. Its focus is on the *forces for change* in police reform in Britain. In this respect the book is essentially a *history* of policing policy in Britain; based largely on literature- and documentary-based research—with some revisiting of interview material from another study (Savage, Charman and Cope, 2000)—it is an attempt to trace origins, sources, influences, and drivers for change and reform in policing. As such the book does not offer a straightforward *chronology* of policy changes as they have emerged in the policing context—which some might find frustrating—rather, the movement is forward and backwards throughout, considering how each area of influence over police reform has impacted on policing over the three decades or so which are the subject of this study.

┌─────┐
│ 1 │
└─────┘

When Things Go Wrong: System Failure and Police Reform

Introduction

Expressions such as 'going pear-shaped' and 'going belly-up'—an equivalent American expression is 'getting whacked'—are common parlance in police-talk; policing is by its very nature vulnerable to 'things going wrong'. The routines, certainties, and predictabilities of bureaucratic decision-making are rarely to be found in police work. Policing decisions, typically involving wide discretion for the officers concerned, often need to be taken in the heat of the moment and with little or no time for reflection, yet might have consequences which are far reaching and, at times, catastrophic. Uncertainty and unpredictability are part and parcel of policing; police activity is never far from 'things going wrong' and the prospect of that happening as a consequence is never far from the mindset of police officers. Policing is associated with 'things going wrong' for another reason. The low visibility of police-work and the nature of the environs within which policing takes place create opportunities for officers to *make* things go 'wrong'. In the catalogue of controversies surrounding policing, episodes of 'rule-bending' or rule-breaking by police officers hold a primary position. In this context 'things going wrong' relates to the fallout when such activities are exposed.

The history of policing, in Britain and elsewhere, is littered with cases of 'things going wrong', otherwise known as 'system failure' (Punch, 2003: 172–3), ranging from police corruption, through to miscarriages of justice involving police misconduct, deaths in police custody, police incompetence and institutionalized racism. The exposure of such system failures in policing has provided valuable insights into the otherwise unknown inner-worlds of the police organization, police-work, and police culture. The exposure of system failure, however, also serves another function. System failure in policing, in its varied forms, has acted as an important *formative* influence on policing and the police organization. If we look to the history of police reform, it is evident that in many areas of institutional change and transformation, system failure as exposed within pre-existing arrangements has played a part, often the critical part, in driving those changes. Whilst system failure, by definition, carries with it negative connotations—of malpractice, of under-performance, of negligence and so on—it can also be a *creative* and productive force; it encourages, even demands, periods of reflection, review, and investigation from policy-makers and from this can flow alternative ways of undertaking the business of policing. Put simply, 'things going wrong' are *forces for change and reform* in policing.

System Failure: A Driver for Reform

System Failure and Reform in the Public Sector

Of course, it is not only in relation to policing that system failure acts as a stimulus for change and reform. Tragic events such as the fire at King's Cross underground station in 1987 (Fennell, 1988) and the Paddington rail crash in 1999 (Crompton, and Jupe, 2002) both stimulated fundamental reforms of the British public transport sector. Similarly, the crisis in the British food and agricultural industries in the 1990s associated with 'mad cow disease' had profound effects on subsequent policy-making in those sectors and other sectors related to them (Forbes, 2004). Indeed, a whole field of study in public administration research is dedicated to the study of what Dunleavy (1995) calls 'policy disasters' and Boin and t' Hart (2000) label 'crises and fiascos'. One rationale for that focus is that 'policy disasters' can be an important stimulus for change and reform, or 'institutional renewal', in public sector institutions. In that sense system failures can offer what has been called 'windows of opportunity' for reform (Keeler, 1993), creating conditions where change and reform become more possible and more likely than would otherwise have been the case (see also Cortell and Peterson, 1999). System failures and the crises they engender provide opportunities for policy-makers to think 'outside of the box', to think the previously 'unthinkable'. This was expressed pointedly by Sherman (1978), in his case concerned with system failure in terms of 'scandals' and what they can lead to:

> Scandal is a mighty weapon. It can topple governments and destroy careers. It can tarnish the reputation of an entire profession. It can cause misery and suffering among the families of its subjects.... *But it can also be an agent of change.* (Sherman, 1978: xv—emphasis added)

Boin and t'Hart (2000) suggest a staged process by which crises within the public sector can lead to 'institutional renewal'. First a stable and established policy sector is faced with problems, generated externally or internally, which seriously undermine the status quo in that sector. Secondly, as a result, the existing or traditional routines and procedures within that sector come under increasing scrutiny and criticism. Thirdly, the authority and legitimacy of policy-makers within the sector are subsequently challenged and an institutional crisis ensues. In turn, this provides a 'window of reform' where institutional change becomes possible, although not certain. If change is to take place then the response to that opportunity might be incremental change ('adaptation' to the problem or 'restoration') or more fundamental reform ('reconstruction').

System Failure, Policing, and Police Reform

It is not difficult, hypothetically for the time being, to apply the staged process outlined above to the police sector, in this case to use the example of public order policing. We might begin with a specific policing operation, a drugs raid on a club in an inner-city area of a major city with a large Afro-Caribbean community. The police in this scenario use force to make a number of arrests for possession of illegal substances and those arrested are taken out of the club and placed in police vans, in view of groups of young black men, who start shouting at the police, complaining that people in the area are being 'picked on' by the police. More people come to the scene of the operation and missiles are thrown at the police officers and police vehicles. A number of arrests are made under public order offences but that only seems to make the situation worse. A major disturbance, a nascent riot, is now emerging. What seemed at one stage a relatively minor and specific police operation has now escalated into a public order problem. It seems to have acted as a 'trigger' or 'flashpoint' (Waddington et al, 1989) for something much bigger. Disturbances continue throughout the night and only subside in the early morning. The national press and television media portray the disturbances as a 'riot', a battle between the police and local black youth. Senior police spokespeople condemn the behaviour of those involved, blaming 'criminal elements' for stirring up others and for exploiting the situation for their own, criminal, ends. Conversely, community representatives lay the blame firmly at the feet of the police, and explain the disturbances in terms of 'aggressive' and discriminatory policing.

Clearly something has 'gone wrong' here, but what follows the set of incidents depends on how the various actors respond to the problem, which may include actors on the national, and most importantly the national political, scene. The problem may be resolved locally, with negotiations between the police, community representatives, and so on. It may simply 'fizzle out' and be seen as a 'one-off', an isolated, if unfortunate, set of circumstances. However, this particular case of 'things going wrong' might also be start of something much, much bigger. These disorders may not be the only ones of their kind, but might be mirrors of similar disorders in other parts of that city or even in other cities around the country; they may be part of what is looking like a *pattern*. Commentators may start making connections between this set of incidents and others of their kind, and begin to construct a case that there is something *systematically* wrong within the police organization and with police–community relations. Politicians may join a growing chorus demanding some form of official *inquiry* into these incidents and others like them; given the right circumstances, a public inquiry might be ordered, to be chaired by an eminent judge and calling on evidence from those directly involved and their representatives, and from academic specialists and others with developed views on the 'problem'. New research may be commissioned to examine particular dimensions of the problem. On examining and weighing the relevant evidence and opposing interpretations of the problem, the inquiry might conclude that indeed the disturbances were not simply a 'one-off' series of events but *indicative* or *symptomatic* of much deeper issues and problems within policing. It might identify and make recommendations to resolve a series of *system* problems and failures, which might include policing methods and styles, policing cultures, police powers and procedures, the management and supervision of officers, police-community consultation, and so on. Faced with the gravitas of a public inquiry, policy-makers might feel obliged to act on its recommendations and launch a programme of *police reform*.

This hypothetical case (although, as we shall see later, not that hypothetical) illustrates the role of system failure in furthering change and reform in policing. 'Things going wrong', in this case in the public order context, can lead to the *delegitimation* of the status quo and those attached to it; there follows a period of review, examination and criticism, culminating in the blueprint of an alternative institutional framework to the status quo, and the makings of institutional renewal. Of course, that is not the end of the matter, and forces determined to resist reform—such as the police staff associations (see Chapter 4)—and their allies may still be able to block or at least blunt the proposed reforms. Nevertheless, system failure at the very least can serve to introduce or lend support to new agendas for change in policing: system failure can be the *midwife of police reform*.

Policing and Vulnerability to System Failure

So what are the system failures most frequently associated with policing, failures which are, in turn, most frequently associated with drivers for police reform? Each policy sector has its own particular configurations of 'stress points' which, for that sector, provide most opportunities and vulnerabilities for 'things going wrong'. For the health sector, that might include outbreaks of infection in hospitals (Martin and Evans, 1984); for the social care sector that would include child abuse cases, such as the Climbie case (Laming, 2003); for the education sector that might include breaches of security for children in the classroom, such as those identified in the Dunblane shootings (Cullen, 1996); for the transport sector, as we have seen, a major stress point lies with the crises associated with collisions and disasters. In terms of policy sectors more closely associated with the police sector, it is evident that the prison sector, for example, is particularly vulnerable to failures surrounding prison disturbances or 'prison riots (Carrabine, 2005), escapes from prison (Barker, 1998) and deaths in custody, such as the killing of Zahid Mubarek (Zahid Mubarek Inquiry, 2005). In all of these cases, system failures are prone to the process of the delegitimation of the status quo, periods of review and criticism, followed by designs for institutional renewal as outlined earlier—and possibly actual reform itself. This leads us to attempt to identify the unique package of vulnerabilities which attach themselves to the police sector.

There is a case for identifying the police sector as particularly prone to 'things going wrong', in the sense that policing carries with it inherent vulnerabilities to things going 'pear-shaped'. To begin with, as we have already seen with the hypothetical case earlier, police-work can position the police in highly sensitive and potentially volatile situations where, either as a result of their own activities and behaviours, or as a result of wider social problems and divisions, police interventions may provoke or at least be the catalyst for outbreaks of social disorder—a relatively frequent form of system failure in the policing context. The potential for public order problems is never that far from certain types of police-work (D. Baker, 2002); when social disorder occurs the police may be blamed for some or all of the problems which become evident. In addition to this level of vulnerability, some police decisions, such as the use of firearms or the hot pursuit of vehicles, have to be taken at short notice and with little opportunity for careful consideration, and yet they may result in death or serious injury to others or the officers themselves; in turn such decisions may become the focus of intense scrutiny, with the potential for exposing a range system failures in such areas as police training, the supervision and management of officers, police communications, and so on. The involvement of the police in such critical incidents, a consequence of the police role, creates a unique propensity for the police sector to be vulnerable to 'things going wrong'. Furthermore, policing is often undertaken in situations where public safety is at issue, and when public safety is compromised police actions and decisions may be identified as causal factors. Perhaps the most notable example of this was the Hillsborough disaster in 1989, when 96 football fans were killed as a result of injuries sustained during crushing on the terraces, and after which the police were to take much of the blame for the ways in which crowd control was handled (Taylor, 1989; Scraton, 2004).

However, in relation to the vulnerabilities to system failure associated with the police sector, it is in the area of *police corruption* where most of the attention on system has been concentrated, and indeed where most of the analysis of the linkage between system failure and police *reform* has been directed (Sherman, 1978; Dixon, 1999; Prenzler and Ransley (eds), 2002; Newburn, 1999; Punch, 2000; Punch, 2003). If anything has the capacity to 'deligitimize' the status quo of the police sector it is the exposure of corruption within the police organisation and the shock waves that can create. In this respect it is important that the classification of what may be called 'corruption' is sufficiently broad and flexible to capture the complexity of police behaviours which can potentially be defined as 'corrupt', not least because different policing systems are characterized by quite different forms of 'corruption'. If we are to understand the role of system failure in terms of corruption in generating or furthering police reform then the nuances of what is called 'corruption' need to be acknowledged.

System Failure as Corruption

Punch (1985) offered an initial definition of 'corruption' which was designed to be as inclusive as possible:

> corruption occurs when an official receives or is promised significant advantage or reward (personal, group or organisational) for doing something that he is under a duty to do anyway, that he is under a duty not to do, for exercising a legitimate discretion for improper reasons, and for employing illegal means to achieve approved goals. (Punch, 1985: 14)

Subsequently, Punch (2000: 304–5) constructed a seven-fold typology of corruption which is fully inclusive in scope:

1. *Misconduct:* Officers breaking departmental rules and procedures—such as sleeping on the job.

2. *Straightforward corruption:* Officers receiving rewards for doing or not doing something, such as bribes to 'lose' evidence against a suspect.

3. *Strategic corruption:* Where the police form agreements or pacts with organized crime to control illicit markets (such as prostitution).

4. *Predatory corruption:* Officers extorting money or taking the lead role in organizing other forms of criminal activity.

5. *Noble cause corruption:* This is otherwise known as 'process corruption' and involves 'rule-bending' or rule-breaking in order to achieve the (legitimate) goals of the police organization, such as pressurizing suspects to sign a confession to strengthen a conviction. This category is critical for our later discussion of *miscarriages of justice*.

6. *Police crime:* Officers committing crimes in the course of their duties; this would include police brutality, racial or sexual harassment, and so on.

7. *State-related police crime:* Where the state uses the police organization, or units within it, for political ends, employing illegal methods, such as political assassinations (Punch, 2000: 304–5).

It is evident from this typology that the system failures associated with corruption are related to quite specific vulnerabilities of the police sector to these forms of 'things going wrong'. Indeed, the policing sector would appear, arguably, to be quite unique in having such a high level of vulnerability to corruption and therefore to system failure as such. By way of developing an explanation of the causes of police corruption, Newburn (1999) surveyed the literature and drew up an inventory of 'constant factors' which are almost universal characteristics of police organizations and which are most relevant to vulnerability to corruption (Newburn, 1999: 16–21):

A. *Discretion:* There is a well-established view that the police organization involves high degree of discretion for officers, particularly at the 'street' level—hence the notion of police officers as 'street level bureaucrats' (Lipsky, 1980). This can create opportunities for officers to use that discretion for gain.

B. *Low managerial visibility:* Police officers work in a way and in an environment which makes it difficult for their supervisors and managers to maintain observation on their movements. This may mean that the possible controls over employee behaviour found in other occupations are missing or weak in the policing context.

C. *Low public visibility:* Much police work takes place away from the public gaze, in one-to-one encounters and/or in 'private spaces', such as police cells or private dwellings.

D. *Peer group secrecy:* Police culture typically ferments an ethos of secrecy which coupled with a culture on intra-group loyalty generates effectively a 'code of silence' amongst officers. A consequence is that behaviours constituting corruption will be able to survive without fear of 'whistle-blowing'.

E. *Managerial secrecy:* Supervisors and managers, because of a mixture of loyalty to their 'own kind' and fear of the consequences the exposure of corruption might bring, are inclined not to 'ask too many questions'.

F. *Status problems:* Police officers, in most nation states at least, are relatively low paid, creating a potential for the lure of corrupt practices to prove too great.

G. *Association with lawbreakers:* Linked to the status problem, the opportunities created by regular, low visibility encounters with criminals present an ever present 'temptation' for police officers.

Of course, such 'constants' do not mean that police officers and/or the police organization will inevitably turn to corrupt practices. Newburn also suggests a number of 'variable' factors which may or may not inhibit corruption (Newburn, 1999: 21–5), these include the strength of corruption controls (forms of accountability), the integrity of police leaders, and the strength of police-community relationships. Nevertheless, the 'constant' factors place policing and the police organization in a position of at the very least of vulnerability to the system failures associated with corruption.

There is little doubting the importance of police corruption—'corruption' here in most of the senses of the term identified above—as a driver of police reform in jurisdictions such as the United States and Australia (Newburn, 1999: 1–2). Sherman's (1978) classic study of the link between 'scandal' and reform in the United States, documents and analyses the interplay between patterns of corruption, their exposure and its impact on the status and legitimacy of the police, and the emergence of subsequent programmes of reform, relating most typically to controlling corruption itself (see also Prenzler, 2002a: 18–21; Newburn, 1999: 31–44). Sherman does this with reference to a number of case studies of corruption within police organizations in America. Most notably, he identifies the extent to which the Knapp Commission (Knapp, 1972), which held hearings into the extent and nature of police corruption in New York during the 1960s and 1970s, served to expose *system* failures in American policing of which corruption was a symptom. This undermined the 'bad apple' thesis of police corruption held to by apologists of the police, whereby corruption was explained away as the errant behaviour of a few 'bad apples' in a healthy organization. In relation to policing in New York Sherman would state:

> The Knapp Commission hearings destroyed the police union's argument that police corruption was confined to a few "rotten apples" in an otherwise healthy barrel... the evidence of corrupt police officers and the evidence they had gathered after being "turned" to work as undercover agents for the commission provided overwhelming documentation of highly organised corruption in almost every area of the department. (Sherman, 1978: xxviii)

Sherman went on to identify how the Knapp Commission in turn made recommendations for police reform which were subsequently acted upon by those responsible for the policing of New York (Sherman, 1978: 160–1), thus linking system failure with change agendas for policing. A similar linkage between corruption and police reform has been identified in the context of policing in Australia by Prenzler (2002a), who traced the impact of two major commissions of inquiry into police corruption in Australia, the Fitzgerald Inquiry into policing in Queensland (Fitzgerald, 1989) and the Wood Commission on policing in New South Wales (Wood, 1997).

This leads us to consider whether police corruption is a major factor in system failure and subsequently a factor in driving police reform in the *British* context. The answer to the question is both 'yes' and 'no'; 'yes' in terms of corruption more broadly defined, 'no' in terms of the popular and traditional notion of police corruption as 'officers on the take'. Police corruption in the latter sense is certainly not unknown in the British context. For example, Reiner (2000: 62–4) has examined the social and political impact of the corruption scandals surrounding Scotland Yard during the late 1960s and 1970s, most notably those associated with the drugs and obscene publication squads as exposed by the *Sunday Times* investigative journalists (Cox, Shirley and Short, 1977). In such cases corruption was widespread and, seemingly, combined corruption in terms of at least two of the categories referred to in Punch's (2000) typology as outlined above—'strategic' and 'predatory'. Most certainly, such revelations, as Reiner has made clear, did much to 'delegitimize' the British police by denting their image as a 'disciplined, impersonal bureaucracy' (Reiner, 2000: 62). The question is whether corruption taking such forms is of major significance in driving change within British policing.

Scandal and Police Reform the British Way: Two Forms of Miscarriages of Justice

Punch (2000; 2003) makes a highly convincing case that there is a significant difference between the nature of 'scandals' which have affected American policing and police reform, and those which have characterized European policing and police reform. The difference lies in the forms of 'problem' scandal is associated with. Put bluntly, in America scandal in policing has tended to be associated with 'corruption on the job', whereas in Europe scandal in policing more typically takes the form of '*corruption for the job*' (Punch, 2003: 173). In other words, corruption in a European country such as Britain is more likely to take the form of '*noble cause corruption*' than corruption traditionally known and as reflected, in the past at least, in the policing of major cities of the United States. Certainly in terms of its impact on police reform, it is 'noble cause corruption' rather than the strategic or predatory corruption which has most left its mark in Britain. Punch argues that even the scandals connected with the strategic corruption exposed in Scotland Yard failed to make a long-term impact on policing; reform which followed in the wake of the exposures, he argues, were largely confined to change within the Metropolitan Police itself and even that was short-lived (Punch 2000: 309). In contrast, as we shall see later, scandals associated with 'noble cause corruption' have led to far-reaching and fundamental reforms of policing in Britain.

However, Punch makes another important qualification about 'scandal' in the European/British context:

> ... in Europe the concerns about corruption and deviance revolve around two matters. First, "noble cause" or "process" corruption, particularly in specialised units, which is oriented to achieving results. And—at the other end of the scale—*non-performance, incompetence and failing to perform adequately.* (Punch, 2000: 308–9—emphasis added)

Punch's identification of two often quite distinct forms of system failure and two differing sources for driving police reform—on the one hand 'noble cause corruption' and on the other organizational incompetence—links to what can be seen as *two forms of miscarriages of justice* associated with policing. It will be argued later that miscarriages of justice have been major factors in driving police reform in Britain; as forms of system failure they have had significant impact on deligitimizing the extant status quo of policing, they have instigated periods of review and reflection about the organization and ethos of policing and, in turn, they have helped generate new designs for alternative frameworks for policing. However, 'miscarriages of justice' is a generic term embracing differing ways in which justice is denied. Walker (2002) has attempted to capture the range of 'failures' associated with the term 'miscarriages of justice':

> A miscarriage occurs whenever suspects or defendants or convicts are treated by the State in breach of their rights, whether because of, first, deficient processes or, secondly, the laws which are applied to them or, thirdly, because there is no factual justification for the applied treatment or punishment, or fourthly, whenever suspects or defendants or convicts are treated adversely by the State to a disproportionate extent in comparison with the need to protect the rights of others, or, fifthly, whenever the rights of others are not effectively or proportionately protected or vindicated by state action against wrongdoers or, sixthly, by the state law itself. (C. Walker, 2002: 506)

As far as policing is concerned, two categories of 'miscarriages of justice' stand out from Walker's framework. Firstly, there are miscarriages of justice caused by 'deficient processes'—this would include, for example, oppressive questioning of suspects by the police, leading to confession evidence which is unreliable. Secondly, there are miscarriages of justice which occur 'whenever the rights of others are not effectively or proportionately protected or vindicated by the state'—for example, the failure of the police to respond adequately to a threat of racist violence against a minority community. These fit well with Punch's division of policing scandals between 'noble cause corruption' on the one hand and organizational incompetence or underperformance on the other. In this analysis both will be referred to as forms of *miscarriages of justice*.

Much of the commentary on and analysis of miscarriages of justice (C. Walker and Starmer (eds), 1999; Rozenberg, 1994; Nobles and Schiff, 2000) has, understandably, focused on 'wrongful' or 'questionable' convictions. 'Wrongful convictions' have a number of sources. Walker, in his review of the miscarriages of justice literature, provides a useful summary of 'recurrent forms of miscarriage of justice' (C. Walker 1999: 52–5) from which we might take the following as being the basis of wrongful convictions in, at least in the British context: the fabrication of evidence; unreliable identification of an offender by the police or witnesses; unreliable expert evidence; unreliable confessions resulting from police pressure or the vulnerability of suspects; non-disclosure of evidence by the police or prosecution; the conduct of the trial (due mainly to the judge's role in the proceedings); and problems associated with appeals procedures (including limited access to legal funds). We shall consider some of these, in so far as they relate to policing—and clearly a number of them do—later in this chapter. However, as has been intimated already, another form of 'miscarriage of justice' is relevant to policing—miscarriages of justice relating to *failures to act or protect* (Savage, Poyser, and Grieve, 2007).

Miscarriages of justice relating to 'failures to act or protect' have arguably overtaken miscarriages of justice relating to wrongful or questionable convictions in the eyes of the media, within political discourse and amongst policy-makers in the police and criminal justice sector. 'Failures to act or protect' in this context relate to actions or inactions (more commonly the latter) on behalf of the police or other agencies within the criminal justice sector which, in some way, create forms of victimization within the community. This would include such things as:

- the failure of the police to properly investigate a serious crime or to misinterpret the nature of the crime—for example, the failure to investigate a racist crime appropriately as a racist incident;
- the failure of the prosecution service to prosecute or construct an effective prosecution of apparently guilty persons;
- the failure of the police and other agencies to protect the community from persons known to be violent—for example, the failure to take appropriate actions relating to a seriously mentally disordered person; and
- the failure of the police or prison services to protect those in custody from other detainees known to be dangerous—for example, placing someone in a cell with seriously violent offenders resulting in injury or the death.

Cases which fall under some of these types of miscarriages of justice will be considered later, including perhaps the most notable case of its kind, the police response to the murder of Stephen Lawrence. What is interesting in this respect is the extent to which the focus of attention on miscarriages of justice, in political and media discourses, shifted quite dramatically during the 1990s. As Rose (Rose, 1996: 1–7) makes clear, from the end of the 1980s, the police and criminal justice agencies found themselves under heavy fire in the aftermath of the miscarriages of justice relating to *wrongful convictions* in the Guildford Four and Birmingham Six cases (discussed later). As Rose puts it: 'After Guildford, miscarriages of justice were suddenly hot property.' (Rose, 1996: 9). This was very much a period providing what was referred to earlier as a 'window of opportunity' (Keeler, 1993) for police reform: the status quo of police was suffering serious delegitimization, blame was being heaped on senior police management (Rose, 1996: 9–10), and, as we shall again see later, a major review of the police and criminal justice processes was under way, in the form of the Royal Commission on Criminal Justice, established in direct response to the Guildford Four and Birmingham Six cases (Rozenberg, 1994: 318–29). However, this opportunity was relatively short-lived—and the reform agenda redirected as a consequence—because the mood change shifted almost as soon as this 'nadir for the police' (Rose, 1996: 10) had been reached. How and why that was the case will be the subject of other chapters in this book—although, as we shall see, the death of two-year-old Jamie Bulger in 1993 was clearly a watershed in this respect (Rose, 1996: 92). Suffice to say at this stage that the mood of the media and political discourse turned quite dramatically from one concerned with wrongful convictions to one concerned for more effective *protection* of the community from offenders; a 'law and order' agenda had replaced the always fragile interest in police malpractice. The 'window of opportunity' had effectively been closed.

As the 1990s progressed the concern over miscarriages of justice had shifted to one more oriented to 'under-enforcement'—such as *failures* to convict—rather than wrongful convictions as such. Furthermore, this shift was also evident across the political spectrum and not just apparent within the right-wing press and the narratives of right-wing politics. Rose's own study *In the Name of the Law* (Rose, 1996) documented not just the catalogue of wrongful convictions of the 1970s and 1980s but also what he termed the 'retreat from prosecution' in the post- Guildford Four era (Rose, 1996: 114–19); procedural rules, occupational cultures, and the inherent deficiencies of the adversarial criminal justice system were conspiring to enable serious criminal operations to go unchecked. The Labour Party, now branded as 'New Labour', had marked its own shift in crime policy with the slogan 'tough on crime, tough on the causes of crime' (Savage and Nash, 2001: 106–7); the 'tough on crime' part of that slogan signalling the new emphasis on stronger enforcement, not something for which the Labour Party was previously known. Anti-racist groups, such as Black Information Link, as well as campaigning against wrongful conviction of black and Asian people, were becoming more and more vociferous about the failure of the police and justice agencies to solve crimes committed against members of the black and Asian communities (<http://www.blink.org.uk> accessed May 2007). In a sense these developments mirrored the shift within left-wing criminology in the 1980s, particularly as reflected within 'left-realism', around the notion of 'taking crime seriously' (Lea and Young, 1984). Traditional leftist discourses, which had focused primarily on abuses by the state (mainly the police) and concerns for the civil liberties for suspects, were challenged with the view that 'crime really is a problem' and one that disproportionately harms vulnerable and powerless communities—as such the left should be concerned to find solutions to crime, not content itself with the critique of state power (Matthews and Young (eds), 1986: Introduction). There seems little doubt that elements of the left-realist case, and the criminological debate that surrounded it, were influential in casting at least some of New Labour's early crime policy (Hopkins-Burke, 2005: 226–7). In that respect both right-wing and left of centre approaches to the police sector became sensitive to the spectre of miscarriages of justice involving 'under-enforcement', failures to act and protect, and so on. In turn this shaped the nature of police reforms which have followed in their wake.

What we now have at our disposal is a range of forms of system failure, including two forms of miscarriages of justice—as involving either wrongful or questionable convictions on the one hand, or failures to act or protect on the other. With this framework in hand we can now consider a number of case studies which bring out the interplay of system failures in policing and the processes of police reform.

System Failure and Police Reform: Case Studies

Confait, Confessions, and the Police and Criminal Evidence Act

The exposure of wrongful convictions, in democratic societies based in principle on the rule of law, can have a catastrophic effect on the standing of the agencies implicated in the miscarriage of justice. Public trust in those agencies can be damaged and the legitimacy of them to deliver fair, transparent, and accountable justice can be destroyed. Yet out of such exposures can come reform which strengthens the rights of citizens, and improves the accountability of those charged with administering justice. Nowhere was this made more evident than in the linkage between the wrongful convictions in the 'Confait' case and what was to become the Police and Criminal Evidence Act 1984 (PACE).

PACE was beyond doubt the most significant set of police reforms emerging out of the 1980s, and arguably one of the most significant set of police reforms, at least in relation to police powers, ever in Britain. It was hugely comprehensive in scope, ranging from police powers of stop and search, powers of entry and seizure, arrest and detention, questioning and treatment of people by the police and evidence, through to the police complaints process and police-community consultation. It had many sources, some of them going back as far as the 1960s, such as debate within the Criminal Law Revision Committee over the rules of evidence in criminal cases (Zander, 2005: xi). It was also undoubtedly a hotly contended piece of legislation, touching as it did a wide range of sensitive and highly political issues (Benyon and Bourn (eds), 1986; Reiner, 1992: 209–10). However, the history of PACE has to include a single case of miscarriage of justice which played a key part in the narrative of this particular package of legislative reform.

Maxwell Confait was strangled in 1972 in a London flat, which was subsequently set alight—the time lapse between the strangulation and the fire would become a crucial issue in the trial processes that would follow. Two boys were convicted of the crime in 1972, Colin Lattimore and Ronald Leighton, both of whom confessed in writing to the murder of Confait and the arson of his flat, as had a third boy, Ahmet Salih, although the murder charge against him was withdrawn before the trial, leaving him with a charge of arson. Lattimore and Leighton both pleaded not guilty to the murder, claiming that their confessions were made under duress, or worse (see Price and Caplan, 1977). Nevertheless, Leighton was convicted for murder and Lattimore for manslaughter on the grounds of diminished responsibility; both, together with Salih, were also convicted of arson. Leighton was 16 years old, but had a reading age of a ten-year-old (Fisher, 1977: 47). Lattimore was 19 years old, but was estimated to have a mental age of a 14-year-old (Fisher, 1977: 53).

The boys' application for leave to appeal was refused by the Court of Appeal in 1973 but, after subsequent investigations carried out on the order of the Home Office in 1974, their case was referred to the Court of Appeal. The Court quashed both the murder and manslaughter convictions, together with other convictions of arson which were attached to the original conviction. The prosecution case rested on there being only a matter of minutes of time between the strangling of Confait and the starting of the fire, and this is what their confessions amounted to. However, the Court agreed that expert pathological evidence now pointed to a time of death more than two hours before the fire started. This not only contradicted the confession evidence but it also opened up an alibi defence, most strongly in favour of Lattimore, who had witnesses to him being at a youth club throughout the time period of Confait's murder. On quashing the convictions as unsafe and unsatisfactory, the Court's judgement also made damning comments about the confessions, stating 'There are . . . a number of very improbable matters in the confessions, and some striking omissions from them' (quoted in Fisher, 1977: 250). Interestingly, one of the Appeal Court judges was Lord Scarman, who was to return to the policing scene in a very different guise some seven years later.

In this context the Home Secretary ordered an official inquiry into the circumstances leading to the trial of the three boys, to be held primarily in private, under the aegis of Sir Henry Fisher, a High Court judge, which reported in 1977. The Fisher Report became a landmark dossier documenting system failures throughout the conviction process, providing what has since become a familiar catalogue of factors contributing to miscarriages of justice (see above and Walker, 1999). One of these was the role of expert evidence, whereby the pathologist appointed by the coroner was thought to have failed to carry out the appropriate tests which would have more accurately estimated the time of death, and who then proceeded to give testimony at the trial which failed to remedy the consequences of this failure (Fisher, 1977: 21–2). The Report also found the prosecution decision-making and evidential processes wanting (Fisher, 1977: 19–21) and it paved the way for the creation of the Crown Prosecution Service, through the *Prosecution of Offences Act 1985*—a form of 'police reform' in the sense that it took responsibility for the prosecution process away from the police.

However, it was police investigative processes which took much of the blame for the miscarriages of justice in the Confait case. The Fisher Report highlighted wide-ranging failures in the conduct of the investigation of the murder, most particularly in relation to the 'interrogation' process—a term which has, symbolically, fallen out of favour in discourse on police investigation in the UK. What the Report identified as failure points in this regard set the agenda for subsequent Royal Commission on Criminal Procedure (Phillips, 1981—known as the 'Phillips Commission') which followed in the wake of the Fisher Report, and PACE, which saw through many of the key recommendations of the Royal Commission (Zander, 1995). In this respect the Fisher Report was hugely predictive. Aspects of the investigative process identified as in need of procedural reform included:

- *Protections for persons under interview.* The Report raised the issue of the appropriate *balance* between 'police effectiveness' and individual rights—with a clear steer towards the latter—and the need for the *codification* of criminal procedure (Fisher, 1977: 13). Both were to become pivotal concerns of the Phillips Commission and subsequently PACE (Zander, 1995).
- *Rights to communicate with a solicitor.* The Report alluded both to the need for access to legal advice to become a formal right for suspects under 'interrogation' and to the need for the development of a *duty solicitor* scheme to guarantee such access (Fisher, 1977: 14–16). Via the Phillips Commission, this proposal found way into the revisions on police powers of detention contained in PACE.
- *The recording of interviews with suspects.* As the Report argued, 'The Confait case lends support to the argument for the introduction of tape-recording for interviews in police stations and the taking of written statements . . . Apart from the additional protection afforded to the individual, tape-recording would constitute a valuable protection for the police themselves . . . ' (Fisher, 1977: 16). As with access to legal advice, the recording of interviewing of suspects was to become a central element of PACE and, arguably, a milestone in the reform of the police investigative practice.
- *The fair treatment of young people and mentally disordered persons.* The Report raised serious concerns about investigations involving the interview of young or mentally disordered suspects conducted in the absence of parents or guardians and, in particular, the reliability of confessions gained under these circumstances (Fisher, 1977: 18–19). Again, this was highly predictive as the shape of things to come in PACE.

In addition to these specific aspects of problematic investigative processes, the Fisher Report also made some telling comments about the need for police investigations to remain *open* even when confessional statements have been made (Fisher, 1977: 29–30) which in some ways constituted a case for what, much later, would become known as *investigative interviewing* (Williamson (ed), 2006—see Chapter 2). This illustrates that, in addition to system failures leading to specific reforms in the form of legislation and policy change, they may also set alight a 'slow fuse' change agenda which works by incrementally changing organizational culture and mindsets, in this case by setting in motion a longer term process of the re-orientation of police investigative 'philosophy' towards greater openness. As has been argued elsewhere (Savage and Milne, 2007), the lack of investigative 'openness' would seem to be the common thread of wrongful convictions involving policing error.

The Phillips Commission was established in 1977 by the Labour government, intent on following up the concerns raised in Fisher, as well as confronting a range of other challenges relating to arcane frameworks for police powers such as the 'Judges Rules' (Zander, 1986: 123–4). The 'theoretical framework' (Reiner, 1981: 35) for the Commission was to strike a 'fundamental balance' between

the 'rights of suspects' and the 'security of the community' in bringing suspects to justice. The Royal Commission on Criminal Procedure (RCCP) reported
in 1981 and was well received by the police and much of the legal profession
(Zander, 2005: xi), but met hostility from civil liberties bodies, including the
National Council for Civil Liberties (now Liberty), on whose behalf one Har-
riet Harman, no less, as then legal officer for the Council, branded the Report
a 'victory for the law and order lobby' (Jones, 1981: 54). However, others on
the left/civil libertarian wing were less dismissive, seeing in the Report's recommendations greater scope for the legal accountability of the police than the
Judge's Rules enabled and a clearer and more definitive framework of police
powers (Reiner, 1981: 34–5). Whatever the divisions amongst commentators
on the Report, its key recommendations were reflected very much in the legislative bill which followed within two years of its publication, the Police and
Criminal Evidence Bill, although with less emphasis on the safeguards to be
attached to the new police powers which Phillips had recommended (Reiner,
1992: 208–9). In addition to the concern that the 'fundamental balance' of
Phillips had transmuted into something much more oriented to the enforcement side than the rights of suspects, opposition to the Bill focused mainly
around provisions for the police to have the right to ask to see doctors' files
and priests' notes drawn from confessionals—bringing with it hostility from
the bishops in the House of Lords. A subsequent version of the bill, with some
homage paid to critics of the first bill (Zander, 2005: xii) was unveiled in 1983
and PACE was eventually passed the following year. One of most controversial
pieces of legislation in Parliamentary history—the Committee stage broke the
House of Commons record for the highest number of sittings—was eventually placed in stature. No small part of that major development was played by
the experiences of the boys originally convicted of the murder of Maxwell Confait.

However, as we have seen, the scope of PACE was much broader than the
reform and codification of police powers. The reconfiguration of the police complaints process and new arrangements for police consultation with their local
communities were amongst the other provisions of the Act. If we are to look for
their origins we find another form of policing system failure becoming evident,
rumbling along almost coincidentally alongside the debate over *Phillips*—the
serious outbreaks of public disorder in Brixton, London, in 1981, which were
to become the focus of attention of another landmark in British policing, the
publication of the *Scarman Report*.

The Brixton Riots, Scarman, and the Rebirth of Community Policing

As with most outbreaks of public disorder, specific events or actions act as the
'spark' which sets more widespread social disorder alight. In the case of the
Brixton disorders this was a stabbing of a young black man on a warm Friday
evening in April 1981 (Scarman, 1981: 17–45). The man, who was being pursued

by his attackers and was obviously distressed, ran towards a police constable who was on patrol duty at the time and the officer tried to stop him; eventually they fell over together at which point the officer noticed that there was blood over his uniform. The youth ran off but the officer, now accompanied by another constable, caught up with him and it became evident that he had suffered serious stab wounding and was bleeding profusely. As they were inspecting the youth three other young black men joined the scene and began shouting 'leave him alone', but despite the officers' attempts to explain that they were trying to help the wounded man other black men began jostling with the officers and the injured man ran off. One of the officers sent out a radio call that a badly injured man was in the area needing urgent medical attention. Meanwhile the injured man had been put into a taxi by a neighbour and the taxi made its way to hospital. Other officers, in a police transit van, who had received the radio message, had seen him being helped into the taxi, followed the vehicle and, when the taxi was held up in traffic, they intervened and administered treatment to him, and decided to keep him there until the ambulance arrived. Suddenly, a crowd of around 40 young, mainly black, youths arrived at the scene and started shouting at the officers, at least one of them shouting 'they are killing him'. They pushed the officers aside and took the injured man away, eventually getting him to hospital. Other officers arrived at the scene and, when the group was pursued by the police, stones and bricks were thrown at them; one man was arrested. A police van arrived with officers carrying shields and they were ordered to charge the crowd, which had now grown to around 100. Police vehicles were targeted by missile throwers and more arrests were made. The disorder lasted for nearly one hour but then calm was restored.

However, that was not the end of the disorders. Rumours spread throughout Brixton about what had taken place, including one that the injured boy was dead. On the following day another specific incident led to further, much worse, outbreaks of disorder. A taxi driver was seen by plain-clothed officers putting a piece of paper down his sock. Suspecting this to be possibly linked to drugs they asked if they could search him, which he agreed to, finding that in fact he was storing bank notes in his socks for safe-keeping. As they were carrying out the search a crowd of around 30, mainly black, youths had assembled across the road and they were evidently becoming hostile. The officers then decided to search the car in any case, in response to which sections of the crowd began shouting that the officers were harassing the taxi driver. As the officers were moving around the vehicle they came into contact with one of the crowd standing close to the taxi who, after some form of altercation, they chose to arrest for obstructing an officer in the execution of duty. This man was eventually put into the back of a police van which had arrived, but by this time the crowd had grown to around 150. As the van moved away the crowd surged around it and began rocking it; missiles were thrown and soon a serious disorder had erupted. As more police support arrived, crowds grew and disorder spread throughout the area, including attacks on police vehicles, looting, and arson.

After more than five hours the disorders began to subside, but by then 82 people had been arrested, 279 police officers injured, 45 members of the public (at least) had been injured, 61 private vehicles and 56 police vehicles were damaged or destroyed, and 145 premises were damaged, in some cases by fire (Scarman, 1981: 36). Further, although less intensive, disorder broke out on the third day, in this case following an attempt to arrest someone for obstruction, and sporadic disorders arose at various points in the area throughout the day. Overall, these events were certainly worthy of their label as 'riots' (Scarman, 1981: 42) and were the worst seen on the mainland in the United Kingdom in many years.

The Brixton disorders sent shock waves throughout what was then Thatcher's Britain, particularly as Thatcher was herself elected on a 'law and order' platform (Savage, 1990—see also Chapter 5). The response of Conservative Home Secretary William Whitelaw, (unfortunate name in the circumstances!) to these events was to set up an official inquiry to be headed by the highly respected, and known liberal, Law Lord, Lord Scarman. Whilst the Scarman Inquiry was underway other serious disorders broke out in Toxteth, Merseyside, and Moss Side, Manchester; although these were not to be included in the Inquiry's deliberations, it was clear that the messages coming out of the Inquiry could extend to other police force areas outside of the Metropolitan Police area. The publication of the Scarman Report (Scarman, 1981) attracted a huge amount of media attention—the report was later published by Penguin Press, such was the level of public interest in Scarman.

The reception to Scarman was mixed (Reiner, 1992: 253–60). Much of the opposition to the Report focused on Scarman's refusal to accept that the Metropolitan police were 'institutionally racist' (Scarman, 1981: 64), although, as Reiner (1981: 258) makes clear, this rested on the particular definition of 'institutional racism' Scarman (1981: 11) employed—when an organisation 'knowingly, as a matter of policy, discriminates against black people'. What is clear is that in so far as Scarman made a number of major recommendations for *institutional reform*, his Report accepted de facto that *institutional racism*, according to the definition which today holds sway (Macpherson, 1999: para 4), was indeed a factor in the disorders in Brixton. Although Scarman interpreted the Brixton disorders as a reflection of wider social deprivation amongst the inner-city community, particularly the black community (Scarman, 1981: 4–11), he laid specific blame at the feet of the police, in terms of episodic harassment of black people (Scarman, 1981: 64), unimaginative and inflexible policing (Scarman, 1981: 66–67), and poor police-community relations (Scarman, 1981: 58–9). Despite its deliberately understated tone—Scarman was anxious not to alienate the police—his verdict was damning, and pointed to fundamental reform as the only way ahead.

The Scarman Report made a wide range of recommendations which had both a direct effect in stimulating specific reforms and more indirect and far-reaching effect, or what was referred to earlier as a 'slow fuse', in shifting the 'problematic' of policing. The specific police reforms which sprang from the Scarman recommendations are in some cases part of a new agenda for policing; in other cases, such as those relating to the police complaints machinery, they build on forces already at work. The recommendations and reforms fall under four main headings: police training; policing styles; consultation and accountability; and discipline and complaints.

Scarman proposed that *police training* be reformed above all with a view to improving police–community relations, particularly in relation to police relations with minority ethnic communities. Training was to be one means by which 'policing by consent' (Scarman, 1981: 62) could be delivered. Scarman proposed that the period of initial recruit training in police schools be extended to six months—it was at the time between ten and 15 weeks only (Scarman, 1981: 80). He also advocated the introduction of focused training on 'community relations' (Scarman, 1981: 82–3)—in effect, race awareness training, and more by way of 'on the job' training (Scarman, 1981: 84), including the placement of tutor constables within minority ethnic communities (Scarman 1981: 82). This pointed to a veritable cultural revolution in police training. In this respect there is little denying that Scarman had a massive effect on the structure and ethos of police 'probationer' training. In addition to the extension of the initial training period, the 'Scarman effect' was evident in a range of training developments:

- 'Human awareness training': this was initially pioneered in the Metropolitan Police training school at Hendon, and combined training in interpersonal skills, self-awareness and community relations (Bull and Horncastle, 1988: 219).
- A change in training methods through the replacement of 'rote learning' (learning by listening) with 'facilitational learning' (learning by doing)—more oriented to skills development than simple knowledge of law and procedure (Poole, 1988); in practice this meant more 'student centred' learning with interactive exercises, such as role play and simulation (Elliot, 1988: 157).
- Structured 'on the job' training once the officer had completed the school-based training and before he or she was fully sworn in as an officer; this took the form of 'street duties' courses and 'tutor constable attachments' (Stradling and Harper, 1988). This initiative, as with the two others, was linked to the wider concern to enhance 'community policing' (see below) in the sense of improving officers' skills in interacting with the community.

The impact of the Scarman Report on police training and those responsible for designing and delivering police training was, however, more than technical or methodological. The Scarman agenda provided an opportunity—a window of opportunity—for progressive thinkers within the police service to more openly challenge the status quo of policing. The adoption of new methods of training was symptomatic of a more fundamental shift in the problematic of policing.

29

The direction in which these new challenges were going was towards the notion of the police as a *service* rather than a *force*. In that respect it was Scarman's views on policing *styles* and *ethos* which had most enduring impact.

Reiner (2000: 204–8) documents how the Scarman agenda was picked up by progressive police thinkers such as Kenneth Newman and used as a trigger for a much wider reorientation of British policing (see Chapter 4). So influential was that trigger that, as Reiner's own research testifies (Reiner, 1991), by the end of the 1980s Scarman's principles for policing had become the predominant source of intellectual guidance for chief constables, evidence of the penetration of the police 'mindset' of the Scarman agenda. That agenda was based on advocacy of 'community policing', the principle of 'policing by consent', and the need for policing to maintain an appropriate 'balance' between enforcement of the law and the maintenance of 'public tranquillity' (Scarman, 1981: 62). In terms of that balance Scarman was quite clear that 'the maintenance of public tranquillity comes first' (Scarman, 1981: 62). Clearly Scarman had been more persuaded by the model of community policing advocated by the then Chief Constable of Avon and Somerset, John Alderson (Alderson, 1979) than most of Alderson's contemporaries.

The Scarman Report did much to energize the debate over whether the police organization is to be seen as a 'force' or as a 'service' (Stephens and Becker (eds), 1994). The case Scarman constructed was that the Brixton disorders were due in large part to policing styles which were enforcement-oriented rather than oriented to the maintenance of order—exacerbated by harassment and heavy-handed policing methods. A consequence of enforcement-oriented policing is that the potential benefits offered by the regular contact between the police and the community associated with, by 'service' roles—befriending, assistance, advice, etc.—are lost, including the development of good police–community relations. Scarman rekindled the principle established when the 'modern police' idea was established in the early nineteenth century (Reiner, 2000: 54–5), that policing is more effective when 'peace-keeping' is given primacy over enforcing the law, when discretion is used to maximum effect and force is kept to a minimum, when preventing crime is seen as a core function of policing and when 'policing by consent' is seen as a cornerstone of the police 'mandate'. All of this ran very much against the grain of a policing system which had drifted inexorably in the direction of valuing reaction to crime over prevention, and rapid response over interpersonal contact with the local community. What Scarman did, following on from Alderson, was confront the extant status quo of policing with an alternative policing paradigm: *community-oriented policing*.

It was noted earlier that some areas of police reform are to do with shifts in 'mindsets' rather than specific policy changes, and the Scarman agenda appears to have generated precisely that. Indeed, it is possible to trace the 'Scarman effect' (and as such the 'Aldersonian' vision) right through to contemporary police reforms such as 'neighbourhood policing' (see Chapter 5), and before that through earlier models of community-oriented policing such as the 'Plus

Programme' in the Metropolitan Police (see Chapter 4)—the 'plus' element being policing over and above law enforcement, i e the 'service' role—and the British version of 'problem-oriented policing' (Tilley, 2003: 317–21). Scarman's re-assertion of the principles of community policing was therefore to have an impact on the shape of police reforms to come as well as those following immediately in the wake of the Report. The disorders in Brixton, and by implication similar disorders in Liverpool and Manchester, served to herald a re-orientation of British policing.

Linked to the advocacy of community-oriented policing were Scarman's proposals regarding *consultation* and *accountability*. At the time Scarman deliberated, the issue of police accountability was a hotly contested one, and remained so for much of the 1980s (Reiner, 2000: 70–1). Scarman found the existing machineries for police accountability to be found wanting, but proposed a solution which would leave the operational *independence* of the police intact (Scarman, 1981: 92–6), stopping well short, therefore, of demands, common at the time, for greater political *control* over policing policy (see Savage, 1984). The 'solution' was to enhance the accountability of the police by making a requirement that the police *consult* with local communities about policing matters. Scarman recommended that there be a statutory requirement on chief officers to establish machineries, in the form of committees, for local police–community liaison and consultation in their force areas. The 'business' of such committees was to be consultation about policing problems in the locality and policing solutions to those problems. The message was that communities should as far as possible *consent* to the goals and styles of policing to be deployed in their area, and that the police should be sensitive to the local community's preferences and priorities for policing in their locality.

The reform which embodied Scarman's recommendations in this respect was to be Section 106 of the *Police and Criminal Evidence Act 1984*. This reform sat somewhat uneasily within a piece of legislation concerned primarily with transforming police powers—it came under 'Miscellaneous'—to such an extent that it is rarely discussed in legal studies of PACE. Around the country, police forces, perhaps not over-enthusiastically, set up what were known as 'Section 106 committees', some of them taking the form of formal committees with participation restricted to committee members, others the form of open, public, gatherings. It soon became clear that whatever the potential for Scarman's vision of community consultation in opening policing to closer, local scrutiny and involving the community in policing decisions (Savage, 1984), in practice '106 committees' became little more than 'talking shops' with little by way of active public involvement (Morgan and Maggs, 1984; Savage and Wilson, 1987). For example, the author, conducting research on the implementation of Section 106, observed one committee meeting where only one member of the public, other than committee members, attended, and when he asked a question he was told it was not the purpose of such gatherings to answer questions from the public!

However, it could be argued that, whatever the distance between Scarman's vision of what community consultation with the police might have achieved and what was achieved in practice, the reform did serve to implant the idea that *community participation* in and with policing is a valuable exercise in its own right. It is interesting that the police reform programme which was to emerge over 20 years after Scarman, in the form of the White Paper *Building Communities, Beating Crime* (Home Office, 2004b—see Chapters 3 and 5), laid great emphasis on building 'a new culture of customer responsiveness within the police service' (Home Office, 2004b: 45) part of the move towards 'community engagement' in policing which was a central platform of the police reform agenda at that stage (see Chapter 5). At the very least Scarman's views on community consultation where ahead of their time; perhaps, however, in this particular area Scarman had planted the seeds of a police reform which were not to bear real fruit until much later.

PACE reflected, partially, another element of the Scarman agenda, in this case that concerned with *police complaints and discipline*. Again, we might see the *Scarman Report* as well ahead of its time. On reviewing the debate over the process of investigating complaints against police officers, concerned that the behaviour of officers in the Brixton context might have been addressed before the damage was done, Scarman stated: 'My own view is that if public confidence in the complaints procedure is to be achieved *any solution falling short of a system of independent investigation for all complaints . . . is unlikely to be successful*' (Scarman, 1981: 118—emphasis added).

PACE was an opportunity to reform the police complaints machinery in the direction Scarman had pointed to—a critical role for independent, civilian oversight in the police complaints process—but it did so only partially. PACE created the Police Complaints Authority (PCA), which replaced the Police Complaints Board (PCB) set up under the *Police Act 1976* (Smith, 2005: 124). Whilst the PCB introduced for the first time an element of civilian oversight of police complaints—the Board was made up of lay members who 'reviewed' complaints investigations—it left no role for independent involvement in the *investigation* of complaints. The PCA on the other hand enabled independent involvement in the investigation process, but in the form of the *supervision* of complaints investigations undertaken by the police themselves. The spirit of Scarman was to an extent evident in this reform, but, as we can see from the above statement, the PCA did not go as far as Scarman recommended; it remained for another system failure, the police investigation into the murder of Stephen Lawrence, to push reform all that way, as we shall see shortly. Nevertheless, again, Scarman seems to have affected the mindset in this area of reform, even if only a small distance.

Scarman was associated with other areas of police reform to those discussed here, for example, his proposal for a lay visitor scheme for police stations (Scarman, 1981: 114) was carried through, originally as a pilot scheme but rolled out nationally following Home Office Circular 12/86. Taken together the impact of

Scarman on police reform was far-reaching and fundamental. In that sense the Brixton disorders served to have a major impact of the shape of police reform and policing in Britain and, as we have seen, that impact may still be working its way through contemporary police reforms. However, it took another system failure, again in London, to push some of these developments further.

Stephen Lawrence, Macpherson, and Police Reform

Reference was made earlier to two forms of miscarriages of justice, wrongful convictions on the one hand and failures to act or protect on the other. The police response to the murder of Stephen Lawrence is the classic example of the latter. The way in which the police handled the investigation into the murder was to become one of the most widely publicized examples of system failure in recent British history and the case become a matter of international interest and concern.

On 22 April 1993 Stephen Lawrence and a friend, Duwayne Brooks, were on their way home from visiting an uncle at around 10:30pm and, as Stephen went out into the centre of the road to see if the bus was coming, Duwayne noticed five or six white youths across the road. When Duwayne called out to Stephen to ask him if he could see the bus coming one of the youths shouted 'What, what nigger?' and the group surrounded Stephen. During this time one of the youths stabbed Stephen twice. The group disappeared down a nearby road and although Stephen managed to run some 100 yards, despite losing blood heavily, he eventually collapsed and died before ambulance staff could move him (Macpherson, 1999: 1–2).

It seemed that the initial police response to the murder was characterized by a 'lack of command and a lack of organisation' (Macpherson, 1999: 62). Decisions made at the scene were not recorded, the officer leading the initial police response left the murder scene without determining what had occurred—and in particular failed to find out what the key witness, Duwayne Brooks, had said—a mobile search of the area was undertaken which was largely pointless, and although cordons of the scene were eventually set up, at least one vehicle, a suspect one at that, was able to drive through it. In the critical hours immediately after the murder the police operation had been badly coordinated and poorly supervized (Macpherson, 1999: 62–5).

Information on those responsible, in the form of written notes, phone calls, and in one case a visit to the police station, including specific names and their involvement in racist attacks in the past, came to the attention of the police within 24 hours of the murder and throughout the weekend following the murder. The police quickly had at their disposal strong intelligence on suspects and a continuing clear message that Stephen's murder was racially motivated. Despite this, a decision, obviously a critical one, was made *not* to arrest those identified but rather to put them under surveillance (Macpherson, 1999: 89–93). However, the surveillance of the premises where the youths were living did not start until the afternoon of 26 April, some four days after the murder, by which time damning forensic evidence could easily have been disposed of. Furthermore, even when one of the youths was seen leaving the premises with a black bin liner seemingly containing clothing, no action was taken by the surveillance team (Macpherson, 1999: 136–9).

These were just some of the critical errors made in the early stages of the investigation, with the undercurrent being the failure to fully recognize Stephen's murder as a racist crime; as we shall see shortly, these errors were compounded by others as the Lawrence investigation continued. Disenchanted with the way in which the police had handled the investigation and with the way in which they personally had been treated as the victim's family, Stephen's parents, Doreen and Neville Lawrence, set out on a long road to campaign for a public inquiry into the affair. They had early support from Nelson Mandela no less, and from a wide range of campaigning organizations and campaigning lawyers (see Savage, Poyser, and Grieve, 2007). However, it was not until Jack Straw, Shadow Home Secretary, pledged that once in office he would call a public inquiry, that real progress on this was made. In July 1997, three months after Labour came into power, Jack Straw, now as Home Secretary, set up the public inquiry under Sir William Macpherson, to inquire into the '. . . matters arising from the death of Stephen Lawrence, in order to identify the lessons to be learned for the investigation and prosecution of racially motivated crimes'. (Macpherson, 1999: *Foreword*). The 'Macpherson Inquiry' reported in 1999 and quickly became a landmark document for British public policy in general and policing in particular. The government established a body dedicated to tracking and overseeing the implementation of Macpherson, the Lawrence Steering Group, which was responsible for producing an annual report on progress across the policy areas covered by Macpherson (see Home Office, 2005c). We shall draw from the wide range of issues raised by the Lawrence case a number of themes of most significance to the police reform process (for an overview see Rowe, 2004; see also Roycroft, Brown, and Innes, 2007).

Institutionalized Racism, Police Investigations, and Training

The most widely publicized matter identified in the Macpherson Report related to the role of 'institutionalized racism' in the system failures surrounding the policing response to the murder and its aftermath. Macpherson adopted a much more inclusive definition of 'institutionalized racism' than Scarman as: 'The collective failure of an organisation to provide an appropriate and professional service to people because of their colour, culture or ethnic origin' (Macpherson, 1999: 28). Significantly, Macpherson included discrimination through 'unwitting' prejudice or ignorance within the catchment of 'institutionalized racism' (Mapcherson, 1999: 28). Applying that concept, in terms of the police investigative process, institutionalized racism, according to Macpherson, was evident at various stages of the investigation of the murder, from initial response—in the failure to recognize the crime as racially motivated (what might be referred to as *case denial* (Savage and Milne, 2007))—to the handling of witnesses and the subsequent treatment of the Lawrence family. As the Report states:

> The failure of the first investigating team to recognise and accept racism and race relations as a central feature of their investigation . . . played a part in the deficiencies in policing which we identify in this Report . . . a substantial number of officers of junior rank would not accept that the murder . . . was simply and solely 'racially motivated'. The relevance of the ethnicity and cultural status of the victims . . . was not properly recognised. (Macpherson, 1999: 23)

The policy recommendations which fell out of this area of concern took a number of forms, including three in particular. First, that the *definition of a 'racist incident'* should be clarified, the proposed definition being ' . . . any incident which is perceived to be racist by the victim or any other person'. (Macpherson, 1999: 328). From the investigative perspective this served to shift the 'judgement' as to whether an incident was to be deemed 'racially motivated' from the *investigator* (as an *outcome* of the investigation) to the victim, or others (as a *premise* of the investigation)—a shift that could, in principle, work to re-orient the whole ethos of a criminal investigation (but see Hall, 2005: 198–9). Secondly, that the Association of Chief Police Officers (ACPO), as a key generator of general policing policy (Savage, Charman, and Cope, 2000), be charged with devising a national 'good practice guide' for the police response to racial incidents (Macpherson, 1999: 329). This was initially reflected in the *ACPO Action Guide to Identifying and Combating Hate Crime* (ACPO, 1999) and, in due course, in *Hate Crime: Delivering a Quality Service* (ACPO, 2005). What emerged in this context was guidance on the definition and classification of hate crimes (ACPO, 2005: 9–12), approaches to gathering 'community intelligence' (ACPO, 2005: 15–17), initial investigations (ACPO, 2005: 38–43), and the treatment of witnesses and victims by investigating teams (ACPO, 2005: 24–32). Thirdly, that *police training* be reformed to reflect more effectively racism awareness and valuing cultural diversity.

It was clear that police training was to become a focal point for the police response to Macpherson, as it was with Scarman previously. The most obvious training response to Macpherson was the introduction for all staff of focused 'race awareness' and 'diversity' training—normally two-day courses delivered by specialist trainers (Rowe, 2004: 61–3). In this and other ways, Macpherson clearly provoked a substantial amount of activity across police forces, although, as the report by Her Majesty's Inspectors of Constabulary (HMIC) *Diversity Matters* indicated, that activity was not always strategically driven, and diversity training was not fully integrated within the training process as a whole (HMIC, 2003: 31–6). Furthermore, the broadcast of the documentary *The Secret Policeman* in October 2003, which showed police trainees, ostensibly trained under the 'post- Lawrence' training agenda, exhibiting explicitly racist behaviour, caused major embarrassment for the police service, and as an issue was consequently picked up for attention by the Lawrence Steering

Group (Home Office, 2005c: 15–16). Despite this, and notwithstanding the shortcomings of 'race awareness training' (Rowe, 2004: 74–7), there is little doubt that the Lawrence/Macpherson agenda has in more subtle ways permeated the 'mind-set' of the police training environment, particularly in terms of the greater role of 'community engagement' in the training of police recruits (HMIC, 2003: 30–1).

Family Liaison and Police Investigations

One of the most disturbing features of the Lawrence case was the way in which Stephen Lawrence's family were treated by the police, in the immediate aftermath of the murder and subsequently in terms of liaison between the family and the police. As the Macpherson Report states:

> ...the family liaison in sensitive and difficult cases of this kind has to be handled with great care and understanding. Things obviously went wrong from the start, and it was the duty of the senior officers in particular to take their own steps to ensure that alternative methods were followed in order to see that the family were kept properly informed and that their relationship with the investigation team was a healthy one. This they signally failed to do. (Macpherson, 1999: 117)

The Report proceeded to make a number of recommendations about family liaison, including the need to establish the role of family liaison officer as a *dedicated role* with specialist training, that senior investigating officers take formal responsibility for ensuring best practice in family liaison and that family preferences and needs should take a full role in investigative decision-making (Macpherson, 1999: 330). Since Macpherson, the critical role of family liaison in the investigative process has been widely accepted, not least in national guidance on responding to hate crime (ACPO, 2005: 27–9). This is not to say that the critical role of family liaison had not been recognized before—the Avon and Somerset Constabulary had shown the way by developing specialist training in this area the year before Macpherson reported (see Grieve and French, 2000). However, what the national guidelines signal is that family liaison has moved from the *periphery* of criminal investigation—as something which took place *alongside*, or even after, the investigative process—to become an *integral* feature of the investigation itself. It also places family liaison as something which not only *supports* families through the process of conducting an investigation, but which values families as sources of *intelligence* around which an investigation might be managed. As expressed in the Association of Chief Police Officers' guidance on hate crime, 'In cases where lifestyle, friends and associates of the victim may hold the key to identifying witnesses or suspects, the family liaison role *is pivotal to the success of the investigation*.' (ACPO, 2005: 27—emphasis added) Of course, there is the potential that the provision of support to families and the pursuit of information from them might not always be compatible exercises, and the message from Macpherson is that the *care* of families should be the primary concern. In this context, the investigative process should ideally be oriented to reducing the degree of suffering by victims as a central goal and in this respect the support role of family liaison is critical. Nevertheless, as a result of Lawrence and Macpherson, family liaison has now attained high status in the 'mindset' and practice of criminal investigation in Britain.

Review of the Investigative Process

What was often downplayed in the aftermath of the publication of the Macpherson Report was that a central concern of the Inquiry was with the actual *quality* of the investigation into the murder of Stephen Lawrence. In part this related to the competency or otherwise of the key players in the investigation, of which Macpherson had much to say. However, it also related to the 'quality assurance' measures at work, or more accurately not at work, throughout the Lawrence investigation. If mistakes or miscalculations have been made at one or more stages of a criminal investigation, it is important that procedures are available and deployable to remedy them at later stages in the process. This was clearly not the case with Lawrence.

It is now accepted that a means of challenging the 'premature closure' of an investigation (Savage and Milne, 2007)—or in this case its parallel, *case denial*—and of maintaining a degree of openness in the investigation is to conduct *case reviews*. Reviews have traditionally been used to re-investigate 'unsolved' major crimes (see Macpherson, 1999: 195). In the Lawrence case, some four months after the murder and the initial investigation, a review was conducted which became known as the 'Barker Review'. The Barker Review involved an assessment of the way in which the initial investigation and sub-sequent decisions were made, and it concluded that 'The investigation has been progressed satisfactorily and all lines of inquiry correctly pursued' (cited in Macpherson, 1999: 199), although it did acknowledge weaknesses in the liaison between the investigating team and the Lawrence family. The Review was heavily criticized by Macpherson as being 'uncritical', 'anodyne', guilty of 'factual errors', and overall as 'flawed and indefensible' (Macpherson, 1999: 200–3). The Report concluded that 'Failure to acknowledge and to detect errors [in the investigation] resulted in them being effectively concealed.' (Macpherson, 1999: 320)

The Macpherson Report made two recommendations relating to review of investigations: First, that 'ACPO devise Codes of Practice to govern Reviews of investigations of crime, in order to ensure that such Reviews are open and thorough.' Secondly, that the Metropolitan Police Service (MPS) 'review their internal inspection and accountability processes' (Macpherson, 1999: 329–30). The message from Macpherson was that a rigorous staged review of criminal investigations should be a key feature of the *quality assurance* of an investigation and the decision-making which an investigation involves. Significantly, this was also a key message coming out of a system failure and inquiry many years previous to Lawrence, the Byford Inquiry into the 'Yorkshire Ripper' murders in the 1970s (Byford, 1982), although not one, apparently, fully appreciated. In effect, Macpherson was calling for greater *openness* in criminal investigations to counter the problem of 'premature closure' in the investigative 'mind set'. Following the publication of the Macpherson Report, HMIC conducted a review of the MPS's approach to major crime investigation, including murder review procedures. This process eventually extended to all other police forces in England and Wales (see Nicol et al, 2004: 9). A momentum had gathered in the wake of Macpherson, which eventually culminated with the Association of Chief Police Officers updating their policy guidance on major crimes in the form of the *Murder Investigation Manual*, a document which aimed in part to institutionalize periodic review of investigations; in turn this has found its way into force-level policy on major crime investigations (National Centre for Policing Excellence, 2005). In practice, reviews range from 'informal reviews' where the Senior Investigating Officer (SIO) reports on progress to the Head of Criminal Investigation and/or another SIO, through 'self-inspection' or 'peer review'—where another SIO checks on progress—through to a 'concluding review', a full re-examination of the evidence and decision-making after all lines of enquiry are completed. Of course, since well before Macpherson, there has also been a practice of one police force reviewing investigations conducted by another, where there are reasons to warrant it. Indeed, this happened in the Lawrence case with the re-investigation of the murder by Kent Police in 1997. However, this sort of review takes place when there are grounds to believe something may have 'gone wrong'—the thrust of the Macpherson case for *institutionalized review* of investigations is to avoid them going wrong in the first place.

Independent Investigation of Police Complaints

The final point to make about the Lawrence case is that this particular miscarriage of justice has also played a critical role in further reform of the *police complaints process*. One of the key recommendations of Macpherson was that consideration be given to a fully independent system for the *investigation of complaints* against the police (Macpherson, 1999: 333). We may recall that this is precisely what Scarman had pointed to nearly two decades earlier and in relation to which the Police Complaints Authority was only a partial measure. In that sense Macpherson may be seen as finally attempting to deliver in full Scarman's vision of police accountability in this particular area.

The Home Secretary pledged to adopt this recommendation and in due course the *Police Reform Act 2002* established the Independent Police Complaints Commission (IPCC), which went 'live' in April 2004. This mirrored the establishment of the Office of the Police Ombudsman for Northern Ireland in 2000—which followed in the wake of the Hayes Report (Hayes, 1997) and was given legal force in the Police (Northern Ireland) Act 1998 (see Chapter 2)—although there is one, perhaps key, distinction between the two systems. The Police Ombudsman investigates *all* complaints against the police, no matter how 'trivial'. However, in England and Wales, there are four levels of investigation (Seneviratne, 2004: 335): investigation by the police ('minor' complaints); investigation by the police supervized by the IPCC; investigation by the police managed by the IPCC; and investigation by the IPCC itself. In that sense the formation of the IPCC still falls short of the *fully* independent investigation of complaints called for by both Scarman and Macpherson. Nevertheless, an interesting factor in these developments is that a new body of 'investigators' has come into being, working alongside the police service. Historically, police opposition to the idea of independent investigation of complaints reflected a logic that 'only police officers' possessed the skills set to effectively investigate complaints or major police incidents. A challenge which the IPCC faces, as the Police Ombudsman did some time before, is whether 'non-police' investigators can demonstrate that the investigative process is as, if not more, safe in their hands than it is with police investigators themselves. If that proves to be the case, it opens up the prospect of extending forms of 'lay investigative' element which might, perhaps as part of the review of investigations, serve to improve the quality of the investigative process overall. As we shall see (Chapter 3), this is indeed what was emerging with the further 'civilianization' of police roles.

These are only some of the police-related reforms associated with the fallout of the Lawrence case. Macpherson also recommended the reform of police powers to stop and search, proposing that police records are kept not just on stops and searches but also on 'voluntary' stops (Macpherson, 1999: 333–4); this was implemented across all police forces in 2005 (Home Office, 2005c: 10). Macpherson further recommended the repeal of the 'double jeopardy' rule, whereby a person cannot be tried for an offence more than once (Macpherson, 1999: 331). This was subsequently adopted in the *Criminal Justice Act 2003* (see Taylor, Wasik, and Leng, 2004: 95–7). Furthermore, it is possible to detect the ethos of Macpherson in the wider police reforms such as 'neighbourhood policing' and its association with 'community engagement' (see Chapter 5), something acknowledged by the Lawrence Steering Group (Home Office, 2005c: 9). Overall, it is difficult to deny that the system failures associated with the Lawrence case had repercussions far and wide throughout the policing world.

At this point, however, it is important to make a qualification to the linkage between system failure and police reform made so far. In most of the examples of this linkage considered so far, change has in a sense been *imposed* on policing; policing has been forced or required to change because of the deficiencies within the status quo of policing which system failure has exposed. However, this is by no means an automatic process. To begin with, system failures themselves have to be exposed, and this might rest on the political will to inquire into them or the power of campaigning groups to influence the body politic in that direction. The Lawrence case for example might never have been the subject of a full public inquiry without a Labour government—the previous Conservative government had refused a public inquiry. That case might also not have been the subject of a public inquiry without the determination of the Lawrence family. We will never of course know the extent of system failures within policing which have yet to be exposed. Furthermore, even when system failures are exposed, there is no guarantee that this will lead to policy change—we have already seen that Scarman's preference for a fully independent system for the investigation of complaints was not accepted, and we had to wait for the momentum of Macpherson to get that far. This is a way of saying that there is a process of *mediation* intervening between event (system failure) and reform, and that process of mediation can forge the shape, direction or even the existence of reforms themselves. The process of mediation involves the balance and configuration of the forces involved in the policy process, and might include the political will and inclination of government (see Chapter 5), the relative influence of, in this case, police pressure groups, and the degree of influence of other campaigning groups, such as civil liberties bodies (see Chapter 4). This is important because it is possible, given the right balance of circumstances, for system failure to be used as an opportunity not for others to impose change on the police, but for the *police* to 'turn the tables' and use the 'window of opportunity' which system failures offer to their own 'advantage'. This, it would seem, is indeed what happened with another system failure associated with miscarriages of justice, once again associated with wrongful convictions.

The Guildford Four and Birmingham Six Cases: Turning the Tables on Police Reform

Although, as we have seen, the role of police conduct in miscarriages of justice had attracted public attention as far back as the mid-1970s, it was the miscarriages of justice associated with Irish terrorism, which only came to light in the late 1980s, which above all turned the spotlight on police conduct and its relationship with miscarriages of justice. This began with the case of the Guildford Four, involving the conviction of Gerald Conlon, Paul Hill, Carole Richardson, and Patrick Armstrong in 1975 for the murder of five people killed in the bombing of the *Horse and Groom* public house in 1974. The case for the prosecution relied almost totally on confession evidence, and at the trial the Four claimed that confessions had been extracted from them by force by the Surrey Police. In 1989 the then Home Secretary, Douglas Hurd, referred the case back to the Court of Appeal, after a lengthy campaign by supporters of the Four, including church leaders. In preparation for the appeal process the case was investigated by the Avon and Somerset Police, and one of the detectives involved found typed notes, heavily edited by hand, from the police 'interview' with Armstrong, whose confession was central to the conviction. The problem was that these amended notes corresponded with the notes presented to the trial as evidence and, it was claimed, they were notes taken during the police interview. The implication was that the police had manipulated the notes after the 'interview' to fit in with the case they wished to present (Rozenberg, 1994:

303–4). These findings led the Crown to concede that the case against the Guildford Four could not be sustained and the convictions were quashed later in 1989.

The miscarriages of justice in the case of the Birmingham Six also pivoted around the extent to which police conduct was a factor in generating injustices (Mullin, 1990). In 1975 Hugh Callaghan, Patrick Hill, Gerry Hunter, Richard McIlkenny, Billy Power, and Johnny Walker were convicted of the 21 murders which arose out of two pub bombings, associated with Irish terrorism on the British mainland, in Birmingham the previous year. Again, confession evidence was central to the case against the Six, and, as with the Guildford Four, allegations were made about maltreatment by the police (in this case the West Midlands Police)—although scientific evidence was also critical. After another lengthy campaign the case was referred to the Court of Appeal in 1990 (the convictions having been upheld at two previous appeals). Electrostatic analysis of interview transcripts suggested that one of the interviews had not been recorded contemporaneously with the police interview, as claimed at the trial. This, together with concerns over the scientific evidence used in the original convictions, caused the Crown to concede that evidence against the Six was not reliable. In 1991 the Court of Appeal duly quashed the convictions of the Birmingham Six (Rozenberg, 1994: 310–14).

It is difficult to overstate the shock to the justice system which the Guildford Four and the Birmingham Six cases created. In particular, the cases pointed an accusing finger at the police as being 'confession oriented' and willing to turn to questionable means in order to obtain such confessions. Ironically, the exposures of past police practices in these two miscarriages of justice came at a time when legislation which would lead to significant controls on police investigations and conduct, PACE (legislation which, as we have seen, was itself driven in part by a miscarriage of justice), was beginning to bed down.

Confronted with the shell shock of the Guildford Four and Birmingham Six miscarriages of justice the then Home Secretary, Kenneth Baker, turned to an institution which had fallen very much out of favour during the Thatcher era, the Royal Commission of Inquiry. Minutes after the acquittal of the Birmingham Six the Home Secretary announced the setting up the Royal Commission on Criminal Justice (RCCJ) under Viscount Runciman. The terms of reference of the Commission however were already moving the agenda away from the specific concerns of miscarriages of justice based on wrongful acquittal towards a wider 'balance' in the justice process between the need for the 'effectiveness of the criminal justice system in England and Wales in *securing the conviction of those guilty* of criminal offences and the acquittal of those who are innocent' (emphasis added). When the RCCJ duly reported in 1993, it was greeted with disappointment from the civil libertarian side as an opportunity lost to tackle root and branch the shortcomings evident in the miscarriages of justice cases (see Sanders and Young, 1995; Rozenberg, 1994: 321–4), but largely welcomed by the police. The reason for this is that not only did the RCCJ broadly endorse current police practice, particularly under PACE, as having already addressed the problems exposed by miscarriages of justice (Sanders and Young, 1995), the RCCJ also gave plenty of ammunition for the police to construct the case that it was *constraints on the conviction* side which was most at issue. In other words, a Royal Commission instigated because of *police failings* fitted into a new policy agenda for *strengthening* the conviction process. The irony of this was stated by one senior police officer interviewed as part of the research by Savage, Charman and Cope (2000):

> the Royal Commission had been set up on the basis that the police were the bad boys and the Royal Commission was going to put that right...I think the police walked away from the Royal Commission with a fairly reasonable clean bill of health whereas the finger was then pointing to the other bits of the criminal justice system which weren't working very effectively. (Savage, Charman, and Cope, 2000: 180)

In one area the RCCJ did make recommendations which more clearly fitted the linkage of system failures and reforms outlined earlier. The Report recommended the replacement of the then existing machinery for reviewing possible miscarriages of justice, which was under the auspices of the Home Office, by a separate and independent 'Criminal Cases Review Authority' (Runciman, 1993: Chapter 11; see also Walker, 2002: 512–13). This was duly implemented in 1997, following the *Criminal Appeals Act 1995* in the form of the Criminal Cases Review Commission (CCRC) (Walker, 2002: 514–16). The CCRC is not as such a 'police reform' but, in so far as it is a machinery for review of all matters securing convictions alleged to be wrongful, it is a form of oversight of police conduct and activity and can serve to call to account police behaviour, by re-opening police investigations and referring cases to the Court of Appeal. In that sense the CCRC fits the cycle of system failure and reform seen in other areas such as the IPCC, in terms of system failures leading to greater regulation and control of police conduct.

However, because the RCCJ had within its remit the need to consider means by which to 'secure the conviction of the guilty' it also opened up a Pandora's Box of debate, research, and bluntly, lobbying, around ways of reforming the criminal justice process in the opposite direction—of *strengthening* the capacity of the police to secure convictions. As we shall see in Chapter 4, the police took the work of the RCCJ as a strategic opportunity to revisit older debates and present 'evidence' based justifications for reforms they would wish to see. One such was around the *right to silence*—the police had long argued that the rules surrounding the right to silence were in effect enabling clearly guilty people to go free, by allowing them to refuse to answer questions during investigations or at trial without that being taken as a possible indication of guilt. The 'police case' was that the right to silence needed amending so as to allow judges to allow jurors to draw negative inferences from the refusal of suspects or defendants to answer questions or provide explanations where requested. The RCCJ actually came out against amending the right to silence by a majority of eight to three, arguing that it might lead to a possible increase in miscarriages of justice (Runciman, 1993: 54). However, the Report only served to heighten the debate and leave the field prey to other agendas. The Conservative Home Secretary, Michael Howard, rejected the majority RCCJ recommendation to retain the existing rules on the right to silence and adopted the *minority* recommendation, a decision announced, significantly, at the now infamous speech to the Conservative Party Conference in 1993 (discussed further in Chapter 5). The *Criminal Justice and Public Order Act 1994* provided that adverse inferences could be drawn from silence whilst under police questioning, subject to the suspect being cautioned (Sch 10, para 61(2)).

In this sense the 'police case' had been accepted and the tables turned on police reform; the amendment of the right to silence was seen as a victory for the police, an outcome of a process which had begun with serious concerns over police misconduct. This was not the only area where the police had, with the obvious assistance of the Conservative government, managed to turn the table on the reform agenda. The RCCJ had also chosen to review the arrangements for the disclosure of evidence from the prosecution case to the defence, given concerns in the miscarriages of justice that vital evidence for the defence case had not been disclosed—the Judith Ward case being one classic example (Rozenberg, 1994: 316–17). However, as well as recommending clearer obligations on the prosecution to disclose evidence to the defendant, the RCCJ also chose to recommend new obligations on the *defence* to disclose its own case to the prosecution, thus enabling the prosecution to ask the police to pursue particular lines of enquiry to bolster the prosecution case (Rozenberg, 1994: 3425). This recommendation was effectively implemented by the *Criminal Procedure and Investigations Act 1996*. RCCJ recommendations also paved the way for the widening of police powers to take intimate and non-intimate *body samples* for DNA analysis, and for the wider retention of DNA-based information on the *DNA data-base* (Wasik and Taylor, 1995: 72–5), all measures sought by the police and all subsequently embodied in the *Criminal Justice and Public Order Act 1994* (Wasik and Taylor, 1995: 72–80). Many items on the police 'shopping list' for change and reform had in effect been delivered at least in part by a Royal Commission set up initially to deal with abuse of police powers. How the police managed to turn the reform agenda around in this way is a matter discussed in Chapter 4.

Conclusion

This chapter has endeavoured to trace the linkage between 'things going wrong' and police reform. In doing that a number of major cases of system failure have been selected on the basis of their comprehensive impact on shaping police reform and/or creating the conditions under which police reform has become possible. This is not to imply that the cases chosen are the only system failures which have been significant factors in police reform. The cycle of system failure, inquiry, and reform can be found in a number of other cases of notoriety. The police investigation of the 'Yorkshire Ripper' case was one such example. Peter Sutcliffe was arrested in 1981, having committed at least 12 murders of women between 1975 and his arrest, despite having been interviewed on a number of occasions over this period by the police. The Byford Report into the police investigation (Byford, 1982)—a document not released to the public or some 25 years—made a number of criticisms and recommendations about police force cooperation and police intelligence systems, and was the driving force behind the introduction of the Home Office Large Major Inquiry System (known as HOLMES), a computerized system for the handling of data and intelligence (Maguire, 2003: 386). The Hillsborough disaster in 1989, when 96 football fans were killed as a result of poor crowd control and the poor physical condition of the stadium, was followed by the Taylor Report (Taylor, 1989), which made a range of recommendations on such things as seating, stadia design, and the availability of alcohol at football grounds. However, the Report was also instrumental in changing policing operations around football stadia and in particular the role of stewarding under police guidance (Frosdick and Marsh, 2005: 175). Finally, the police role prior to and since the 'Soham murders'—the murders by Ian Huntley of Holly Wells and Jessica Chapman in 2002—was one of the subjects of the Bichard Inquiry. The Bichard Report (Bichard, 2004: 13–17) paid particular attention to the police failings in information management, the handling of intelligence, and police vetting of persons applying to posts which would bring them into close contact with children. All of Bichard's recommendations were accepted by government, including the establishment of a national information technology system for the police intelligence (Bichard, 2004: 13), and their implementation is, as Bichard also recommended, the subject of annual progress reports by the Home Office (Home Office, 2006a). These and other examples of system failure linking to police reform are primarily concerned with particular reforms and developments. The system failures discussed at more length here, are those which have been responsible for more comprehensive police reform agendas.

In this respect it is necessary to make two concluding points. First, to return to the qualification referred to earlier, the linkage between system failure and police reform is by no means an automatic one, but is *mediated* by the play of forces and influences which are at work at the time. It is the configuration of these forces and the balance between them, which will determine whether and how specific system failures transmute into police reforms, or not. A classic concept in political science is that of 'non-decisions' (Bacharach and Baratz, 1969); as well as understanding how decisions and policies are made, we also need to understand how decisions are *not* made, typically as a result of the power and influence of those that have an interest in those decisions not being taken. An illustration of this was the 'non-decision' to move to the independent investigation of complaints as recommended by Scarman considered earlier; the less radical option of the PCA model was adopted rather than more radical option preferred by Scarman, perhaps, as Smith (2005: 127) has argued, as a reflection of the balance of power between the interested parties at the time. System failures, assuming they have been exposed in the first place, may become 'decisions' (reforms) or 'non-decisions' (non-reforms) depending on the balance of power and influence holding at that conjuncture.

A second concluding point to make, again referred to earlier, is that system failures can impact on police reform in varying ways. They might entail a one-to-one relationship between the failure in question and the eventual reform—diversity training for police officers as a response to Lawrence and Macpherson is a good example of this. System failures may also, in addition, affect police reform over a much longer period, by changing a problematic or mindset in policing ideology, and have consequences for many years to come as a result. This was the sort of long-term impact of Scarman's vision of community policing, which set in motion the growing interpretation of policing as more of a 'service' than a 'force', which still has a resonance in more contemporary forms of police reform such as 'neighbourhood policing' (see Chapter 5). Linked to this is the extent to which system failures may serve to move the police reform agenda 'step-by-step' towards more fundamental change. The history of the police complaints process, as we have seen, is an example of this: Scarman helped move the system further in the direction of civilian oversight, but it took Macpherson to see that process through to the more radical model encapsulated in the formation of the IPCC. What determines how and why system reform can have these differing forms of impact are the political forces and the balance of power at work at the time, and that is the subject of later chapters in this book.

2

Import Duties: Police Reform and Influences from Abroad

Introduction

One potential source of influence in changing policing in any nation state is the multitude of alternative policing models, systems, styles, and approaches which exist elsewhere on the international scene. Those alternative policing forms have been shaped by nationally specific configurations of law, politics, social structures, cultures, and histories which generate variation and difference across nation states in the way policing is organized, oriented and activated. There are, as a consequence, many different examples offered from the international environment of the way the business of policing is undertaken, some of which might be taken on board by governments and/or police organizations as better ways of doing policing business.

Of course, the very fact that policing is done differently in other places can be one reason why those alternative policing forms are *not* attractive as models of better practice. 'It couldn't work here' is a sentiment often expressed when practitioners are presented with other ways of going about their work. In some ways policing in particular is a sector which clings doggedly to its own traditions; in Britain, for example, it is clear that dimensions of policing still reflect principles, such as 'policing by consent', which were first laid down in the first half of the nineteenth century (Morgan and Newburn, 1997: 75–6). If the police organization has been resistant to wider social changes taking place elsewhere within the same country, it seems unlikely that it would be responsive to alternative models from other countries.

However, there is also a sense in which policing can also, potentially at least, be *pervious* to influence from abroad. Unlike most other public services, policing is routinely exposed to the international scene, and increasingly so, because of *operational* involvement. Cross-border crime, machineries for the sharing of information and intelligence and coordinated activity across states, such as *Interpol* and *Europol*, and other ways in which policing beyond the nation state is driven, serve to expose police services to the workings and ways of policing systems elsewhere. They may not be impressed with what they see, but, because of operational exposure, they do have opportunities to see it, in a way that would not apply to other public services. Of course, there are other channels of exposure to alternative policing systems, and these are also applicable to most other public services. International conferences, study and fact-finding visits, exchange programmes, professional and academic journals and periodicals, and so on, are all vehicles by which policy-makers and practitioners can learn about how their services are organized and delivered in other countries and what might be better ways of doing their line of business. International aid programmes (discussed later), are another way in which ideas travel, in this case typically *from* developed *to* developing and/or transitional societies.

In the policing context there are numerous platforms for the exchange of ideas. For example, the International Association of Chiefs of Police (IACP), which has over 17,000 members, holds annual conferences—usually in highly attractive venues—where senior police officers from around the globe meet and exchange ideas about policing. The Association also publishes a journal, *Police Chief*, which disseminates information and ideas about policing worldwide. The Academy of Criminal Justice Sciences (ACJS), based in the United States, is another body for ideas exchange on an international scale, which has law enforcement as a core concern. What ICAP and ACJS could help cultivate is what Jones and Newburn (2007: 149–50) refer to as a 'trans-national policy network', frameworks of contact and exchange between policy actors from a multitude of nation states, including policing 'elites', decision-makers and opinion formers in the policing sector—the notion of 'policy networks' is discussed at length in Chapter 4.

In this respect there are particularly strong channels for ideas exchange between Britain and the United States on policing matters, furthered no doubt by a common language, a degree of cultural commonality, and legal systems which bear the same origins and principles. The Fulbright Fellowship scheme has facilitated a programme of study-visits and officer exchanges which have enabled the dissemination of alternative policing practices and approaches across the Atlantic. The John Jay Institute in New York had housed a number of British officers as Visiting Lecturers and Professors, which, as well as exposing American police students and staff to British ways of policing—not that they took too much notice—had provided opportunities for British officers to travel the United States and discover alternative policing approaches, which can find their way back across the Atlantic. Given the huge range of police organizations in the United States, there were many models on display. Officers selected for the Fulbright and John Jay exchange programmes were often regarded as 'high fliers' and future opinion formers in their own organizations. Some of them were to become what has been called 'policy entrepreneurs' (Jones and Newburn, 2007: 28; see Chapter 4), officers who subsequently played a key role in leading and driving future policy change. The same applied to what was known as the 'Bramshill Scholarship' scheme (Savage, Charman, and Cope, 2000: 101–3), whereby British officers were seconded to UK universities to undertake full-time degrees. Although this scheme was not directly concerned with capturing ideas about policing from abroad—it was more concerned to improve the numbers of graduates in the police service—it did enable some officers at least to study and research alternative and emerging notions about policing, and bring those back into policing after graduation. What the Bramshill scheme may also have done in some small way was, by enhancing the educational awareness of a number of officers 'destined for the top' (Savage, Charman and Cope, 2000: 104–5), help to generate a policing environment more receptive to new ideas about policing, one which could include ideas from abroad. The framework for the penetration of British policing by alternative models of policing from abroad was therefore in place.

In the wider study of public policy-making and shaping there is an established literature around the cross-national processes of policy influence, which Jones and Newburn (2007) have attempted to develop as part of the 'meso-level' analysis of policing policy making. In that literature, now captured by the concept of 'policy transfer' (Dolowitz and Marsh, 2000), various policy-shaping processes are embraced. That includes the notion of *'lesson drawing'* (Rose, 1991), the 'voluntary' means by which policy actors in one country learn from policy development (including what was seen in Chapter 1 as 'policy disasters') in other countries and shape their domestic polices accordingly. It also includes the concept of *'policy convergence'* (Coleman, 1994; Bennett, 1991), a deeper-lying process that relates to the ways in which policies across nation states can tend to take similar forms—without any necessarily conscious realisation that this might be happening or deliberate decision to emulate policy forms evident elsewhere (Jones and Newburn, 2007: 23–5). Policy convergence, according to Bennett (1991: 218) can mean convergence along five possible fronts: policy goals, policy content, policy instruments (eg a regulatory framework), policy out-comes, and policy styles. Policy convergence is particularly appropriate as a model to account for broad-sweep developments such as the rise of 'new public management in policing' across nation states (see Chapter 3), which relate more to wider issues of state formations and globalization, than direct 'cross-influence' or 'cross-fertilization', the major focus of this discussion, although the notion of policy convergence will be referred to at various points in this chapter.

Dolowitz and Marsh (1996: 344), primary architects of policy transfer theory, define the policy transfer as:

a process in which knowledge about policies, administrative arrangements, institutions, etc. in one time and/or place is used in the development of policies, administrative arrangements and institutions in another time and or place.

Dolowitz and Marsh (2000: 10) also identify the range of *policy actors* who might be engaged in the policy transfer process: elected officials; political parties; civil servants; pressure groups; policy entrepreneurs and experts; trans-national corporations; think tanks; supra-national governmental and nongovernmental institutions; and consultants. In the policing context and from the perspective of this discussion, it is the role of 'policy entrepreneurs' (Mintrom, 1997—see also Chapter 4) and experts which has been most significant—key individuals, adopting the role of 'policing thinkers', who have played critical parts in the policing policy transfer process, both within the 'donor countries', where the policy in question originated, and in 'recipient countries' where the policy is transferred to. Policy entrepreneurs may have operated within the 'donor' country as the *policy initiator*, the person or persons who initially forged the policy in question. Policy entrepreneurs may also have operated as the key players who have identified a policy already developed abroad as having promise, and who have then acted as what might be called the *'policy courier'* and who have 'imported' the policy into the 'recipient' country. In this respect, as will be seen later, individual police officers have played important roles as 'policy couriers' in transferring policing policies from abroad into policing in Britain.

In addition to the question of policy actors, Evans and Davies (1999: 368) map out an inventory of *policy levels* at which policy transfer can operate: international, national, regional, and local. For the purposes of this discussion it is the national and local dimensions which are most relevant; policy transfer in the context of British policing has exhibited various patterns by which the 'donor country' has interfaced with the 'recipient' country, and these have involved various dimensions of national and local policy processes. As will be seen, some *local* policing policies from abroad (eg policies that have been developed within one city) have transferred into *national* policing policies in the UK; alternatively, some *local* policies from abroad have also transferred only into *local* policing polices in the UK (ie have only been adopted in one or two police forces, not on a national scale). This variation in levels of policy transfer is important to the understanding of the impact of influences from abroad on British police reform, because this driver of policy change tends to be more fragmented and focused in impact than the other policy drivers considered in this book. This is due in part to the fact that policy transfer in the policing context is not typically part of a *programme* of reform, of the sort that, for example, a government might seek to launch, whereby the reforms in question might be part of a wider agenda for change in the police sector or public sector as a whole. Policy transfer is more likely to be policy-specific, relating to one discrete area of policy, and be subject to a 'one-off' process and, as has already been noted, very dependent on the key individuals who bring those policies 'home'.

On this basis a number of areas of British policing policy and police reform will be identified as bearing the fingerprints of processes of policy transfer, even if other factors have also been at work in influencing the destiny of the policies in question. This will begin by focusing on the ways in which *American* policing policies and/or ideas about policing have shaped British policing.

Born in America: From 'Over There' to 'Over Here'

It has already been noted that there has been a particularly strong linkage between American and British policing and thus a high degree of permeability of British policing to American approaches to policing—although perhaps rather less by way of influence in the opposite direction. As Newburn (2002: 172–7) has argued, the strength of the linkage might be due in part to a deeper symmetry between American and British political and social cultures and within that spheres of 'ideological proximity' around visions of crime control and the 'politicization of crime' (see Chapter 5). The influence of American thinking about policing goes back a long way. For example, the introduction of *unit beat policing* in Britain in the 1960s mirrored very closely the development of what has been called, pejoratively, '911 policing' in the USA (Kelling and Coles, 1996: 89–102). Unit beat policing was introduced in Britain in the mid-1960s and was a policing model built around the apparent virtues of rapid response to police calls, the 'deterrent' effect of car patrols in the community and the 'efficiency' of such patrols in covering large geographical areas with limited numbers of officers (Weatheritt, 1986: 88–9). It was given full governmental backing in 1967 with a Home Office circular which promised direct central financial support for the purchase of cars to underwrite what was then heralded as the most fundamental change in operational policing since the formation of the police in the nineteenth century (Weatheritt, 1986: 88). In essence, however, unit beat policing replicated the policing model which had emerged in the late 1950s and early 1960s in the USA under the rubric of 'scientific policing' organized around technology (Kelling and Coles, 1996: 79) which had placed the emphasis on centrally controlled police patrols, based on car patrol and oriented to rapid response to calls from the public—through the '911' emergency call line. The enthusiasm with which the British government had embraced unit beat policing mirrored closely the enthusiasm with which their American counterparts had welcomed the ethos of '911 policing'. This was a form of policy transfer across the Atlantic of a policing model that was to have profound effects on the status of policing in the United Kingdom and even the quality of police–public relations in the years to come (Reiner, 2000: 60–1).

However, given the time frame on which this book is based, it is policy transfer in the context of policing policy since the end of the 1970s which is the focus of this discussion. In that respect three policing approaches will be highlighted: *policing by objectives, problem-oriented policing,* and *zero tolerance.* All three may be seen as having roots in the USA and subsequently to have found their way, unevenly and even untidily, across the Atlantic.

Policing by Objectives: The Emergence of 'Planned Policing'

At various points in this study the notion of policing as 'special' relative to other public services, or the 'sacredness' (McLaughlin, 2007: 39; Loader and Mulcahy, 2003: 4–7) of the role of (British) police officer relative to other occupations, has been considered. The basis of these notions in that policing is somehow a 'special case' when it comes to debating reform and that arrangements which may be in place for the other sorts of organizations, private sector and public sector, are not transferable into the police organization; policing is *different*. As discussed fully in Chapter 3, one line of argument that policing is a 'special case' has been used to challenge attempts to apply *management* principles, developed for other sectors, to the police organization; that given the special conditions under which policing operates (as essentially a service which *reacts* to *unforeseen demand*—Waddington, 1986), models of managing organizations which might work elsewhere, in the private sector or in some other parts of the public sector, simply would not hold water when applied to policing. What provoked that line of argument in the context of British policing more than anything, was the attempt in the early 1980s to introduce a model of police management into Britain known as *policing by objectives*. That model was first developed in *America* and arrived on the British scene in a classic case of policy transfer.

Policing by objectives (PBO) in a sense stands as an American import twice over. Its origins lie in the wider concept *management by objectives*, which was also initially developed in the USA and which then found its way into public sector management philosophy in Britain—mainly in terms of local government—well in advance of its policing counterpart (Glendinning and Bullock, 1973). The general ideas within which PBO was situated were already in circulation in British public policy almost a decade before PBO itself landed ashore, as a second wave of American inspired thinking on management, in this case focused on policing. Management by objectives (MBO) itself emerged in the mid-1950s in the USA as industry attempted to find ways of improving effectiveness and efficiency in an increasingly competitive domestic and international economy, and management gurus such as Drucker (1955) began to advocate management frameworks which were based on clear objective setting in terms of production, finance, and so on and the gearing of organizations to achieve those objectives—MBO was the label this approach was given. At the core of MBO is the notion of a continuous and cyclical process of management involving a number of stages (Glendinning and Bullock, 1973: 2):

- A *strategic plan* forged by senior management which defines the corporate aims and objectives of an organization in key areas of its business;

- A *tactical plan* which identifies courses of action and the resources required to meet these objectives;
- *Unit objectives* which defines what managers of individual departments and organizational units are to achieve and what outputs are to be sought;
- After a period of time has elapsed systematic *reviews* are carried out to assess the performance results;
- Objectives and output requirements are updated—and the cycle begins again.

The first full application of MBO principles to the police organization came with the publication of *Policing by Objectives* by the American academics Lubans and Edgar (1979). Their starting point was the message from a leading MBO thinker Dale McConkey, about the problematic culture in many such organizations:

> Management of non-profit organisations has no landed right to be ineffective, to ignore managerial productivity, to ignore the 'profit' motive, or to fail to evaluate new or revised approaches to management... (McConkey, quoted in Lubans and Edgar, 1979: 3)

Lubans and Edgar (1979: 2–5) argued that a combination of economic constraint on public services, which was placing greater onus on public service managers to demonstrate efficiency, and the emergence of a 'new breed' of police officers, better educated and more inclined to show initiative and sensitivity to 'social and cultural issues', was creating pressures for structural and operational change in the police organization. PBO was, they argued, the means to achieve this; PBO was MBO but it was 'tailored to the needs of police managers and takes into account the unique features of the police enterprise'. (1979: 5). In PBO, 'the basic MBO principles of planning, execution and review, and results-orientation have been applied to the police experience' (1979: 6). They argued that PBO was different from 'familiar' police management in four fundamental ways:

- PBO is highly systematic
- PBO is goal-oriented—about achieving results
- PBO makes use of talent from all levels of the organization and involves as many members of departments as possible
- PBO places emphasis on planning and assessment.

To translate MBO into PBO Lubans and Edgar took the primary steps of MBO—'mission', 'departmental goals', 'objectives', 'action plans', 'implementation', and 'assessment'—and located them within the decision-making and operational frameworks of the police organization. They did this through what they called the 'PBO Linking Pin Principle' (Lubans and Edgar, 1979: 22–3). The 'Linking Pin' involved the following stages. First, the community and local government, together with senior/executive police management in an 'executive planning group', develop the police organization's *mission*. Secondly, the senior management team work with middle/command management in a 'command planning group' to draft *departmental goals*. Thirdly, middle management works with line managers to develop *unit objectives*. Fourthly, line management, working with front-line officers, turn those objectives into *action plans*—and the service is delivered. Once implemented, action plans and outputs are reviewed and assessed periodically and a final review is undertaken, after which the whole process may be revised. For Lubans and Edgar PBO is a 'top-down' and 'bottom-up' process in the sense that broad 'guidelines' are sent *down* the organization but organizational units and sub-units are *active* in determining action plans and on feeding back *up* the hierarchy progress made.

Interest in the American experience of PBO began to grow within senior police circles in Britain in the late 1970s and early 1980s. The most significant of these was Kenneth Newman, who had three unbeatable opportunities to influence the course of British policing, first as one of Her Majesty's Inspectors of Constabulary, then as Commandant of the Police Staff College at Bramshill, and later as Commissioner of the Metropolitan Police (see Chapter 4). Newman had toured the USA in the late 1970s and had been impressed with the MBO/PBO framework. He subsequently preached the virtues of MBO in his various roles; in the case of the Metropolitan Police, the MBO paradigm soon became apparent on the force planning process. For example, in 1983, one year after Newman took office as Commissioner, an 'Area Strategic Plan' was produced which was explicitly based on MBO (Metropolitan Police, 1983). The document was littered with terms such as the 'planning cycle', 'objective and action plans', and so on. Interestingly, it also spelt out the virtues of *devolved management* and referred to the 'division' as the 'prime unit of policing' (1983: 6); as is made clear in the following chapter, these are both principles which were to become a key part of subsequent management thinking and policing policy, the latter taking the form of 'Basic Command Units'. Already, it seemed, MBO had gained a foothold in the largest police force in Britain.

The growing influence of MBO was given a further boost with the publication by Tony Butler of *Police Management* in 1984—which had a Foreword by Sir Kenneth Newman. Butler was at that time a middle ranking officer but one very seen much as a 'high flier'—he was later to become Chief Constable for the Gloucestershire Constabulary and a leading chief within ACPO. Butler had visited the USA and met with Lubans and Edgars who gave Butler his first 'introduction' to PBO (Butler, 1984: vii). Significantly, Butler spent time on the staff of Bramshill Police College, under Newman, and used the opportunity to assist the Northamptonshire Police in introducing POB into that force (see the following chapter). For Butler the case for PBO in the context of British policing was bolstered by the challenges then facing the police service. Two fundamental lines of public questioning were confronting the police, despite the general level of satisfaction the public have with the police (Butler, 1984: 7). On the one hand were groups looking for change and improvement in the way the police go about their tasks—these were 'effectiveness' and 'efficiency' concerns. On the other hand, given the climate of the time with heated debates around the issue of police accountability (see Chapter 5), were groups looking for more community involvement in the making of policing policies. According to Butler the answer to this dilemma, one which Johnston (2000: 84) has argued is about responding to criticisms both on the right (police 'inefficiency') and on the left (lack of police accountability), lay with the PBO paradigm.

Butler claimed that the evidence from the United States on police forces which had gone down the road of MBO/PBO supported the view that police organizations can deal with such challenges more successfully than those which had not (Butler, 1984: 9). Butler took a number of themes from the Lubans and Edgar framework and painted them in British colours. These included the 'Linking Pin' model (Butler, 1984: 162), the PBO 'management cycle' (1984: 15; 160), and the framework of performance measurement (1984: 25–40). Butler's work on the latter is particularly significant given that at the time the very idea of measuring police 'performance' was questioned by some—as shall be seen in the following chapter. Butler had provided a practical basis, and one which was linked closely to the logistics of policing in the British context, on which the American notion of PBO could be worked into the fabric of British police management.

Weatheritt, in *Innovations in Policing* (1986), reviewed the impact of this particular American 'import' on the mindset of British policing at that time. She identified a number of features of PBO which could, at least potentially, contribute to the positive development of British policing, particularly within the context of what was then the deeply ingrained traditionalism associated with it (Weatheritt, 1986: 118–20). First, because of the emphasis in PBO on planning, measurement, assessment, and review, it offered a *'rational/empirical'* approach to police decision- and policy-making, as Weatheritt (1986: 120) puts it '[PBO] is an argument for good research as a precondition of good policing'. Secondly, PBO offered a *dynamism* in the sense that the PBO cycle writes continuous *change* into police decision-making. Furthermore, in this respect, because of the role within PBO of *devolved* decision-making and its 'bottom-up' as well as 'top-down' processes, it presented opportunities to engage those at the lower ends of the police organization who would otherwise be major *obstacles* to change. Thirdly, PBO presented an 'uncompromising emphasis in the importance of results'; it offered the approach that 'nothing is sacred: the unthinkable can be thought' (1986: 120). Policing activities have, under PBO, to be *justified, measured, reviewed*, and overall be *questioned*. It offered an approach to policing which was preferable to maintaining the status quo for the sake of it. To critics of PBO (Waddington, 1986) Weatheritt could respond, at least policing by *objectives* is better that policing by *subjectives* (Weatheritt, 1986: 118).

Innovations in Policing also reviewed the impact in Britain of another 'import' from America which was appearing on the British policing landscape: *problem-oriented policing*.

Problem-Oriented Policing: Community Policing Meets Intelligence-Led Policing

It was noted earlier that policing models such as 'unit-beat policing' reflected an attempt to develop 'rational' approaches to policing, focusing on improving the 'efficiency' of the police by exploiting 'new' management approaches to resource allocation and the exploitation of technologies such as communication systems. The case for such policing models, as has been seen, was developed initially in the USA and then 'imported' to Britain. However, soon after such approaches to policing were being 'picked up' in Britain, a *critique* of such strategies also began to emerge within the USA, and as part of that critique a new term was introduced which, a decade and a half later, was also to be influential in British policing—*problem-oriented policing* (POP). In a paper published in 1979, Herman Goldstein, the architect of this particular policing model, began to map out the basics of a case for a move away from policing approaches such as unit-beat policing and the rationale which underpinned them (Goldstein, 1979).

Goldstein began stating his case with the oft quoted example, ironically, of a London bus service. As a way of demonstrating the tendency in public services to let the *means* take priority over *ends*, he reported the following tale:

> Complaints from passengers wishing to use the Bagnall to Greenfields bus service that 'the drivers were speeding past queues of up to 30 people with a smile and a wave of the hand' have been met by a statement pointing out that 'it is impossible for the drivers to keep to their timetable if they have to stop for their passengers'. (Goldstein, 1979: 236)

Goldstein was critical of then recent police reforms in the USA which had emphasized improving the *means* by which policing had been delivered—management systems, upgrading personnel, modernizing equipment, and so on—whilst neglecting what the *ends* of policing are about and how well they are being pursued. He argued that police managers and those who direct them 'have succeeded in developing a high level of operating efficiency [but] have not gone on to concern themselves with the end results of their efforts [and] the actual impact that their streamlined organizations have on the *problems* the police are called upon to handle'. (Goldstein, 1979: 239—emphasis added). Goldstein then lists the 'troublesome situations' or *problems* that prompt people to turn to the police—some of which, such as vandalism, were 'police problems' because no other means had been found to solve them—including street robberies, burglaries, battered wives, speeding, runaway children, accidents, and acts of terrorism (Goldstein, 1979: 242–3). In response he argued that what was needed was a 'systematic' process for dealing with such problems—hence the term 'problem-oriented policing'—which at this stage was articulated in the form of a series of questions the police should ask (Goldstein, 1979: 243):

- What are the problems that citizens look to the police to handle?
- What do we know about the problem in question?

- What more could we know about the problem with further research?
- Should the problem be a proper concern for the authorities?
- What resources are available for dealing with it?
- How do the police currently deal with the problem?
- Taking a holistic view, what might be the most intelligent response?
- If a new response is adopted, how might its effectiveness be evaluated?

In many ways this line of questioning reflects a similar ethos to the mindset of 'new public management' discussed in Chapter 3, but Goldstein's approach was essentially police-specific: how the police can respond to the wide and varied calls on their time in such a way as the produce the best *end-product*—solving problems. This earlier framework was later developed into a full-blown policing model (Goldstein, 1990; see also McLaughlin, 2007: 68–72 and Tilley, 2003). In this model a number of themes were emerging which were to have symmetry with other policing models to emerge in parallel, such as *intelligence-led policing* (see Chapter 3). First, there was call for the police to 'group incidents as problems' (Goldstein, 1990: 32–4); this meant that incidents coming to the attention of the police should be analysed in order to build up a 'picture', say, to determine whether there is a *pattern* making up a 'problem' wider than the individual incidents themselves, for example, whether burglaries are concentrated in certain areas of a city—what have been called crime 'hot spots'. Secondly, there was a demand for 'systematic inquiry' (Goldstein, 1990: 36–8), the use of multiple sources of information on which to base a policing response (or a response involving various agencies). This was a form of what was later to be termed 'evidence-based policing' (see Chapter 3). Thirdly, Goldstein argued that where appropriate that response should concentrate attention 'on those individuals who account for a disproportionate share of the problem' (Goldstein, 1990: 104). This reflected the notion of targeting repeat and prolific offenders (Heaton, 2000) which was to become a core feature of intelligence-led policing and a central feature of the Audit Commission's recommendations for improving the effectiveness of police investigation in Britain (see Chapter 3). Finally, Goldstein's model of POP emphasized that a critical role in the whole process should be played by *front-line* officers who are best placed to become aware of community problems, how they might relate community problems and be understood, and how they might best be addressed. More generally, front-line officers are better placed to undertake *proactive* and *preventative* work which is central to the POP philosophy.

In a later paper Goldstein (1996: 10) illustrated some of these themes with a concrete example from San Diego:

> Two officers were assigned permanently to a neighbourhood in which street prostitution had been a long-standing problem. They undertook—over a period of several months—to study the problem: the characteristics of the prostitutes and their customers; the varied interests of local businesses and residents; the pattern of prostitution; and past efforts at dealing with the problem.

Having identified a group of prostitutes who most commonly frequent the area, they then explored the feasibility of obtaining injunctions that would restrain the conduct associated with their solicitation. Using the records of prior convictions of the prostitutes and documentation of their current activities, the officers engaged the merchants in the area in petitioning a local court for restraining orders and, ultimately the issuance of injunctions that specifically prohibited the named individuals from engaging in specified behaviour commonly associated with solicitation. Under threat of being held in contempt, the enjoined prostitutes left the area. The merchants, brought together through this action facilitated by the police, were left stronger as a community. The officers made inquiries—before and after—about the volume of business, the hours merchants were keeping their businesses open, and the investment being made in private security measures. On the basis of their observation of street activities and these measures, they concluded that prostitution was dramatically reduced, and the area, in its use and economy, was revitalised.

This example has been cited at length because it exhibits more than an illustration of a technical process for policing. Goldstein argued that POP was a policing approach running much deeper that simple 'problem-solving': 'More broadly, it is a *way of thinking about the police job* (Goldstein, 1996: 7—emphasis added). If we consider the range of tasks contained in the example above it is clear that the model of 'police officer' on view and aspired to within the POP framework is one well beyond the straightforward 'law enforcement officer'. Even at the front-line level this example implies that the police officer should be seen as multi-functional and (ideally) multi-skilled; the functions involved are:

- The police officer as *researcher*: officers should gather data and information on problems and processes relating to those problems.
- The police officer as *analyst*: officers should make sense of and interpret data, crime and otherwise, the causes of the problems confronting them and the community, the possible courses of action which could be made as responses to them, and conduct post-response evaluation of their impact.
- The police officer as *mobilizer of the community*: the officer should be placed to harness community resources and steer them in appropriate directions in order to further community cohesion.

In some respects this vision, clearly an optimistic one, of the role of the police officer restated, perhaps unknowingly, Alderson's vision of policing and the police officer as 'community leader', as discussed in Chapter 5. As will also be seen in Chapter 5, these particular dimensions of POP were also to be restated in the related notions of *'neighbourhood policing teams'* and *'community engagement'* in the police reforms under Labour in the early years of the twenty-first century. Goldstein's version of POP was about fundamental ways of orienting not just the police role but also the mindset about policing itself and the relationship between the police and the community. In this respect the community would not be passive consumers of policing services: communities would be central to the processes both of identifying problems—things that the public are concerned about—and in marshalling responses to those problems, responses which would engage the community itself wherever possible.

Perhaps inevitably, Goldstein's philosophy of policing, when translated into a framework for practitioners and as a policy instrument, became somewhat simplified, perhaps *over* simplified. Eck and Spelman (1987), through trials adopting POP in Newport News, USA, worked POP into a four-stage process, know by the acronym (acronyms always being a popular device for a police audience) *SARA*, which stands for:

Scanning: the process of gathering information and knowledge of incidents in order to identify patterns of related incidents and, subsequently, problems.

Analysis: the process of investigating further the nature of the problem and, if possible, causes of the problem; part of the analysis may relate to features of the victim (such as incidence of victimization in the past), features of the location of the incidents (a crime hot spot?), or features of the offender (repeat offender?)

Response: deciding upon and carrying through strategies tailor-made to tackle the problem—multi-agency responses.

Assessment: evaluating the impact of the response or responses to the problem and drawing lessons which might be learned for the process overall.

At this stage POP was still an American framework for American policing problems. However, POP was to be adopted as good policing practice across the Atlantic. Certain chief officers, such as Charles Pollard, then Chief Constable of Thames Valley Police, a force which had a reputation for innovative policing approaches, embraced the model with enthusiasm. In an article for *Police Review* (28 June 1996) Pollard praised the 'holistic' approach to crime and disorder advocated by the 'father of POP', Goldstein, and its proactive and preventative ethos; he announced that 'The POP method may well become a major part of policing strategy as we move into the next millennium' (see also Pollard, 1997). The theme of POP began to clutter the pages of *Police Review* in the months following Pollard's article—in July of 1996 senior officers of the West Midlands Police and Leicestershire Constabulary made public their own adoption of the model (*Police Review* 12 July 1996). Significantly, given what was stated earlier as the key role of 'elite networking' in disseminating ideas about police innovations, ACPO made POP a central theme of its 1996 Summer Conference and invited Goldstein to make a keynote speech to the assembly (*Police Review* 12 July 1996). The ACPO Summer Conference was the main opportunity for ACPO to 'showcase' British policing—it was also a gathering of both chief officers and their local police authority chairs—and the choice of Goldstein as key speaker was most significant.

The Home Office was keen to act as sponsor to the spread of the POP philosophy across police forces in Britain. On behalf of the Home Office, Leigh, Read, and Tilley (1996 and 1998) followed through a number of schemes in Britain which have sought to implement POP, in most cases using the SARA process, in various local areas across a range of police forces. In one force, Leicestershire, a pilot POP scheme was set up by the Home Office research team and its progress was monitored carefully. Using one Basic Command Unit (BCU—discussed in Chapter 3) for the pilot, the intent was to model the implementation of a POP scheme as closely as possible to *Goldstein's* vision (Leigh, Read and Tilley, 1996: 14). In this respect the scheme involved the following:

- the early involvement of as many beat officers as was possible;
- 'bottom up' approach for both the identification of problems and decisions on best responses;
- the involvement of a wide spread of officers, geographically and in terms of functions;
- comprehensive training programmes for officers;
- the analysis of incident patters undertaken by officers with direct knowledge of beats;
- the provision of bespoke information technology to support officers in problem identification and decisions on responses;
- the assessment of all responses and an evaluation of the scheme as a whole; and
- the continuing involvement of the public in problem identification and responding to them (Leigh, Read, and Tilley, 1996: 14).

Although the eventual results of the pilot were somewhat negative—some beat officers embraced the POP approach with enthusiasm and produced some quality work, but many officers were 'cynical' about the scheme, failed to operate fully in accordance with it and tended to fall back on 'traditional' methods (Leigh, Read, and Tilley, 1998: 18–20)—the project team remained optimistic about the potential for POP in the future. The work of HMIC and the Audit Commission (see Chapter 3) furthered the cause of POP. Also, by this stage, Labour had introduced the *Crime and Disorder Act 1998* (see Chapter 5), legislation which was very well suited to the thinking behind POP. With later reforms around the notion of *community engagement* (also discussed in Chapter 5), the momentum was well under way for this model of policing to become institutionalized within British policing.

There was an irony in the timing of the growing interest within policing and political circles with the notion of POP. At almost the same time as POP began to take off in British policing, in the mid-1990s, a policing model or style quite different from POP, or at least from Goldstein's particular brand of POP, was to travel across from the USA. This model had its own distinctive way of 'problem-solving': *enforcement*.

Broken Windows and Zero Tolerance Policing:
Importing Intolerance

In the study by Leigh, Read, and Tilley (1996: 25–6) it was noted that in one force which had adopted the POP scheme, Cleveland, that scheme had over-lapped with another policing style *zero tolerance policing* (ZTP). The Cleveland force had argued that whilst POP was an important policing model for long-term problem-solving, ZTP was also important as a means of tackling *short-term* problems (Leigh, Read, and Tilley, 1996: 26). The two could live side by side and were not incompatible. Whilst this was highly debatable (see Tilley, 2003), it is fair to argue that there is some common ground between the two models, not least because both stress the importance of 'low level' disorders as 'problems' in their own right, even if what to do about them is an issue on which they tend to part ways, as shall be seen. Both POP and ZTP can be seen as models to tackle 'quality of life' problems, of which low level disorders seem to be paramount. ZTP, however, has its own slant on how such problems should be confronted.

ZTP is a policing model which has the distinction, unlike most other models, of being virtually a household name: it has also been one of the most controversial policing developments in recent times (see Dennis (ed), 1997; McArdle and Erzen (eds), 2001; Bowling, 1999; Jones and Newburn, 2007: 106–42; McLaughlin, 2007: 117–25). The architects of ZTP, both theoretically and practically, were American, and include academics, politicians, and police chiefs. However, it is necessary to disaggregate two strands of thinking associated with ZTP because they do not necessarily come as a package, and in terms of American influences over British policing policy this is particularly significant. Those two strands are on the one hand *Broken Windows theory* and on the other zero tolerance itself. The reason this disaggregation is important from the British perspective is that Broken Windows theory is more widely accepted as a basis for policing than ZTP. For example, Pollard, whilst prepared to acknowledge the influence of American academic theory in terms of Broken Windows theory—'I well remember its impact on my own thinking... when I studied it for the first time at Police Staff College, Bramshill, 15 years ago.' (Pollard, 1997: 46)—was at pains to disown ZTP itself:

> The 'Broken Windows' principle is sound. Where however it becomes more complex and difficult is in the solutions it proposes, and it is here that we need to identify the distinctions from 'Zero Tolerance'. The expression 'Broken Windows'—and the theory behind it—is essentially about identifying and describing a complex problem... 'Zero Tolerance', on the other hand, is concerned purely with solutions. The expression imparts both the idea of tackling low level crime and disorder; and of doing so in a particular way, namely through aggressive, uncompromising law enforcement. (Pollard, 1997: 47)

Pollard was not alone, even if he was more passionate in his objection to ZTP than most. Leigh, Read, and Tilley (1996) noted that ZTP was not openly supported by any chief officer in Britain (see also Jones and Newburn, 2007: 110), although it did have support at lower levels, as shall be seen. Although ZTP was attractive *politically* (see below) it did not enjoy 'respectability' as a policing model in senior police circles in the way POP clearly did. This was perhaps some measure of the depth of changes in police mindset, at least at senior levels, in favour of community-oriented policing and community-sensitive policing discussed in the previous chapter. In the wake of Scarman, a policing model which advocated aggressive, enforcement-oriented policing was hardly likely to win support amongst the police elite (Jones and Newburn, 2007: 142)—Broken Windows theory perhaps, with its emphasis of prioritizing low-level disorders which communities were typically most concerned with, but not zero tolerance.

Going back to the USA, it was Broken Windows theory, rather than ZTP, which had the longest pedigree. Kelling and Coles (1996: 16–17) trace the theory to Kelling's Newark Foot Patrol Experiment in the mid-1970s. At a time when foot patrol was very much out of fashion with politicians and chief police officers alike—this was, after all, the era of '911 policing'—this research allowed close observation of the work of police officers on foot and it revealed some surprising features of the depth of the role of such officers within local communities:

> Foot patrol officers kept abreast of local problems, assumed special responsibility for particular locations or persons, developed regular sources of information (apartment managers, merchants, street persons), became regulars at local restaurants, checked 'hazards' such as bars...and in other ways came to know and be known on the beats. (Kelling and Coles, 1996: 17)

The research also revealed that foot patrol officers established 'rules of the street' which were accepted and respected by both 'respectable' and 'street' people. These rules covered and controlled behaviours such as 'panhandling', public drinking, and lying down or congregating in public spaces. Not only were officers exerting informal controls within communities—and were respected by local people for doing so—it also meant that much police time was being spent, *to good effect*, on 'non-crime', quality of life, issues:

> Although foot patrol did not reduce the incidence of serious crime, residents of foot-patrolled neighbourhoods felt more secure than did those in other areas...[and] believed crime to have been reduced. (Kelling and Coles, 1996: 18)

What was happening, it was argued, was that the police on foot were controlling *disorderly behaviour*, which if *not* controlled, would generate other problems, including *crime*. Soon after the Newark research was published, Kelling teamed up with James Q Wilson, and together they articulated the findings of the research into a theory: Broken Windows, which they spelt out as follows:

> serious street crime flourishes in areas in which disorderly behaviour goes unchecked. The unchecked panhandler is, in effect, the first broken window.

> Muggers and robbers...believe they reduce their chances of being caught or even identified if they operate on streets where potential victims are already intimidated by prevailing conditions. If the neighbourhood cannot keep a bothersome panhandler from annoying passersby, the thief may reason, it is even less likely to call the police to identify a potential mugger or to interfere if the mugging actually takes place. (quoted in Kelling and Coles, 1996: 20)

Kelling and Coles also identified the prime suspect for creating the conditions under which this process had taken place: *911 Policing*. In a wide-reaching critique of 911 policing (Kelling and Coles, 1996: 89–102) they also claimed that the growth, from the 1960s onwards, of policing based upon rapid response to incidents and car-based patrols, had damaged the former capacity of the police to engage in preventative policing and maintain close working relationships with communities. One consequence was that policing low-level disorders, a vital link in the wider battle against crime, had all but disappeared: Broken Windows were no longer being repaired.

The reception of such aspects of Broken Windows theory, along these lines, by Pollard and others involved in policing policy in Britain, did have an element of irony. Not only had British policing been seduced into adopting unit beat policing in the first place by models (911 policing) coming out from the USA—it was now adopting the *critique* of such policing models in turn! The British police had imported both thesis and antithesis from the USA. What was less readily adopted was what followed Broken Windows theory: ZTP.

Kelling and Coles (1996: 158–9) advocated that the way to 'win back the streets' after the failures of '911 policing' was to employ the policing style of 'aggressive order maintenance'. By 'aggressive' in this context they do not mean physical aggression but rather uncompromising, determined, comprehensive, and relentless approaches to restoring order on the streets. It is this notion of 'aggressive order maintenance' which brings Broken Windows theory into the province of ZTP itself and it is to the experiences of New York City in the 1990s that advocates of ZTP normally relate.

The story (Bratton, 1997; Kelling and Coles, 1996: 108–56) began with the appointment of Rudolph Giuliani as Mayor of New York City. He was appointed after an election battle in which he focused very clearly on restoring order to the city. It started on the underground train system known as the subway. Over the years on the subway, graffiti had increased, disorderly behaviour was rampant and petty crime was evident in all areas. Conditions began to deteriorate and where possible passengers used alternative means of transport. The authorities initiated a 'Clean Car Program', if any of the trains from the subway had any graffiti painted on them, they would be removed from service or cleaned within two hours. The 'taggers' (graffiti artists) would then never see their work or their 'tag', thus reducing the importance and significance to the offenders. Within five years the authorities had gone from a situation where their trains were completely covered in graffiti to one where there was an entirely clean fleet.

With this success behind them, the authorities then moved on to disorder in the subway. At this point Commander William Bratton took over in heading the Transit Police Department having previously worked in Boston. Bratton described graphically his first impressions of New York:

> I remember driving from LaGuardia Airport down the highway into Manhattan. Graffiti, burned-out cars and trash seemed everywhere. It looked like something out of a futuristic movie. Then as you entered Manhattan, you met the unofficial greeter for the City of New York, the Squeegee pest. Welcome to New York. This guy had a dirty rag or squeegee and would wash your window with some dirty liquid and ask for or demand money. Proceeding down Fifth Avenue . . . unlicensed street peddlers and beggars were everywhere. Then down into the subway where every day over 200,000 fare evaders jumped over turnstyles while shakedown artists vandalized turnstyles and demanded that paying passengers hand over their tokens to them. Beggars were on every train. Every platform seemed to have a cardboard city where the homeless had taken residence. This was a city that had stopped caring about itself. (Bratton, 1997: 34)

It was estimated that 2,000 people were sleeping rough in the subways every night. 'Taking Back the Subway' was an initiative to eject disorderly people from the subway. This included informing people of their behaviour, warning them, and ejecting them. Ejections tripled within months. This operation was working in tandem with attempts to stop fare-beating. The results of this were that one in ten people stopped for fare-beating were carrying weapons or held outstanding warrants. A consequence of this was that serious crime was also found to decrease in the subway (Kelling and Coles, 1996: 133). Opportunities for crime were also reduced within the subway using situational measures by changing broken light bulbs and closing rarely used passageways. The subway experience became a much more pleasant experience for the people of New York City and the strategy had reduced both disorder and crime in the subway.

Meanwhile crime was still rampant overhead, in the streets. The subway strategy had become a blueprint for restoring order across the entire city. The first group to be targeted were those involved in 'squeegeeing', people who wait at junctions or traffic lights on the roads and clean the windscreens of cars as they approach. They are usually cleaned without the owner's consent and it is assumed that money will be paid for the job, some are aggressive, use filthy water and intimidate people in their cars. By aggressively policing those involved in squeegeeing, the activity died out within weeks and other groups were then targeted, including others involved in disorderly behaviour. Bratton's approach was strongly oriented to decentralized decision-making and he devolved responsibility for policing to the 76 precinct commanders—in effect what was established was 76 'mini-police departments' (Bratton, 1997: 35). Those commanders were given strict performance targets and had to be prepared to present the results for their area at any time and face challenging questions about their department's performance. The cornerstone of the police operations was the twice weekly Compstat (Comprehensive Computer Statistics) meeting where results were compared area by area. The Compstat process involved, 'timely intelligent data, rapid response of resources, effective tactics and relentless follow-up' (Bratton, 1997: 38). The detailed and demanding accountability of police managers which Compstat created was seen as critical to the effectiveness of the police strategy overall.

Bratton could then point to the results of the New York Police Department's strategy—which *others* rather than Bratton labeled zero tolerance policing—in terms of a 37% drop in the official crime rate between 1994 and 1996 and a drop in the homicide rate of 50% (Bratton, 1997: 40–1). Not surprisingly, the New York experience attracted huge interest from elsewhere, including the UK. As Jones and Newburn (2007: 110–11) have made clear, leaders of both of the major political parties in Britain were keen to demonstrate their enthusiasm for the notion of ZTP. They were fired no doubt by the prospect of any political benefits this model of policing might accrue in the battle over the politics of law and order, given the power of the language which surrounded ZTP within the discourses of 'law and order politics' (as discussed in Chapter 5). Jones and Newburn (2007: 127–8) refer to the stream of 'policy tourists' who beat a path to New York to witness the marvels of the policing in the city, including Jack Straw, then Shadow Home Secretary, who went several times in the mid-1990s. However, politicians did not have to go that far to sample ZTP: Britain had developed its own New York—in Cleveland.

In 1994 Ray Mallon was appointed as a new head of crime strategy in Hartlepool, Cleveland. He set out with a mission to reduce crime by establishing what he subsequently called 'confident policing' (Dennis and Mallon, 1997). In essence 'confident policing' meant 'zero tolerance policing' because it was about tackling low level disorders in an 'assertive' fashion. In an article for *Police Review* (13 September 1996) Mallon explained what this approach was about:

> Criminals, like house burglars, have a career path which starts with anti-social behaviour so we decided to concentrate our resources on tackling that. I told the officers to get intimate with this sort of behaviour and yobs. Where appropriate, they should arrest people, but also just confront them. When they see 10 yobs on a street corner and get abuse they should get out of the patrol car and confront them to let them know we're there. It's a simple strategy that has led to crime figures tumbling down. When you hassle known offenders criminal offences are less likely to happen...It gets the message across that we're there and it brings some discipline to the streets which has been lost.

Mallon and his approach attracted widespread media attention at the time and his message was quickly picked up by those with particular axes to grind, including the right-wing think tank the Institute of Economic Affairs (Dennis (ed), 1997), which had already shown interest in Bratton's policing strategy (Jones and Newburn, 2007: 121). Politicians who had travelled to New York to identify themselves with ZTP there, now headed for the North-East of England to be seen with Mallon and be associated with the populist pull of ZTP, Cleveland style. Michael Howard, then Home Secretary, openly praised Mallon's work (Jones and Newburn, 2007: 111). Jack Straw was also anxious to capture the political capital on offer and both he and the Leader of the Opposition Tony Blair paid a visit to Cleveland. Straw had himself dipped into the ZTP agenda, at least in terms of rhetoric, with his own attack on 'squeezee merchants' and pledged to tackle social disorder:

> In conjunction with tackling the underlying causes of crime, the community has the right to expect more responsible and less anti-social behaviour from its citizens. That means less intimidation, bullying and loutish behaviour on the streets and in our towns and city centres. (Straw, 1995)

Mallon and Bratton became identified as two sides of the same coin, and they and their close colleagues began to exchange ideas with one another, and after a visit to Cleveland in 1996 Bratton declared how 'impressed' he was with Mallon's policing strategy (*Police Review* 13 September 1996). ZTP seemed to be the flavour of the month. However, despite the media clamour surrounding Mallon and the political interest in ZTP, senior police officers in Britain refused to be drawn into the fray. As Pollard was to put it, 'coming down heavy on enforcement is just not best for us' (*Police Review* 28 June 1996). Even when there were isolated schemes, such as those in the Metropolitan Police area and in Strathclyde, which have might have been seen as broadly in line with ZTP, senior officers associated with them were keen to disown the label of 'zero tolerance' (Griffiths, 1997: Orr, 1997).

For this and other reasons Jones and Newburn (2007: 130–42) have urged caution in assuming that ZTP has been part of a process of policy transfer from the USA to Britain. Even where ZTP took root (for a time at least) in Britain, in Cleveland, that was happening on a *parallel* basis rather than a flow of ideas from the USA across the Atlantic—Mallon started his campaign before being exposed to Bratton's system. What is more significant, however, is that ZTP never really established itself as a widespread policy form in Britain. It that sense it does not stand fully as an example of police reform in the way other policy measures discussed in this book have. Nevertheless, policing oriented to tackling low-level disorders *has* become part of the tapestry of British policing. In this respect the case made by Jones and Newburn (2007: 140–2) is highly convincing: that whilst ZTP is not clearly an example of policy transfer *Broken Windows theory* is.

> ... although British policing has not been significantly affected by the political interest in the New York experience, the rise of New Labour's anti-social behaviour agenda does owe something to North American ideas and practices, most particularly to Wilson and Kelling's 'broken windows' thesis. (Jones and Newburn, 2007: 142)

The *Crime and Disorder Act 1998* stands as some expression of this. Amongst other things, the Act launched Labour's 'antisocial behaviour' agenda, with the creation of 'anti-social behaviour orders'. Anti-social behaviour was defined in Section I of the Act as behaviour 'which causes or is likely to cause harassment, alarm or distress', aimed clearly at 'quality of life' issues such as noisy neighbours, rowdy youth, intimidating behaviour, and so on. This agenda was reinforced subsequently by the *Anti-Social Behaviour Act 2003*, a piece of legislation given over almost totally to quality of life problems and 'solutions'. This was closely associated with the *'Respect'* agenda, concerned amongst other things with 'respecting the street and public places' (Home Office, 2003b: Foreword). The addition to this package of 'reassurance policing', which also emerged in the wider police reform programme of the early years of the twenty-first century and which focused on improving citizen confidence and sense of safety (discussed in Chapter 5), was further evidence of the permeation of 'Broken Windows' thinking—coupled with the ethos of POP—around British policing.

The influence of American ideas about and practices of policing on British policing policy and police reform should thus be apparent. Policing by objectives, problem-oriented policing and Broken Windows theory, all American inspirations, have each left their mark on the British policing scene and the mindset of those responsible for policing policy, within and without the police service. There have also been other policy initiatives which have found their way across the Atlantic. *Neighbourhood Watch* schemes, whereby the citizen becomes the 'eyes and ears' of the police in terms of keeping watch on their own neighbourhood and which involved various forms of police-community mobilization programmes, began in Britain in the early 1980s and by the mid-1990s had totalled over 130,000 individual schemes (Laycock and Tilley, 1995). The notion of neighbourhood watch originated in the USA in the mid-1970s (Washnis, 1976) and was then 'imported' into Britain as a new means of involving citizens in crime prevention activities (Husain, 1988). Similarly the now nationwide *Crime Stoppers* programme, whereby citizens can offer information on unsolved crimes anonymously by phone or on-line, and which involved joint working between the police and the media to access the public, began in the UK in 1988 but originated as a concept in the USA in the late 1970s (Lippert, 2002). One can also detect an American influence in changes in the way the British police began investigating rape in the 1980s. In the wake of the controversy following the broadcast of the 'fly-on-the-wall' series *Police*, based on the Thames Valley Police—where detectives investigating the case treated the woman making the allegation virtually as a suspect—Ian Blair, then as a middle-ranking officer, visited the USA to see how the police operated in the treatment of rape victims. He found practices there much more oriented to treating rape victims *as* victims and wrote up his findings in a book (Blair, 1985), that was itself to be influential in developments such as the establishment of victim examination suites (Gregory and Lees, 1999). The influence of American ideas and practices on British policing ranges far and wide. Although American influences are also apparent in other European policing systems—such as in the Netherlands, which has also picked up on models such as POP, Broken Windows theory, and elements of ZTP (Punch, van der Vijver, and Zoomer, 2002)—the linkage back to Britain has been particularly strong.

However, if American ideas and practices stand out as the major overseas influences on British policing they are not the only such source. Influences from policing initiatives from neighbouring policing systems, although less extensive than those emanating from the USA, can also be identified.

Closer to Home: Policy Transfer from Neighbouring Systems

British policing has not tended to draw widely from models and best practice in policing from its neighbouring policing systems in Europe. This is due to a number of factors, including the differing legal and justice frameworks within which most European countries operate (inquisitorial rather than adversarial judicial systems; the subordination of the police to the public prosecutor, and so on (Pakes, 2004)), differing structures of policing in Europe (in most cases involving a national policing system and the direct control of policing by central government) and, of course, language barriers. However, it could be argued that one area of police reform in Britain did have some roots in the wider Europe, in this case from the *Netherlands* and involving *police community support officers*.

Going Dutch: The Emergence of Police Community Support Officers

The police in the Netherlands have a long tradition of community-based policing and have experimented extensively with differing means of furthering community policing (Punch et al, 2002). In the 1990s two 'policing' forms were established by some local authorities in the Netherlands which were set up to enhance the quality and extent of visible policing, and develop policing in a way which was more closely in touch with local communities and their concerns (Hauber et al 1996). On the one hand there were the *Stadswacht* or 'city wardens', and on the other the *Politiesurveillant* or 'police patrollers'.

The city wardens were created in 1989 and the role exploited the general right of Dutch citizens to act in ways to uphold the law. They did not have any of the formal powers of a police officer and their duties involved providing information and assistance to the public and intervening to 'talk' to perpetrators of offences. In some towns and cities the city wardens wore uniforms, in others not. In some cases the management of the wardens was undertaken directly by the police, in others by police officers working for the city authorities on secondment, but in general they worked closely with the local police—they were to be the 'eyes and ears' of the police (Morgan and Newburn, 1997: 168). The 'police patrollers', set up during the early 1990s, were given the general powers of the regular police officer but were created as a new 'lower rank' of officer one rung below the 'normal' police constable (Hauber et al, 1996). Their purpose is to increase citizens' feelings of safety by providing visible 'surveillance' on the streets. They patrol on their own or in pairs and are tasked to assist the 'normal' police with mainstream public order policing, helping the public with information and various traffic control duties. They wear full police uniform, with the exception of a distinguishing badge, carry radios, and handcuffs but unlike the full constable, do not carry firearms (Morgan and Newburn, 1997: 168).

Morgan and Newburn (1997: 164–70) proposed that the Dutch system of *auxiliary policing* should be considered positively as a means of enhancing the visibility of patrols in the British context, in the light of public demand for more visible policing and the constraints on police expenditure, and they advocated that experiments should be undertaken on such auxiliary policing schemes by local authorities in Britain. Their preference was for the 'police patroller' model rather than the city warden (Morgan and Newburn, 1997: 168). Their examination of auxiliary patrolling mirrored the review of police patrols which had been undertaken by the Audit Commission (Audit Commission, 1996) and which will be considered in the following chapter. As shall be seen, the Audit Commission concluded that the creation of auxiliary patrols was not viable, even if attractive in some ways. However, the case for auxiliary patrols was not going away. Although highly sensitive politically, not least with the Police Federation, representing the rank and file of the service, who were ready to jump on any scheme for auxiliary policing with the accusation of 'policing on the cheap'. What the schemes in the Netherlands offered in this context was evidence of how auxiliary policing might be set up and to what effect.

The new Labour government elected in 1997 came in with determined plans for police reform, even if, for the reasons outlined in Chapter 5, they were cautious in advancing them too assertively during their early years. However, a number of visits to the Netherlands were made by Home Office officials in the late 1990s to review the operation of auxiliary patrol in a number of Dutch cities. Similar visits were also made by officers from the MPS and it does seem that at the very least, what was to follow in Britain in terms of auxiliary policing was 'inspired' by developments in the Netherlands (Jones and Newburn, 2006: 46). Neighbourhood warden schemes were boosted in 2000 with a joint funding initiative by the Home Office and the Department of Environment, Transport and the Regions (Jones and Newburn, 2006: 46) but the major push for auxiliary policing came with the Government's White Paper on police reform, *Policing a New Century: A Blueprint for Reform* (Home Office, 2001b). The White Paper is discussed at more length in Chapter 5, but for the purposes of this discussion one proposal was significant. It was announced that police support staff, under the command and control of the chief officer, will 'be given powers enabling them to carry out a basic patrolling function in the community, providing an increased and visible presence and exercising the powers necessary to deal with anti-social behaviour and minor disorder' (Home Office 2001b: 31). They would become known as '*community support officers*' (CSOs), later '*police community support officers*' (PCSOs). The White Paper also proposed that staff from outside the police service would also have similar powers, subject to them being 'accredited' by the police (Home Office, 2001b: 31). The then Home Secretary, David Blunkett, explained the role of auxiliary officers as ensuring that the regular police 'can use the eyes and ears and the presence of other people to enhance and support the surveillance and communication which the police need' (*Police Review* 7 December 2001).

The proposal was met with much hostility, most predictably by the Police Federation, which, as has been noted, could label the CSO scheme 'policing on the cheap' and the start of 'two-tier policing'—a survey undertaken by the Federation of local Federation branches found that 29 out of 31 branches responding were opposed to the idea (*Police Review* 26 April 2002). The Conservative Shadow Home Secretary ridiculed the idea of CSOs as being about 'plastic officers doing plastic jobs' (*Police Review* 24 May 2002). However, the initiative was welcomed at senior levels within the police service. In part this was instrumental, as Chris Fox, ACPO spokesperson on community policing, indicated: 'We want more police officers and that is what the public tells us, but if there is no money for officers and there is money for CSOs then the majority of chiefs will work within that' (*Police Review* 26 April 2002). However, some were more philosophical about the significance of the notion of CSOs. Sir Ian Blair, then Deputy Commissioner of the Metropolitan Police Service, had taken part in a Home Office working party on neighbourhood wardens and that, as well as his role on the MPS (one of the early adopters of the scheme), made him one of the architects of the CSO framework. He claimed that the CSO development heralded nothing less than a 'new era in policing', stating 'We have reached a watershed in the evolution of the system of command and control and law enforcement. One system of policing ends and another one takes its place' (*Police Review* 29 November 2002). This 'new era' was alluded to in the MPS response to the 2001 White Paper, which, broadly supportive of the Government's proposals, referred to auxiliary officers and other 'accredited' officers as part of the *'extended police family'* (Metropolitan Police Service 2001). Ian Blair had coined a term which was to become part of the new vocabulary associated with this 'new era' of policing. If policing was to be delivered increasingly by a *range* of workers, regular officers, auxiliaries under police command, volunteers, local authority employees and private security staff, along the lines of what has in academic terms been called *'plural policing'* and the 'mixed economy of policing' (Crawford et al, 2005; Jones and Newburn, (eds), 2006), it was not to be a matter of the *fragmentation* of policing. The notion of the 'extended police family' was designed to counter the assumption that the existence and growth of multiple providers of policing services necessarily means the fragmentation of policing, because it paints a picture, however fanciful, of a possible *unity* between providers and a sense of common purpose, both no doubt made possible by having the public police in charge.

Whichever way, the CSO initiative was now well and truly anchored in government and police thinking. A number of force areas were used as trials for the

CSO scheme (including the MPS—see Johnston et al, 2004) starting in the summer of 2002, and the *Police Reform Act 2002* gave the legislative framework for what were by now called Police Community Support Officers to go nationwide. The model of auxiliary patrol which was to emerge, one which, as will be made clear in Chapter 5 was to become a key part of Labour's wider police reform programme and particularly the 'public reassurance' agenda, was broadly along the lines of the schemes in the Netherlands but in a hybrid way. If we take the Dutch schemes of city warden and police patroller, the PCSO model probably lies somewhere between them, in the sense that they were *not* given the general powers of a regular police officer like the police patroller, but they were to be much more an integral part of the *police organization* than were the city wardens in the Netherlands, because they were under the authority of the chief officer. PCSOs were given limited powers—to detain someone until a constable arrives, to direct traffic and remove vehicles, and to issue fixed penalty notices for 'anti-social behaviour' (see Chapter 5). PCSOs are now very much part of the British police scenery (Johnston, 2005). Indeed the concept was subsequently extended to the police *investigative* function, with the creation of *investigative support officers*, auxiliary officers who support detective work with tasks such as statement taking (Home Office, 2006b—see also Chapter 3). The a*uxiliarization* of the British police was now well and truly entrenched.

Other sources of 'overseas' influences on British police reform were also to come from somewhere much closer than mainland Europe, indeed from somewhere not even technically 'abroad': Northern Ireland.

The Irish Solution: Patten and Police Reform

In the Introduction to this book it was made clear, given the unique and specific circumstances surrounding it, that police reform in Northern Ireland would not be included in the framework of police reforms discussed in this study. However, police reform in Northern Ireland is significant in another way: as a source of *influence* over police reform in the rest of Britain. It has been argued for some time that Northern Ireland has been a form of testing ground for policing in Britain but primarily in terms of *repressive* policing and legislation, grown out of policing and controlling terrorism, which then finds its way back across the water to the rest of Britain (Hillyard, 1997). As Mulcahy (2005) has argued, this thesis needs qualifying, not least in the light of the possibility that some of the lessons from Northern Ireland might be more *positive* than the testing ground theory assumes. In particular, Mulcahy cites the work of the Patten Commission and its advocacy of 'human rights policing' and new forms of accountability as an example of this (Mulcahy, 2005: 204–5). In 1998, as part of the Good Friday Peace Agreement, the *Independent Commission on Policing in Northern Ireland*—which became known as the *Patten Commission*—was established with the goal of serving to develop what in the words of the Agreement was 'a police service capable of attracting and sustaining support from the community as a whole' (Patten, 1999: 4). Of course the primary focus for the Commission was the past and future of policing in Northern Ireland, but in many ways it became something of a 'Royal Commission on policing', not just for Northern Ireland but for policing more generally. It was an opportunity to stand back and review policing as a concept and consider the range of alternatives available to secure good policing in democratic societies. It was particularly useful for generating ideas about policing in the rest of Britain, because although policing in Northern Ireland had its own distinctive features (Mulcahy, 2006), it did share much in common with policing elsewhere in Britain, making the Patten Commission's work of great significance across the water (and, some have argued, for the South of Ireland as well (Irish Council for Civil Liberties, 2003). The potential impact of Patten on wider police reform was made even more likely given the Commission's membership, which included progressive thinkers on policing, both academic (such as Clifford Shearing) and professional (such as Sir John Smith, former Deputy Commissioner of the MPS). The Commission reported in 1999 and contained recommendations on a wide range of policing matters (Patten, 1999). Three aspects of those recommendations were particularly significant for police reform in other parts of Britain.

Firstly, Patten endorsed fully the role of the *Police Ombudsman* for Northern Ireland as a cornerstone of police accountability, which had been recommended by the Hayes Report on police complaints (Hayes, 1997), and which was made responsible for the independent investigation of complaints against the police (as discussed in Chapter 1). Furthermore, Patten recommended that the scope of the Ombudsman's office be extended to enable it to 'take initiatives, not merely react to specific complaints received. He/she should exercise the power to initiate inquiries or investigations even if no specific complaint has been received.' (Patten, 1999: 37). This opened up the possibility that the independent oversight body might also have a role in influencing *police policy* and not just be restricted to dealing with complaints. However, Patten's endorsement of the Ombudsman model added weight to the case for a fully independent system for the investigation of complaints against the police for England and Wales, a case which had been building for some time but which was boosted by the Macpherson Inquiry into the death of Stephen Lawrence, which the Patten Report itself acknowledged (Patten, 1999: 37fn) and which was discussed in Chapter 1. Both Patten's endorsement of the Ombudsman model, and the fact that the Police Ombudsman stood as an example of a fully functioning independent investigative body which appeared to work, could not but help the case for an independent investigative body for England and Wales.

In due course the *Police Reform Act 2002* created the Independent Police Complaints Commission (IPCC), which became operational in 2004 (see Chapter 1). If not a case of policy transfer form Northern Ireland—the momentum after Macpherson seemed unstoppable—it was at least a case of 'lesson learning', as outlined earlier. The lesson was that independent investigation of police complaints can be undertaken effectively—given the right conditions—thus undermining the long-standing concern amongst critics of the idea that it was not practically viable. It was also, perhaps, Patten's recommendation that the Ombudsman adopt a *policy* function which lay behind the decision by the government to grant the IPCC the role of 'guardianship'. The *Reform Act* decreed that the IPCC remit extend beyond the investigation of specific complaints against the police and embrace a 'guardianship role' which has been defined as 'those aspects of this responsibility to increase public confidence that do not relate specifically to its own investigative and casework functions'. (IPCC, 2007). Guardianship was to have four elements, which mirror closely the recommendations for the Northern Ireland Ombudsman presented by Patten (Patten, 1999: 37–8):

- Setting, improving, reviewing, monitoring, and inspecting standards for the operation of the police complaints system;
- Promoting confidence in the complaints system as a whole amongst the public, and national and regional stakeholders;
- Ensuring the accessibility of the complaints system; and
- Promoting policing excellence by drawing out and feeding back lessons arising from the IPCC's work (IPCC, 2007).

The decision to grant the IPCC a 'guardianship' role further strengthens the machinery of what has been called 'regulatory governance' or the 'regulatory state' (Hood et al, 1999), discussed in Chapters 3 and 5. In the development of that machinery no small part was played by the Northern Ireland experience. However, this was not the only example of arrangements for police accountability in Northern Ireland having influence elsewhere in Britain. The second area of recommendations from Patten to find their way across the water related to *localized accountability*.

One of the key recommendations from Patten was that accountability mechanisms *below* the level of regional level accountability structures (provided by the 'Policing Board', also one of Patten's reforms) should be developed in Northern Ireland:

> The Policing Board will be the central institution for democratic accountability. But an important theme of this report is that policing should be decentralised, and that there should be constant dialogue at local levels between the police and the community. (Patten, 1999: 34)

The report recommended the establishment of *district policing partnerships boards* (DPPBs), one for each District Council, and coinciding with police District Command Units—the Northern Ireland version of Basic Command Units (as discussed in Chapter 3)—which would be 'advisory, explanatory and consultative'. The membership of the DPPBs would involve just over half elected members, reflecting the balance of the District Council, with the remainder being independent members representing business and trade union interests and others with expertise in community safety. They were to have more 'teeth' than the existing police-community consultative committees (see Chapter 1) and, in addition to providing forums for information exchange and consultation, were to have a role in helping set *local policing priorities* with the divisional command team. The proposal was rolled out during 2003/4 with the establishment of 26 DPPBs across the region (Northern Ireland Affairs Committee, 2005: 1).

However, the notion of DPPBs did not stop at Northern Ireland. One senior police officer, Peter Neyroud, had argued that the Patten/DPPB model should be given serious consideration for England and Wales, and could move local involvement in policing beyond what is possible with the established scheme of Police Community Consultative Groups (PCCGs—see Chapter 1):

> The Patten proposals [on DPPBs] seem to provide a building block worth developing [in England and Wales]. ... The key shift that Patten has provided is from a passive meeting that receives information (the PCCG) to an active, statutory body that has both a clear remit to hold local communities to account and some scope ... to add a significant local twist to the priorities of policing. (Neyroud, 2001: 15)

Drawing on Patten, the West Mercia Police Authority (where Neyroud had been Deputy Chief Constable) had changed its local consultation framework from PCCGs to local Policing Boards along the lines of the DPPBs recommended by Patten. Furthermore in the government's Green Paper *Policing: Building Safer Communities Together* (Home Office, 2003a: 23) a framework for governance was set out which proposed three levels of police accountability: *neighbourhood panels* (to operate at the level of the 'parish' associated with 'neighbourhood policing teams'—see Chapter 5); *local policing partnerships/community safety boards*; and the *strategic policing boards* (to operate at the level of the police force). It is the 'local policing partnerships' proposal which most closely follows the DPPB model. It was proposed that they operate at the level of the Basic Command Unit and build on the work which was already being undertaken by the Crime and Disorder Reduction Partnerships (CDRPs), set up by the *Crime and Disorder Act 1998* which brought together the various agencies involved in furthering community safety (Fielding, 2005: 127–8). The subsequent White Paper *Building Communities, Beating Crime* (Home Office, 2004b), in making a case for more 'community engagement' in policing (see Chapter 5), reinforced this view by proposing that there be a new 'requirement for CDRPs to *oversee the delivery of neighbourhood level priorities* agreed with local communities' (Home Office, 2004b: 68—emphasis added). This was essentially the mode and level of accountability which lay behind the DPPBs in Northern Ireland, and which prioritized community engagement in local policing priority setting and police–community consultation at the level of the police command unit. Another Patten recommendation had been reflected in the police reform programme for England and Wales.

The third area of influence of the Patten recommendations will be noted here because it is discussed in more detail in Chapter 5. It was stated earlier that one reason why developments in policing in Northern Ireland 'travel easily' across the water to England and Wales is that the policing systems have much in common. One such common element has been the principle of 'operational independence', the constitutional thesis built up over time that chief officers in Britain are fully independent of political authority when it comes to matters of policing policy and operational matters (Savage, Charman, and Cope, 2000: 193–6). The concept was deemed to apply to all chief officers in Britain, including the Chief Constable of Northern Ireland. Patten challenged the notion of 'operational independence' head on and recommended that it be formally replaced with very different doctrine of 'operational responsibility' (Patten, 1999: 32). Although this particular recommendation was not adopted in subsequent reforms in Northern Ireland, the 'sanctity' of the principle of 'operational independence' had been split open by Patten, a matter of significance for policing in the rest of Britain. As will be seen in Chapter 5, and as anticipated by Savage, Charman, and Cope (2000: 207), Patten's alternative concept of the 'operational responsibility' of chief officers was also to emerge in Labour's 'radical' police reform programme in the early years of the twenty-first century.

In these ways developments in Northern Ireland have had an impact on policing, or at least thinking about policing, elsewhere in Britain. Taken together with policy transfer from the Netherlands, and the wider-reaching policy influences coming out of the USA, it can be seen that police reform in Britain has been shaped in part by 'imports' from abroad. However, it has not all been one-way traffic. It would be misleading to end this discussion with consideration only of policy transfer *into* Britain. In the final part of this chapter it is appropriate to reflect on policy transfer *out* of Britain: *export policing*.

Export Policing: British Policing Models on the Move

It has already been noted that policing models can 'travel' through international channels of communication and networking, such as the International Association of Chiefs of Police. *British* models of policing can travel in just this way. As shall be seen below, British models of police investigation have indeed been influential on approaches taken in other countries and this has come about, in part, through international conferences and seminars focused on the topic. However, British policing models have also travelled through other mechanisms. Of course, one way in which, historically, British policing has been 'exported' was through British imperialism, when countries coming under the British Empire had policing forms imposed on them with the explicit function of maintaining control and imposing discipline within the colonies, such as Ireland and Hong Kong. A task facing police reform programmes in the former colonies has been how to move *away* from those British models of policing, and shed the legacies of colonial policing and its ethos of coercion and control (Anderson and Killingray (eds), 1992). That form of 'export policing' has since given way to a very different framework within which British policing models can be 'shipped abroad': through *international aid* programmes. British governments, as with other governments in the developed countries (Bayley, 2001), have, through agencies such as the Department for International Affairs (DFID), engaged in extensive aid programmes around the globe to challenge poverty and/or to assist post-conflict and transitional societies in economic, political, and social regeneration. One dimension of these programmes has been 'security sector reform' (see DFID, 2005), which includes *reforming the police*. In this respect one policing model above all has 'travelled': *community-oriented policing*.

Community-Oriented Policing: British Policing Styles Reinvented Abroad

Brogden and Nijhar (2005: 1–10) have documented how community-oriented policing (COP), as well as being central to Anglo-American police thinking and policing styles, has also become the dominant policing model which some overseas aid programmes have sought to implement in restoring order in 'failed', transitional and post-conflict societies; as they state with some flourish:

> ... it is in *failed* and *transitional* societies that COP is the new cargo cult, as the Western missionaries promote a policing elixir that will resolve a range of social ills. Where such societies are characterised by rising recorded crime rates ... [and] by delegitimation of older criminal justice agencies ... police reform is perceived as the essential bedrock of social and economic progress. In that theatre of social change, COP is cast to play a key role. (Brogden and Nijhar, 2005: 3—emphasis in original)

Aid programmes from donor countries to transitional societies will often prioritize *police reform* as being critical to developing the social stability and order necessary for economic growth and the move towards democracy. Police reform can take many forms, as can be seen throughout this book, but a core component of reform programmes within transitional societies, as encouraged and furthered by donor countries through financial support and the direct engagement of overseas personnel from donor countries in consultancy and training, is COP. Brodgen and Nijhar (2005: 9–13) talk of the '*globalization*' of COP, facilitated by the involvement of Western—mainly North American and Northern European—states in the processes of furthering police reform in other nation states, ranging from Central and Eastern Europe post- the collapse of the Soviet Union, through to sub-Saharan Africa and onwards to South and East Asia (Brogden and Nijhar, 2005: 84–104).

However, it is the specific role of *Britain* and of British policing models in furthering the development of COP in other countries, which is of most significance. This can operate through British participation in international aid organisations which have police reform on their agendas. A notable example of this is *Saferworld*, a London-based aid agency which has been highly active in

Africa, Central and Eastern Europe, and South-East Asia. *Saferworld* is an independent, non-governmental body which works to prevent armed violence and create 'safer communities'; one of its main goals is 'to develop integrated security sector reform and access to justice strategies that are able to enhance safety and security for local communities' (Saferworld, 2007). Central to this goal are programmes of police reform and a core feature of those programmes is COP. In a set of guidelines on police reform issued jointly by *Saferworld* and the *International Peace Academy* (Groenewald and Peake, 2004: 3–4), the central role of COP within development strategies is made clear:

> Community-based police reform can contribute to a wide poverty reduction strategy . . . Community-based policing, through its partnership approach, aims to ensure that the safety and security needs of all groups in a particular community are addressed. In this way, the police can facilitate people's access to justice, regardless of their social or economic status. Addressing local needs while effectively combating crime improves safety and security, and with it, strengthens the conditions for development to take place.

With this 'orthodoxy' as a basis for its police reform activities—some measure of the 'globalization of COP' which Brogden and Nijhar have identified—*Saferworld* coordinates training and consultancy operations in developing and transitional societies, including the use of British experts, such as serving and retired police officers. In doing this it works closely with British governmental agencies which have a statutory brief to provide development support overseas. This relates to the more direct means by which British ideas about policing can be influential abroad. As has been noted, a core concern of DFID is 'Security Sector Reform' (DFID, 2005) and central to that process is police reform. Working often closely with the British Council—which tends to focus its support of development in the policing context by sponsoring exchanges of officers and study visits by officers and policing experts—DFID has supported a wide range of police reform programmes as part of its wider assistance agendas for developing countries. In this context, COP again makes an appearance. For example, in its *Human Rights Review* of 2004 (DFID, 2004: 62), the role of COP is identified as part and parcel of the pursuit of 'responsive and accountable policing':

> DFID's focus on accessibility and responsiveness to the needs of the port has encouraged the development of various activities to facilitate communication between justice institutions and local communities, for example, through the adoption of a community-policing model.

The *Review* cites one case of this in practice, the Bangladesh Public Access to Justice Project in 1999, one part of which aimed 'to increase police efficiency and responsiveness through training, in particular on investigations [and] implementation of a community policing approach.' (DFID, 2004: 63). COP appears to be part of what British governments 'export' when their agencies work abroad on policing projects. Brogden and Nijhar have argued that this has evidently been the case in support given to post-Apartheid South Africa, where the UK and Commonwealth Advisory Team undertook an extensive, and expensive, programme of community policing projects (Brogden and Nijhar, 2005: 12), and also in the Ukraine, where the British Council employed British experts to attempt to develop community policing in that state, clearly not an easy or even viable task (Brogden and Nijhar, 2005: 194).

However, not all British development projects around police reform set out so explicitly to implant COP in the countries receiving assistance; they probably don't need to. The people that are commissioned by DFID and the British Council to work on the reform programmes have in most cases themselves already accepted the orthodoxy of the virtues of COP. The former police officers and seconded officers who undertake much of the reform work overseas for DFID and the British Council will themselves have been brought up as police officers within the 'post-Scarman' consensus (Reiner, 1991; see also Chapter 1)—COP will be in their blood. It would be difficult to imagine police experts from Britain working on overseas projects *not* advocating COP when they have the opportunity to do so. Those retired and seconded officers—and perhaps their academic counterparts who also are brought in to support police reform projects in developing countries—will be key agents for the exportation of British policing models abroad, what Jones and Newburn (2007: 128) have called 'policy tourists', although they would be tourists on commission. The gentle steer from HM Government to push police reform in developing or transitional countries in the direction of COP would normally be matched by a mission of those out in the field of reform to move things along in the direction of COP. The outcome can be a reformed policing system or a policing ethos bearing remarkable similarities to British policing back home.

A case in hand of this is the Botswana Police Service. The Botswana Police—note at that stage referred to by title as a 'service'—were the subject of an assistance programme from the British government which started in the late 1990s and which had two primary dimensions. On the one hand the British High Commission in Botswana sponsored a programme of management development, focused mainly on an organizational change programme around organizational 'mission' and identity, management structures, and performance management regime. A new 'top team' of the Botswana Police emerged, most of whom, significantly, had also attended courses at Bramshill Police College in Hampshire, England. The second dimension involved a training development programme, funded by the British Council, and using the services of Centrex, formerly National Police Training, the national police training and development agency for England and Wales. This part of the reform programme was targeted at training methods and styles, and used former staff from training schools in the UK, and also academic advisors (of which the author was one). After a period of more than four years, the programme was completed. What was left in place was a new model of policing, core elements of which were remarkably familiar. The Botswana Police formally changed its name to the Botswana

Police *Service* (shades of what happened with the MPS in the 1980s here). It had adopted a new *vision* which read: 'We, the Botswana Police Service, are committed to providing a professional law enforcement service for a peaceful, safe, and secure nation, *in partnership with the community*' (Botswana Police Service, 2003: v).

Reference was made in the organization's Mission Statement of the goal of maintaining 'security and public tranquillity' and of 'increasing public confidence in the police by developing a community style of policing which entails both consultation and partnership with the community' (2003: v). Emphasis was to be placed on foot patrols and beat patrol areas, and on 'problem' solving approaches to crime prevention (2003: 17), use is to be made of 'community consultative forums' (2003: 23) and 'partnership' was identified as core to the community policing strategy (2003: 24). Of course, some aspects of the new policing approach adopted by the Botswana Police may reflect policy *convergence*—such as problem-solving approaches, which is an international development in policing—but the language and ethos of what became the new policing philosophy of the Botswana Police is clearly strongly 'British' in orientation. This is but one example of a process of policy transfer, in this case COP, as policing exported out of Britain and into states receiving assistance from Britain. Police reform and police policies have moved outward as well as inward.

However, it is not only COP which has been 'exported' from Britain. The DFID Human Rights Review mentioned earlier also made reference to another policing approach which had been developed mainly in Britain and had since been shipped overseas. Referring to police reform under DFID in Malawi, note was made of:

> ...training of the police to operate in the new constitutional order and meet new standards, integrated as part of the police reform programme. This includes training in *investigative interviewing techniques* to avoid excessive use of force and torture in gathering evidence. (DFID, 2004: 62—emphasis added)

This relates to another area of 'export policing' coming out of Britain: police *investigative interviewing*. If investigation is a core function of policing, then interviewing is a primary tool in the investigative process. As a consequence the ability to undertake interviews is a critical issue for policing: 'The investigative task is [a] core aspect of policing today and what emerges from that core task is the key element of the ability to interview.' (Evans and Webb, 1993: 37).

Investigative Interviewing: Exporting Investigative Technique

It is interesting that of the range of measures taken by Britain's Foreign and Commonwealth Office to undertake security sector reform and peace support in post-War Iraq, one was training for the Iraqi police in *interviewing techniques* (Defence Select Committee 2005). Training in police interview techniques in the form of 'investigative interviewing'—which, as shall be seen, is an approach to police interviewing which amongst other things emphasizes the humane and non-oppressive treatment of suspects, and an open-minded approach to investigations—is something which became part of the armoury of reform measures HM Government could offer as part of police reform programmes overseas, including DFID's reform framework, as indicated above. Police organizations in receipt of British assistance would, as part of a police reform programme, be offered the opportunity to develop their investigative capacity by accessing an interview training model, known as PEACE (see below), which had become a standard feature of training for police investigators in Britain as a means of getting the principles of investigative interviewing across. Police forces in developing countries, that had in the recent past, as matter of routine, forced confessions out of suspects through force, were now being advised and encouraged to turn to an approach to police interviews (*not* police 'interrogations') which even the police in North America were finding too 'gentle' for their own purposes (St-Yves, 2007).

Investigative interviewing, however, is not only being 'exported' from Britain through overseas assistance programmes. Two international conferences, the first in Canada in 2004 and the second in the UK in 2006, brought together academics and practitioners from many developed countries to further the cause of investigative interviewing nationally and internationally, and in particular to attempt to draw up international protocols for the approach for adoption in various nation states (Milne, Savage, and Williamson, (eds) 2007). An international network for the growth of investigative interviewing had emerged. So what was so significant about investigative interviewing?

The background to investigative interviewing in Britain lies with the miscarriages of justice during the late 1970s and 1980s and the legislation of police powers which followed in their wake, as discussed in the previous chapter. These events and developments served to place police interview methods in the spotlight, not least because, with the tape-recording of interviews with suspects which came about as a result of miscarriages of justice, those techniques became more transparent and open to public scrutiny (Milne, Shaw, and Bull, 2007). As a consequence the *training* on which police interviews are to be based also came into focus. A training framework was available in the form of the 'Reid' model (named because it was developed by the Reid Organisation) (Buckley, 2006) which still has currency in North America (St-Yves, 2007), and, at one time, was influential in British investigative practice (Walkley, 1987)—but this was hardly a model to inspire those more oriented to human rights policing, given that it suggested, amongst other things:

- The 'interrogator' tells the suspect from the outset that they have committed the offence, and if the police have no evidence that this is so the interrogator should pretend that they do
- The interrogator is to stop denials from the suspect by persistently interrupting those denials and telling them to listen

- When it looks as if the suspect's resistance is breaking down the interrogator is to show signs of sympathy and understanding
- The suspect is encouraged to make self-incriminating admissions by being asked to choose from two highly incriminating options.

Not surprisingly perhaps, commentators have challenged this approach to interviewing on the grounds of its over-reliance on confessions—rather than on what might actually have happened—and its vulnerability to false confessions (Gudjonsson, 2006). At some points it does indeed amount to encouraging trickery on behalf of the police interviewer. In the British context, stirred to move in particular by research highly critical of the standards of police interviews then applying (Baldwin, 1992), the Home Office, with ACPO, set out in the early 1990s to develop an alternative model for interview training, one more oriented to the '*search for the truth*' and '*open investigations*' (Milne, Shaw, and Bull, 2007). The model to emerge was in many ways the opposite of the Reid model: *investigative interviewing*. Crawshaw, Cullen, and Williamson (2007: 249) summarize the investigative interviewing approach as involving:

- Keeping an open mind, searching for the truth and the gathering of as much reliable information as possible
- Conducting thorough pre-interview investigations and information gathering before the interview is conducted
- Thorough preparation and planning prior to the interview
- Establishing a rapport with the interviewee and treating the interviewee with respect and cultural sensitivity
- Allowing the interviewee 'free recall' of events without interruption
- Starting with 'open-ended' questions before moving to more closed/focused questions
- Trying to achieve a positive 'closure' to the interview so as not to jeopardize any future interactions between the interviewer and interviewee

Clearly this model was not based on the investigative style of DCI Gene Hunt of *Life on Mars*. In fact it drew in part on the framework developed by two American psychologists Fisher and Geiselman (1992) and subsequently advanced by British psychologists (Milne, Shaw, and Bull, 2007), the *cognitive interview* (CI). The CI is a technique for interviewing which allows the interviewee to recall events and things in their own way and at their own pace and then uses 'memory enhancing tools' to maximize recall and the quality and quality of information from the interviewee. Investigative interviewing also drew from other British psychological research on 'conversation management', which aimed to find ways in which interviewers could overcome resistance in interviews (Shepherd, 1988).

For practical purposes, ACPO and the Home Office sought to translate the principles of investigative interviewing and the notion of the CI into a technical model and training package which could be used as a national basis for achieving standards across the police service in interview skills. Although there would subsequently be a number of levels or 'tiers' at which this training would be pitched, ranging from introductory/awareness levels to levels appropriate for specialists (Milne, Shaw, and Bull, 2007), the main instrument to emerge was to become known as the '*PEACE*' model (National Crime Faculty, 1996). PEACE is an acronym—always popular in police training as a learning tool—for the main stages of conducting an investigative interview, which were to be:

Planning and preparation: getting ready for the interview, gathering information, analysing evidence, clarifying legal frameworks for the interview, etc.

Engaging and explanation: establishing rapport with the interviewee and explaining the purpose of the interview, etc.

Account: the process of allowing the interviewee to present their own account, including the use of CI techniques

Closure: ensuring that there is mutual understanding of what has taken place, checking that the issues have been covered and what will happen in the future

Evaluation: evaluating the information obtained during interview, how the information sits within the overall investigation and how well the interview was undertaken (self-evaluation)

The PEACE model was duly rolled out across England and Wales through nationwide programmes of 'PEACE training' (Crawshaw, Cullen, and Willamson, 2007: 251–8). The model, conveniently simple and easily translated into training packages, was subsequently to become a part of what was referred to earlier as the 'exporting' of British police thinking on investigative interviewing through overseas assistance programmes. However, investigative interviewing itself has also been 'exported', through the international network cited above, to developed countries as well. Fahsing (2007) has documented how in Norway, following a case revealed in court as being based on a false confession (after an interview by a police officer thought to be one of the best interviewers on the country), conditions were created which demanded changes in the way in which police interviews with suspects were undertaken. One police officer was seconded to the UK to undertake postgraduate study in forensic psychology and visits were made to Norway by British academics specializing in investigative interviewing. This eventually led to the launch of pilot schemes for the training of police investigators along the lines of the PEACE model. Investigative interviewing was subsequently rolled out nationally as the core model on which such training and practice would be based, as it was also in other Nordic countries (Fahsing, 2007). Given its close association with humane treatment of suspects and 'ethical investigation' (Denmark, 2005), investigative interviewing seems destined to spread even further as policing systems seek to ally themselves more closely with human rights-based and ethics-based policing (Neyroud and Beckley, 2001).

This chapter has focused on the movement of policing policies and 'thinking about policing' between and across nation states. The policies in question have been the subject of varying degrees of *policy transfer, lesson learning*, and *policy convergence*. These processes often overlap and combine. Policing policies which emerge in one nations state may have taken the *forms* they have because of policy transfer and lesson learning, whereby ideas and practices in the policing field are 'picked up' by policy entrepreneurs and imported elsewhere; however, the deeper forces of policy *convergence* may have created the *conditions* for their acceptance elsewhere. Two cases from earlier discussions in this chapter illustrate this point. PCSOs may have appeared in Britain because of practical models on display in the Netherlands which could provide indications of what *form* auxiliary policing might take—in that sense the policy came through policy transfer and/or lesson learning. However, the *conditions* for the acceptance of auxiliary policing were already in place with the growth in British policing over the two decades prior to their introduction firstly of *civilianization* of police roles and later with the push to differentiate between 'core' police functions and 'ancillary' police roles. This relates more to process of policy *convergence* whereby policing systems in various nation states are responding to increased demands on their resources and rising expectation from the public by moving in the direction of 'plural policing'. Similarly policy and practice around *policing by objectives* may have been directly influenced, through policy transfer, by specific police management techniques developed in the USA; however, the adoption of PBO in Britain at that time had much to do with wider processes associated with the emergence and rise of *new public management*, a movement which spanned nation states and which affected virtually every developed society in due course—more in line with policy *convergence*. It is these deeper forces underpinning police reform which will be the subject of the following chapter.

3

Policing as a Performing Art? 'Value for Money' and Police Reform

Introduction: Value for Money Thinking

In Chapter 1 the ways in which police 'mindsets' or paradigms can change was discussed, in that context in relation to the emergence in the 1980s of the ethos of 'community-oriented policing' and the repositioning of the police which that change in mindset entailed. What also began to appear in the 1980s, and very much accelerated into the 1990s, was a mindset change of a somewhat different dimension, involving ways in which the police organization should be *managed*. This paradigm shift has been a process of police reform in its own right—it was about changing the way the police organization went about its 'business'—but it also set in motion or influenced a range of other reforms of the police service, from 'civilianization' to 'intelligence-led policing', and as such constitutes an important 'force for change' in police reform in the way the term has been used in this study. Central to this paradigm-shift was the emergence and rise of the *performance culture* within and around policing, associated with the mantra of *'value for money'*.

'Value for money' (VFM), simply put, is about achieving the best results ('effectiveness') at the lowest cost ('efficiency' and 'economy'). In that sense it is fair to claim that British policing has for a long time been exposed to forms of VFM measures. For much of its history, the 'effectiveness' of policing has been measured by the recorded crime statistics and those statistics have been one way in which the police have been called to 'account' in terms of how well or how badly they are doing. Furthermore, as was seen in Chapter 2, initiatives such as the introduction of 'unit beat policing' in the 1960s were driven by the desire to make patrol more 'efficient', in the sense of maximizing the scope of police patrols with fewer, or static, police numbers. Added to this was the use of 'targets' and 'measures of effectiveness', in the form of maximum and average 'response times', which could be used to judge how well a police force or division within a force was doing in comparison with others. It would be a mistake to assume that the language and mindset of VFM was something totally new to policing when the push came in the mid-1980s to extend the ethos across the service. However, it is also important to recognize, as has been noted at a number of points in this study, that the police sector in Britain was, relative to other parts of the public sector, allowed some protection by government from the full blast of the VFM agenda for a great deal of time. In that sense, what emerged in the mid-1980s in terms of the VFM ethos as it confronted the police service was of major significance to the shaping of policing policy and the reform of the police organization.

Before going on to flesh out the VFM agenda and its association with the 'three E's'—Effectiveness, Efficiency, and Economy—it will be useful to set the scene in terms of the context within which the VFM movement emerged under the Thatcher government. Until the 1970s, many commentators agree, British public policy was dominated by the 'post-war consensus' or the 'post-war settlement' (Farnham and Horton, 1993: 9–13; Hay, 1996). The 'settlement' had three dimensions. First, a mixed economy based on Keynesian demand management policies, with state ownership of key sectors of industry (Gamble, 1981: 24–5). Secondly, a welfare state funded by high levels of public expenditure, defined as:

> the totality of schemes and services through which central government together with the local authorities assumed a major responsibility for dealing with all the different types of social problems which beset individual citizens. (Marwick, 1990: 45)

Thirdly, a political consensus within which the major political parties accepted the mixed economy and the notion of a welfare state and the state's role in relation to it, as Marshall (1965: 97) expressed it, involving a:

> measure of agreement on fundamentals ... There is little difference of opinion as to the services that must be provided and it is generally agreed that ... the overall responsibility of the welfare of citizens must remain with the State.

The post-war settlement came under increasing pressure during the 1970s, a key development being the international recession caused by the sharp rise in oil prices following the Arab-Israeli War in 1973–4 (Gamble, 1981: 184–5). This, together with other crises of the early to mid-1970s, such as the IMF crisis of 1976 (when the then Labour government were forced to accept the stringent terms of the International Monetary Fund, including major cuts in public expenditure, as a condition of financial assistance (Jenkins, 2006: 2–3)), and industrial unrest and political protest (Loader and Mulcahy, 2003: 8–9), all served to undermine the economic, political, and social foundations of the post-war 'consensus'. From the point of view of this discussion two consequences followed. First, as the economic basis on which public expenditure had expanded over the post-war period had been all but shattered, governments were forced to turn the tide of public expenditure and seek drastic cuts where possible; the Labour government took the initial steps in this direction, cutting state expenditure from 55.1% of gross domestic product in 1975–6 to 48% in 1978–9 (Gough, 1979: 128). The era of 'economy' in public services had well and truly arrived, one which the incoming Conservative government of 1979 would take significantly further. Secondly, the *political* basis on which the consensus of the post-war settlement was built began to dissipate and new political forms began to emerge. Prominent amongst these was the rise of the 'New Right', associated with the politics of 'Thatcherism' (Gamble, 1988; see also Chapter 5), which challenged many of the basic assumptions of the post-war consensus, from its approach to economic policy—and particularly the extended role of the state in economic and industrial affairs—to its commitment to the welfare state (Gilmour, 1992: 13–22). Of the many dimensions of the New Right and Thatcherism (Riddell, 1989: 1–13) one is of particular significance here: the belief that the *private sector* and private sector (market-based) mechanisms offer the best models of business and organizational behaviour. If we are to look for ways in which the public expenditure associated with the public services can be contained or reduced, so the New Right argued, we should emulate private sector ways of working and 'doing business' (Farnham and Horton, 1993a: 13–16). If the 'party was over' on expenditure for the public sector (with the exception, for a time at least, of the police—see Chapter 5), the management approaches found within private sector would be offered as the way to come to terms with that.

In this sense, from the perspective of the police service the emergence of Thatcherism must have sent out mixed messages. On the one hand, as we shall see in depth in Chapter 5, the politics of Thatcherism made what to the police were reassuring noises—the pre-election of 1979 slogan was, after all, 'less tax and more law and order' (Savage, 1990: 89). That dimension of Thatcherism which commentators have called 'neo-conservative' or 'authoritarian', which emphasizes the need for a *strong state* when it comes to maintaining social and moral order (Gamble, 1988), offers comfort to those, like the police, in that line of business. In this way the police were to be an important pillar of the Conservative's plans to solve 'Britain's problems'. On the other hand, that dimension of Thatcherism closer to 'neo-liberal' thought (Gilmour, 1992: 36–7) saw *rolling back the state* (Self, 2000; Gamble, 1988) and extending or 'freeing up' the *private* sector as vital to economic success. As indicated, this dimension triumphs private sector models of organizational behaviour and in that sense presents a challenge to public sector managers, the police included, although they might not have realized it at the time Thatcher came to power. However, it was not long before this aspect of Thatcherite ideology was employed in reforming the public sector. It took the form of the 'Financial Management Initiative' (FMI).

The FMI grew out of an initiative which began soon after Thatcher took office in 1979 when she appointed Derek Rayner from Marks & Spencer as a part-time advisor on 'efficiency' and head of what was called the 'Efficiency Unit', located within the Prime Minister's Office. The Unit was charged with promoting efficiency and reducing 'waste' in Whitehall departments by carrying out scrutinies (thereafter known as the 'Rayner Scrutinies' (Atkinson, 1990: 14–15)) of departmental processes, but the Unit was also intended to raise the status of *management* within the Civil Service, changing the ethos from one of 'administering' their departments to *managing* them, effectively importing business practices used in the private sector into the management of public service departments (Horton, 1993: 134–5). These were early signs of what was to be called 'new public management', which will be examined later in this chapter. The FMI took that a stage further and was a government initiative designed to improve the allocation, management, and control of resources throughout central government; in the 1982 White Paper launching the initiative it was stated that this was to be achieved by:

> promoting in each department an organisation and a system in which managers at all levels have (a) a clear view of their objectives; and means to assess, and wherever possible measure, outputs or performance in relation to those objectives; (b) well-defined responsibility for making the best use of their resources including a scrutiny of output and value for money (Cmnd 8616)

The key elements of the FMI evident in this statement were: *objectives-based management*, otherwise known as 'management by objectives' (discussed in Chapter 2), *performance measurement*—an essential component of *performance management*—and *value for money*. Linked to this was a call for more *devolved management* as a means of increasing the responsibilities and accountabilities of managers lower down the organizational hierarchy and enhancing the flexibility of management overall. These were all core elements of the 'new public management' which the Thatcher government was seeking to spread throughout the public sector and which, in due course, was to arrive at the door of the police service. 'New public management' (NPM) however, was a development which stretched well beyond Britain (Ranson and Stewart, 1994) and was, and still is, an expression of the extent to which nation states of the developed world have restructured themselves in order to remain competitive in the 'global marketplace' (Dahrendorf, 1995: 41). One reflection of 'globalization' (Giddens, 1993: 528) is the tendency for state organizations to adopt, or be forced to adopt, management styles and approaches which emphasize efficiency and effectiveness, along the lines of management of private sector organizations, as a means of maximizing 'value for money'. NPM is the label given to this trend in public sector management.

NPM has a number of dimensions and is by no means a coherent and consistent 'model' of management (Hood, 1991; Dunleavy and Hood, 1994; Pollitt, 2002). As summarized in Savage, Charman, and Cope (2000: 32–6) NPM has four main primary dimensions. First, NPM often embodies an ideological assumption of the superiority of *markets* over state monopolies of service provision, and where the state is the provider NPM asserts that *market mechanisms* and market forces should be injected into the sector—known as 'quasi-markets' (Bartlett and Le Grand 1993)—to drive up effectiveness and efficiency. Secondly, NPM embraces the notion of a separation between the bodies responsible for policy and budgets and those responsible for actual delivery. Famously, Osborne and Gaebler (1992: 34) have called this the separation of *'steering'* and *'rowing'*: where once central government departments both made policies/set budgets *and* were responsible for service delivery, there is now an increasing tendency for them to concentrate on the former ('steering') and to leave the delivery side ('rowing') to other agencies and bodies. Thirdly, linked to this, NPM *decentralizes* the public sector by dispersing delivery to a plethora of agencies, including private sector organisation, other public agencies (for example, local authorities) and voluntary bodies. One apparent advantage of such decentralization—this has also been called 'disaggregation' of the public sector (Hood, 1991)—is that it brings service providers in closer contact with *consumers* (Foster and Plowden, 1996: 52–3). Fourthly, NPM reflects the view that *competition* between public and private sectors and also within the public sector itself, leads to greater efficiency in service provision and makes the sector as a whole more responsive to consumer preferences. Pollitt (2002: 276) captures these features of NPM more concisely and lists the key features of NPM as:

- Being close to its customers;
- Being performance-driven (targets, standards) not rule-bound;
- Displaying a commitment to continuous quality improvement;
- Being structured in a 'lean' and 'flat' way—highly decentralized with 'street level' staff who are empowered to be flexible and innovative;
- Tight cost-control with commercial style accounting systems;
- Performance related systems for recruiting, posting, and rewarding staff.

The FMI was a means of initiating change within the public sector along at least some of these lines, although other reforms were needed—such as the creation of the Audit Commission in the 1980s and the 'best value' agenda in the 1990s, both discussed later—to push the public sector further in these directions. McLaughlin and Murji (1995, 2001) have attempted to draw the implications of this movement for the police service in particular in terms of what they have called the 'managerialization' process. We shall return to the specific applications of this process to policing shortly, but it is useful at this stage to outline what this process entails for the public sector generally before doing that. McLaughlin (2007: 96–7) offers the following as features of the manageri-alization process, which builds on the elements outlined above:

- creation or appointment of professional managers who are required to extract maximum value from specified resources;
- setting of measurable standards and targets;
- explicit costing of all activities;
- development of performance indicators to enable the measurement and eval-uation of efficiency;
- publication of tables showing comparative performance against these indica-tors;
- increased emphasis on outputs and results rather than processes;
- rationalization of the purpose, range and scope of organizations through the consolidation of core competencies and the outsourcing of peripheral activi-ties;
- adaptation to a competitive environment characterized by full or quasi-market relations, service contracts, and agency status;
- separation of finance from provision, a split between providers and purchasers of services, and client-contractor relationships;
- reconfiguration of the recipients and beneficiaries of services as 'customers' and 'consumer-citizens'; and
- overhauling of the work culture to improve productivity, accountability, and representativeness.

Such inventories of NPM, or the 'new managerialism'—a term that is often used in a pejorative way—reflect the ways in which the value for money agenda has developed and become nuanced since its arrival in the early 1980s in the more basic form of the FMI. Furthermore, as the reforms which have embodied these elements of NPM have been rolled out we have, perhaps, begun to view them as 'natural' features of the police organization—mission statements, policing plans, performance targets, league tables of police performance, the 'extended police family', and the like. However, it is easy to forget how very *inapplica-ble* to policing the NPM agenda seemed to many when it was launched, and for some still does seem inapplicable (Waddington, 1999: 236–50). Apart from those objecting to NPM and new managerialism as a matter of principle, as inap-propriate for the public sector as a whole (see Farnham and Horton, 1993a), a case has been constructed which holds out policing as a special case of public service provision, one simply not amendable to the ethos of NPM and certainly not to 'business' models of organizational management.

The 'special case' argument has a number of strands. In part it draws on what have become widely accepted interpretations of the nature of policing itself—accepted even by those who feel quite comfortable with the NPM agen-da. Two features of police work stand out in this respect. First, and something noted at various points in this study, policing is characterized by wide *discretion* at the lower levels of the organizational hierarchy (Sanders and Young, 2003), with a key role in service delivery played by 'street level bureaucrats' (Lipsky, 1980). At the very least, this makes 'managing down' the organization difficult; the police officer, particularly the patrol officer, enjoys a relatively high degree of freedom from direct supervision by line management and as such a degree of autonomy in the 'workplace' not typically found in other organizations. Secondly, linked to this, is the *unpredictability* of police-work in the sense that police actions are driven largely by unforeseen demands and calls on police time: policing is to a great extent a *reactive* service which takes its 'priorities' from what comes in its direction, and that is notably difficult to predict or anticipate in advance (Waddington, 1999: 235). If this is the case, organizational management oriented to objective-setting and resource allocation based on achieving those objectives cannot sit that easily with the realities of police work. For some, this means in effect that the ethos of NPM is simply inapplicable to policing and doomed to fail if an attempt is made to operate on that basis. The most ardent advocate of that view has been P.A.J. Waddington, who engaged in a revealing and protracted debate in the mid-1980s with Tony Butler, who, as we saw in Chapter 2, had developed the model of policing by objectives in the context of British policing; the timing of that debate was significant, because it coincided very much with the early stirrings of NPM within the police organization.

The principles of PBO were outlined in the previous chapter but for the purposes of this chapter its ethos is nicely summed up by Butler who, in an article for *Police Review* (7 September 1984) stated: 'police work should have some of the mythology stripped away and should be subject to the *same rational and analytical processes* that have been the hallmark of successful commercial organisations for years' (emphasis added). This stance challenges head-on the notion of the police as a 'special case' when it comes to models of management and seeks to undermine the assumption that policing is somehow so 'unique' as a public service, that it must stand outside of any attempt to apply 'business' models of management to the public sector, as the FMI seemed to be doing. What follows, according to the logic of PBO, is that policy-making and decision-making in the policing sector can indeed be organized around the notions of priority-setting, resource allocation, measurements of performance, evaluation of effectiveness, and so on which are standard concepts in the management of commercial organizations.

Waddington (1986) took issue with the rationale of Butler's call for PBO on the grounds that policing could not be 'shoehorned' into the management by objectives model of management. There were two primary reasons for this, it was argued. First, that policing, as has already been noted, is an activity that is essentially *reactive* and reactive to *unpredictable demand*. To seek to run policing on the basis of *a priori* objective-setting is folly because police work simply cannot operate in that way. If policing 'follows' anything, it these unforeseen and unpredictable calls on police time rather than objectives set out by management in advance. Waddington was to restate this view some years later (1999: 242), when he challenged 'rational police management' as the 'pursuit of chimera' and, in answer to a self-posed question of whether this implies that policing is 'unmanageable' or 'uncontrollable', stated:

> The answer is yes, if management and control is taken to mean the issuing of directives, guidance or any other means of influencing police behaviour *in advance* of the situation they deal with. Policing is largely reactive and attention should be given to how those reactive interventions can be improved. (Waddington, 1999: 242—emphasis in original)

The second concern with the PBO ethos which Waddington (1986) and others have raised is with the measurement of police 'performance'. There are in fact two issues here which relate to the nature of police work and the extent to which its 'effectiveness' is something that can be captured by measurement as such. On the one hand, PBO assumes that police activity can be measured as if it is about the carrying out of 'tasks', whereas much police work, particularly patrol, is about a public *presence* as a symbol of authority. Policing, so this argument runs, is as much what the police *are* as what they *do*, so that policing may be 'working'—in terms of order-maintenance (Reiner, 2000: 112–15)—simply by officers 'being there'. The symbolic role of the police is something which does not lend itself easily to measurement in the way PBO assumes it can. On the other hand, measuring the 'effectiveness' of policing along PBO lines, might mean evaluating police performance by 'outputs' over which the police have little control or impact. The classic case of this is recorded crime, which not only presents a distinctly partial picture of 'actual' crime rates (Bottomley and Pease, 1986), but, in so far as recorded crime measures crime at all, it measures something largely out of the control of the police, because crime is as much an index of social conditions as it is of police activity. These are of course well established criminological principles, but when applied to the specific question of police management they have a particular resonance, because they might challenge the notion of police 'performance' as something which lends itself to measurement at all.

The case constructed by critics of PBO, and by extension of the application of NPM to policing as a whole, does draw on some convincing and well established axioms on policing and the nature of the police role. However, the question is whether these characteristics of policing constitute grounds for rejecting the application 'rational' management approaches to policing altogether. A number of counter arguments can be offered. Take the case that the 'special' nature of policing renders this particular public service foreign to the notions of objective setting and performance measurement. Precisely the same sort of argument has been made in relation to other public services, where parallel claims for 'special status' have been made. For example, a case against the application of 'managerialism' to higher education has been made on the basis that 'hierarchical management' (ie where managers rather than employee set directives!) would destroy the uniquely 'collegial' and 'self-governing' nature of decision-making in the university sector (for a discussion see Farnham and Horton, 1993: 244–6)—perhaps just a touch of idealism here. There is perhaps a tendency for each area of the public sector to be seen as 'special' or 'unique' in some regards, and from some quarters, particularly the trade unions and staff associations within those sectors, that claim may be part of a strategy of resistance to change (in the context of policing see Chapter 4 in this respect). For the professions at the 'receiving end' of the new managerialism, claims of special status may be one way of seeking to protect the status quo and 'win space' from the encroachment of management on what has been their own, semi-autonomous, 'territory'. 'Uniqueness' seems to be a strangely common trait!

It is also possible to challenge the particular features of the 'special' case of policing. Take the question of the 'reactive' and 'unpredictable' nature of policework. Policing is not the only public service which has to live with this condition. Hospital emergency services have to respond to demands which are externally driven—illness, accidents—and which are equally 'unpredictable'. Fire-fighting services similarly have to react to what comes their way in terms of fires, accidents and other unforeseen events. Even local authorities are confronted with calls on their time which they cannot always predict and to which they are required to react—such as flooding, for example. Indeed, as they take on more and more 'community safety' responsibilities (Crawford, 1999; see also Chapter 5) the scope for 'unpredictable' demands on their resources are increasing all the time. The point here is that much public service work is reactive and forced to cope with uncertainty and unpredictability—policing is not unique in this respect. Perhaps the *range* of demands on policing is wider than in other service areas, and this has to be recognized in management terms, but reactivity itself is not unique to policing.

We can go further in this respect. Although a level of unpredictability does exist with demands on police time, it is not always a case of 'out of the blue', unforeseen, events. Just as the hospital emergency services might not know exactly what is coming their way but can know for certain *in advance* that Saturday night will be busy for them, so too the police will know with relative certainty when 'pinch points' will occur. Football crowds arriving before and departing after matches are known sources of *potential* problems for the police to deal with; closing times of pubs and clubs are a similar challenge. Without knowing for sure whether the 'wheel will fall off', experience and analysis shows when problems are likely to escalate or not. Resources can be, and to an extent always have been, deployed accordingly. It is possible to overstate the 'reactive/unpredictable' case. This is even more so when it is acknowledged that much police work does not fit this model of reactivity. 'Desk based' police-work such as case-file preparation, the supervision and oversight of officers, police training, intelligence analysis, to mention just a few, are tasks which are not characterized by high levels of reactivity and unpredictability, even if all does not go strictly according to plan—but then that is so for the public services as a whole and even, I dare say, the commercial sector as well; again, the 'special case' thesis is overstated.

The message here is that indeed each sector is 'special' or 'unique' in certain respects—that is why they are different sectors in the first place. This does not necessarily mean that management styles and processes used as standard elsewhere cannot as a matter of principle be applied to those services. The real challenge is whether such processes as objective-setting, planning, measurement of 'outputs' (even if not called 'performance') can be crafted in such a way that they best fit the particular features of the sector in question and are sensitive to the nuances of that sector. In the policing context, that would involve the appreciation of the richness and diversity of police work *as well as* the need to maximize effectiveness and value for money. Since the early days of the new managerialism, and particularly with the work of such organizations as the Audit Commission (see below), there is evidence that such an appreciation has been forthcoming. At this point, however, we should return to the FMI as the first significant movement in the direction of NPM and consider how it was introduced into the policing world.

FMI Meets Policing: Circular Thinking

In Chapter 5, the processes by which the Home Office has, over time, accumulated greater influence and control over policing at the local, force, level will be considered, particularly in terms of its use of self-awarded powers to draw up national *priorities and plans* for policing around the country. If we go back to the early 1980s, a very different picture emerges, one in which the Home Office had far more limited spheres of influence over local policies and decision-making. As Burrows (1989: 23) made clear, the instruments of Home Office 'control', if that is what it can be called, at this stage were twofold, one direct the other indirect. Direct power over the police service was exercised by the payment of the police grant and the provision of support services (forensic science, police training, and so on). Indirect influence over the police could be carried out through the force *inspection* process involving Her Majesty's Inspectorate of Constabulary. It could also be exercised by the issue of Home Office Circulars which historically provided central 'guidance' to forces on policing matters. The FMI was visited on the police service by the combined use of these two indirect instruments of influence, and together they were to make a more powerful weapon of central control than either had separately before. Circular 114/83 was the vehicle for that.

Circular 114/83 began with a clear indication that, as far as police expenditure was concerned, 'the party is over' (Burrows, 1989: 22), in the sense that, as far as the Home Office was concerned, the levels of expenditure enjoyed between 1979 and up to the issue of the Circular in 1983, could no longer be sustained. In the wording of the Circular: 'The restraints in public expenditure at both central and local government level make it impossible to continue with the sort of expansion which has occurred in recent years' (Home Office, 1983: para 2). The issue of 'the party is over' is addressed in detail in Chapter 5. The Circular then went on to advise, in terms more assertive than has been the case in the past with such documents, that police managers should, in that environment, be clear about their priorities and how resources are to be directed to meet them:

> Her Majesty's Inspectors are now adopting in their inspections an approach which is more specifically directed towards ways in which chief officers . . . identify problems, set realistic objectives and clear priorities, keep those priorities and objectives under review, deploy manpower and other resources in accordance with them, and provide themselves with practical means of assessing the extent to which chief officers are achieving their objectives. (Quoted in Leishman and Savage, 1993: 216)

This statement is significant in a number of ways. First, it signals an 'enforcement' role for HMIC on behalf of the Home Office in the sense that force inspections are to become both more challenging and 'on message' with government priorities. This will be discussed further below. Secondly, it is fully in accord with the ethos of the FMI as outlined earlier and evidently expressed in the language of NPM. It should however be noted that the 'objectives' and 'priorities' in question are a matter for *chief officers* and not, as was later to become increasingly the case, the objectives and priorities of *central government*—as discussed later. At this stage all government was seeking to do was ensure that the police *had* objectives and worked to them—the determination of those objectives was left to the police themselves.

The significance of Circular 114/83 may not have been appreciated by all initially—a search of the *Police Review* for 1983 found no reference to it at all—but the subsequent high level of scrutiny devoted to it (Burrows, 1989: 22) is some indication of the Circular's importance. In effect, it heralded a new era of thinking about policing, even if the service did not respond in full for some significant time after its release. A new 'mindset' was emerging through a combination of 'push' from government and 'pull' from inside the service itself, the latter in the form of PBO as outlined previously. This movement was nicely captured in a statement from the Chief Constable of Northamptonshire, Maurice Buck, in 1984, commenting on the new 'language' which had emerged within his own force:

> terms such as effectiveness and efficiency, devolved management, participative management, systematic approach to problem-solving, prioritisation, are becoming commonplace in the police vocabulary (*Police Review* 9 November 1984)

Another Home Office Circular issued in the 1980s provided even more 'push' from government but in this case the push was far less permissive, one sign of a growing interventionism of central government that was to become most explicit in the 1990s. Circular 105/88, *Civilian Staff in the Police Service* (Home Office, 1988) took the VFM agenda further by promoting the policy of *civilianisation*. Civilianisation is the process by which roles and functions to date undertaken by warranted officers are passed on the civilian employees of the police service (Jones, Newburn, and Smith, 1994: 166–74), and is a process that neatly captures many of the themes of the new managerialism. It was, and still is, driven by a concern to make efficiency gains by having tasks undertaken by less well-paid staff and which, in principle at least, enables the 'freeing up' of warranted officers to undertake roles which only they can fulfil. It involves asking questions about the nature of the work in question, the 'skills set' necessary to carry them out, and the recruitment and deployment of staff accordingly. The driving question (and it did relate to driving in every sense because one post which has been civilianized is that of driver for senior officers!) is this: is it necessary for a fully trained and expensive warranted officer to undertake this role? If the answer is 'no' then that post can go out for civilianization.

Civilianization is however about more than efficiency, despite the perennial claim (particularly by the likes of the Police Federation (see Chapter 4)), that it is about 'policing on the cheap'. As Leishman and Savage (1993:225–7) have argued, it can also be about the provision of more *effective* services, because the appointment of civilian staff to undertake specific duties can involve the use of *specialists* in that area of work, and staff who are more likely to carry out that role as part of a *career* path, not something they do for a few years before moving on to something totally different, as has typically been the case with warranted officers. An example of this is the personnel function. The civilianization of personnel work allowed the recruitment of specialist professional personnel officers to posts which had previously been given to police officers, who undertook the role as (more or less willing) 'amateurs' before moving on to another area of work—and 'moving about' in terms of role changes is part and parcel of the police 'career' path, rightly or wrongly. In this sense 'civilianization' may in some respects be in effect 'professionalization'

Nevertheless civilianization was a controversial issue when the Home Office first started to drive police forces in that direction. This began in 1984, when, in the discussion document *Criminal Justice: A Working Paper* (Home Office, 1984), which called for greater efficiency and effectiveness from the criminal justice services, it was made clear that additional police numbers would only be approved at force level if the Home Office was satisfied that the force in question had maximized the use of officers on 'operational' duties; in relation to this the document advised giving more roles to civilian staff (*Police Review* 18 May 1984). Circular 105/88 took this case much further. It did not just advance the general case for civilianization, it actually identified a number of functions which forces should look to civilianize and charged HMIC with the task of inspecting forces to see whether this recommendation was being carried through; HMIC duly took as one part of their remit the role of reviewing the extent to which individual forces were 'toeing the line' on civilianization—failure to do so led to critical comment in inspection reports and would be followed up in later inspections. The functions which were the earliest recipients of civilianization included finance and personnel (mainly at senior levels), press and public relations, and administration at sub-divisional level. Soon to follow were semi-operational posts, such as photography, counter assistants, and gaolers. Despite such developments, the civilianization agenda, as will be seen in Chapters 4 and 5, was to become much more radical as time went on, particularly as associated with the Posen Review of core and ancillary functions in the mid-1990s. From the perspective of the 1980s, however, it was radical enough already.

Civilianization was and still is an important area of police reform in its own right. However, what is most interesting is the extent to which it is also a reflection of a much more fundamental reform of policing, one about a changing *mindset* in British policing: NPM in the policing context. It involved the emergence and development of a different way of *thinking about policing*, parallel and even compatible in some ways (although very different in others), with the changing mindset identified in Chapter 1 in terms of community-oriented policing. Loader and Mulcahy (2003: 289) refer to this change of mindset towards managerialism as the process of making the police 'profane', by which they mean the shift from the notion of the police as what has here been called a 'special case', or the notion of the 'sacredness' of policing, to one in which the police are 'no different from any other bureaucracy, and, able, like them, to learn from organisations that have to compete and survive in the marketplace'. Civilianization is one expression of making the police 'profane', in the sense that it challenges the view that the 'special' nature of policing requires that 'only police officers' can undertake roles which, from an outside and particularly commercial perspective, look just like roles undertaken in other organizations by 'ordinary' employees. Civilianization also reflects the commercial principle that organizations should minimize the costs of employment and only buy in levels of skills necessary for the work in question. The question managerialism asked in this regard was why the police sector used well-paid and expensively trained sworn officers to perform tasks, which in other sectors would be undertaken by staff paid much less, according to the workings of the labour market.

The new mindset of managerialism was given further impetus by a process already referred to but which became much more powerful as the late 1980s gave way to the early 1990s: the rise of *inspection and audit* in British policing.

Inspecting Morse: Audit, Inspection, and Regulatory Governance

Reference has been made as to how, throughout the 1980s, Home Office Circulars were becoming increasingly 'directive' in tone, and the way in which that was coupled with an enforcement role for HMIC. This was indicative of a wider shift in the role of HMIC during the 1980s and beyond, one linked to the rise of 'regulatory governance' or the 'regulatory state' (Hood et al, 1999) in general. It has already been noted that a core feature of NPM is the development of a separation between 'steering' and 'rowing' (Osborne and Gaebler, 1992: 34) in the delivery of services: central government increasingly concentrates on steering the direction of services in terms of policy and budgets, whilst a plethora of other agencies are given responsibility for the direct delivery of services—'rowing'. As shall be seen in Chapter 5 and in the Conclusion, this is associated with 'governing at a distance', in the sense that central control over public services is maintained not through direct provision of those services, but through regulatory machineries which monitor, inspect, and audit the 'performance' of delivery agents. In the policing context HMIC have become a key part of that machinery, a means by which government can seek to influence through regulation what happens at force level, without direct central 'control' as such.

It is now widely agreed that HMIC, from the early 1980s onwards, became an increasingly assertive if not directive instrument of central government policies and preferences (Hale, Heaton, and Uglow, 2004: 293–5; Savage, Charman, and Cope, 2000: 136–8; Loader and Mulcahy, 2003: 294–5). Prior to the rise of the VFM culture within policing, HMIC inspections were in effect a matter of 'going through the motions', a form of annual ritual the outcome of which, the signature of the 'certificate of efficiency', was a forgone conclusion. Traditionally, HMIC was populated by retired chief constables—Reiner (2000: 191) called it the 'House of Lords for the police'—who were appointed as a reward for a distinguished police career, or to get them out of harm's way if they were not performing well. Force inspections were on all accounts leisurely affairs little concerned with a testing scrutiny (Reiner, 2000: 191–2). A number of changes, through the 1980s and 1990s, in the Inspectorate regime changed all of that (Savage, Cope, and Charman, 1997). First, the FMI exercise itself, as reflected in Circular 114/83, changed the role of force inspections from one of 'ritual' to one of *enforcement*; annual inspections now had clear frameworks for action—such as monitoring progress on civilianization—on which to base judgement as to whether forces were 'efficient' or not. Inspectors now had stated policies against which to audit force-level activity. This was to be enhanced, as will be seen, with the arrival of a suite of *performance indicators* for policing in the mid-1990s. Secondly, HMIC started a range of 'thematic inspections', on top of its annual inspections, which took a sample of forces for in-depth scrutiny in order to monitor performance in areas such as equal opportunities and training (Hale, Heaton, and Uglow, 2004: 293–5). Additionally, it was decided to publish all HMIC reports, a means of adding to the pressure for forces to comply with Home Office wishes. Thirdly, inspectors were appointed from the ranks of in-service senior officers, who were viewed as at their peak or even on the way up, rather than at the end of their operational policing careers. Increasingly, HMIC was being staffed by officers who had themselves demonstrated the new managerialism in their own organizations. Linked to this was the establishment of 'lay' inspectors to HMIC, senior civilian staff with specialist expertise in areas such as financial management and personnel management (Savage, Cope, and Charman, 1997). In these ways HMIC developed into a more 'professional', corporate, and assertive body, a key element in the process of reforming the police along the lines desired by central government. Force inspections would become a constant reminder to senior officers to think VFM principles in the management of their own organizations.

If the regime of *inspection* was to be strengthened, regulatory governance was further enhanced with the rise of organizational *audit*. In this respect a major contribution to the rise of NPM within the police sector has been made by the *Audit Commission*. The Audit Commission was created by the *Local Government Act 1982* as the body responsible for auditing all local authorities and police authorities. This involved two primary functions (Hale, Heaton, and Uglow, 2004: 295; Cope and Goodship, 2002: 34). On the one hand the Commission was to audit the organizational accounts of those bodies to ensure that they are making proper arrangements for securing economy, efficiency, and effectiveness. On the other hand, the Commission was to undertake *studies* of the organizations in question so that it can make recommendations for *improvements* along the lines of the Three Es and extending VFM. The staff who carried out those studies were in most cases people with a background in senior management, often with a commercial organization. It is this second function of the Audit Commission, more about *policy development*, which is of most significance in the analysis of police reform, because it is the Commission's studies of policing which have been highly influential both in terms of furthering specific reforms and in assisting to change the 'mindset' of police management.

The Audit Commission began its work on the police in the mid-1980s when it undertook its first study on the police organization on administrative support for operational police officers. This study (Audit Commission 1988a) was presented as the first in the series of what became known as the 'Police Papers', which together (there were to be over 20 of them) constituted a form of 'managerialist audit' of the police service, at least in terms of local policing bodies—interestingly, the opening statement of this Police Paper was 'Policing is big *business*' (Audit Commission, 1988a: 2—emphasis added). At the time the Commission began to work on the Police Papers, however, they were not dealing with an audience as receptive to their recommendations as it was later to be. Not only was the NPM 'mindset' in its infancy within the police sector, but this was the mid-1980s which, as shall be seen in Chapter 4, was an era in which chief police officers were still often 'maverick' types (Loader and Mulcahy, 2003: 234) who resented *anyone* 'telling them what to do', let alone people they could dismiss as a 'bunch of accountants'. They could turn to the 'special case' argument considered earlier and in this context challenge the *legitimacy* of an exercise involving 'outsiders' coming in to the world of policing and having the audacity to recommend change. This mood was nicely captured by a senior member of the Audit Commission, interviewed for the research under-taken by Savage, Charman, and Cope (2000), who reflected on the early days of the Commission's work with the police, referring to chiefs

> ...who didn't welcome our involvement at all because, not because we were the Audit Commission, just because we weren't police officers...there was a case of 'What do you know about policing? You've never walked the streets of Bolton at night' or 'You've never had to control an animal rights demonstra-tion, so what can you possibly tell me about how to do my job?'

This environment was to change to one much more positive about what the Commission had to offer, not just because a 'new breed' of chief officer was emerging, less individualistic and more open to new ideas (Savage, Charman, and Cope, 2000: 86–9; Reiner, 1991: 304–8). The environment also changed because of the strategic way the Audit Commission went about winning over the 'hearts and minds' of the police service, one so successful that one Audit Commission member, also interviewed as part of the study by Savage, Char-man, and Cope (2000: 133), stated that: 'The take-up of our recommendations is much higher in the police world than it is in the rest of the local authority sec-tor or in the health service.' The approach the Commission took was to move by stealth—start on what might be seen as peripheral areas of policing, both to appear as non-threatening and to 'earn their stripes' by demonstrating that they were talking sense, and then move more and more to the 'core' of polic-ing. This pattern was evident in the span of work contained in the Police Papers over time. Having started on the area of administrative support, it then moved on to study and make recommendations on the fingerprint service (Audit Com-mission, 1988b) and vehicle fleet management (Audit Commission, 1989). Only later did it attempt to embrace areas of policing more obviously 'core' to polic-ing, such as criminal investigation (Audit Commission, 1993) and police patrol (Audit Commission, 1996), and, as core issues, potentially much more sensitive to tackle. An indication of the success of that strategy to win legitimacy for the Commission in the eyes of senior police officers was the statement of an ACPO officer made in the research by Savage, Charman, and Cope (2000: 134–5), in which it was said:

> we accept them [the Audit Commission] now as I think they are an extremely useful, competent, objective body who do the job they do in a focused way, looking at particular issues and where we can actually get something of real benefit...if the Audit Commission produces something we take it on board quickly and fairly strongly.

Having cleared the ground and won legitimacy within the police service with its earlier studies, the Audit Commission then moved to more core policing functions. In *Helping With Enquiries: Tackling Crime Effectively* (Audit Commis-sion, 1993), it reported on its study of *crime management*, which in the words of the Commission, is 'an activity which many people view as the primary role of the police' (Preface). Most significantly, this study tackled the thorny issue of *criminal investigation* and the *detective function*, the area of police work with the most 'sacred' status, so much so that it is deemed beyond the 'understanding' not only of 'outsiders', but also of those police officers not fortunate enough to have been detectives. This hallowed status of criminal investigation within the police organization is commented on by the Commission, when it remarked on how BCU commanders without detective experience (which is most of them) 'lack credibility' with detectives under their command and as such find it difficult to manage detectives properly (Audit Commission, 1993: 21). In the typically understated style of Audit Commission reports—the sub-text seems to be that things are in an awful mess, but the words do not quite state that—*Helping With Enquiries* identified weaknesses in then current practices in criminal investigation and crime management, and made a number of key recommendations, highly imbued with the NPM ethos, which were to become highly influential in reforming policing in these areas. These included:

- Police forces should make clear how tackling crime sits in relation to other areas of police work in terms of organizational *objectives and priorities*. In particular, the appropriate balance between investigating crimes committed and *crime prevention* should be determined, the message being that the status of the latter should be enhanced and the status of the (mainly uniformed) officers responsible for it enhanced accordingly (Audit Commission, 1993: 41–3).
- The role of Criminal Investigation Department (CID) work should be more clearly defined, as should the question of which crimes are to be deemed 'serious', and steps should be taken (a) to ensure that detectives should be restricted to the investigation of serious crimes and (b) to allocate the investigation of crimes falling outside of this remit to uniformed officers, who should in turn be given more training in the investigative function. This is a message about *rational resource allocation*.
- Police forces should consider using *'crime desks'*. Crime desks are crime management units which seek to rationalize the response to crimes coming to the attention of the police (Audit Commission, 1993: 47–8). They decide on the initial response to the crime—questioning whether an immediate response is required, or whether the response could be 'graded' as suitable for a delayed action on behalf of the police, again, based on rational resource allocation; the issue of graded response was initially flagged up in the Commission's earlier Police Paper on improving police communication rooms (Audit Commission, 1990: 9–11). This was an approach which, over a decade later, was reflected in the creation of the 'non-emergency' police call number (911) to separate out emergency and non-emergency calls from the public. Crime desks were also to be responsible for monitoring the progress of investigations ('quality assurance'), for keeping victims ('customers') informed of the progress of investigations, and for offering direct advice to victims, such as how to secure a car after a theft.

- There should be more effective *management* of police investigations (Audit Commission, 1993: 50–4). In particular, detective sergeants, who oversee detective constables, should have a better grasp of fundamental management functions such as leadership, motivation, delegation, project management, and performance appraisal. These were not the sort of skills traditionally associated with detective work. The chat over a pint in the pub was no longer to be the management style of the more senior detective, and detectives were no longer to be free agents following their 'natural instincts'.
- Greater weight should be given to *intelligence* in police investigations; investigations should be *intelligence-led* (Audit Commission, 1993: 54–8). This was to involve the appreciation of uniformed officers as a key source of local intelligence, the enhancement of the role of 'support' staff as crime *analysts*, the critical role of information technology in such processes as crime mapping, the systematic use of *informants* in intelligence-gathering, and an overall re-orientation towards targeting the *criminal not the crime*. This was a call for *proactive policing*, coming not from the stocks of community-oriented policing, in the way discussed in Chapter 1, but from the mindset of NPM, with its emphasis on 'market research', management information systems, and the 'targeting' of markets for focus and activity. Just as it is unwise and wasteful to spread the marketing of top-range cars to all sectors of the community, so too is it unwise to spread the work of detectives thinly across all sectors of crime: targeting is the key. If less than 1% of the population can afford a Rolls Royce, marketing activity of this particular product should focus on them; if 7% of the male population account for 65% of criminal convictions (Audit Commission, 1993: 54) criminal investigations should prioritize them. Richard Branson, rather than Inspector Morse, was to be the role model as NPM, in the form of the Audit Commission, was visited on the CID.

Helping With Enquiries was in these respects ways an important step along the way to the reform of the police in areas such as 'graded response', 'crime management units' and intelligence-led policing. For a service that was ostensibly so 'demand-led', here was an agenda for cutting into the heart of the policing function and challenging some of the 'untouchables' of police work. Objective-setting, rational resource allocation, and management information systems were to be the drivers of this new approach to even this core activity of the police. However, another 'core' policing activity was to come under the gaze of NPM: *police patrol*.

Following on the heels of the Audit Commission's review of police investigation came *Streetwise: Effective Police Patrol* (Audit Commission, 1996). It was no accident that police patrol was to be left late in the Audit Commission's timetable for its scrutinies of policing, for here was an area which if anything was even more 'sacred' than detective-work as something 'unique' about policing. This is the undeniable territory of the 'British Bobby'. Despite this, the Audit Commission was by now emboldened to make three major criticisms of the use and work of police patrols (Audit Commission, 1996: 5). First, that public expectations of policing in this area are 'unrealistic' and as such doomed to remain unsatisfied unless expectations are matched more realistically with what can be delivered. Secondly, that the deployment of patrol officers is not well managed in the sense that time is wasted 'waiting for things to happen' and/or that officers are dealing with incidents which do not merit police involvement. Thirdly, that patrols are not properly targeted and that the basis on which the effectiveness of patrols is monitored is inadequate.

The Audit Commission's recommendations for addressing these problems—recommendations that, significantly, were 'broadly welcomed by the police staff associations' (*Police Review* 8 March 1996)—were an interesting mix of 'standard' NPM solutions and some quite 'police-specific' proposals, some of which were later to become mainstream features of the police reform agenda set up by the Labour government (discussed in Chapter 5). The 'standard' NPM recommendations included:

- Setting up objectives for patrol and developing performance indicators and targets to monitor achievements against those objectives;
- Better management of police officers' shift patterns, in terms of increasing the flexibility of officers' time, and reducing sickness absence;
- 'Screening' out incidents that do not require police attendance and responding to them via help desks where civilian operators offer assistance over the telephone.

The more 'police-specific' recommendations included:

- Recognizing the importance of *partnership* between the police and local authorities in maintaining *community safety* by putting partnership work on a statutory footing. This was in effect what happened under Labour's *Crime and Disorder Act* of 1998 (discussed in Chapters 2 and 5).
- Developing a closer link between the police and the community with the police responding more to the preferences of local communities in the setting of local policing objectives, and a commitment to improving *public reassurance*; these were to be central features of *neighbourhood policing* within Labour's later police reform programme.
- Better *targeting* of patrol around geographical locations which intelligence indicates are problem-areas; this is another call for *intelligence-led policing*.

However, it was the recognition in *Streetwise* that personnel other than the regular police carry out 'policing' and the case for the greater use of special constables which was perhaps the most significant contribution made by the Audit Commission to reform in the area of police patrol. It set out a framework it called the 'community safety spectrum' (Audit Commission, 1996: 56) on the grounds that 'the police are the most important, but not the only, contributor to community safety'. The spectrum included the regular police, private security guards, local authority patrol officers, parks police, traffic wardens, special constables, and auxiliary patrol officers. Although *Streetwise* did not come out strongly in favour of an 'auxiliary tier' of policing (perhaps on political grounds, as the logic of the report clearly pointed in that direction), it did this in part by arguing for the greater and more inventive use of specials to increase visible police presence on the streets. Furthermore, the spectrum was an earlier version of what was subsequently labelled the *extended policing family*, as discussed in Chapter 2 and later in Chapter 5. At the very least, the Commission was 'softening up' the police service for what was to come in terms of the *auxiliarization* of British policing.

What the work of the Audit Commission did, through the Police Papers, was make NPM alive in the policing context through focused studies of police work based on well-established commercial-style management perspectives and principles. The Commission did not necessarily invent new ways of managing and delivering policing—many of the practices recommended, as the Papers openly acknowledged, were already happening somewhere in the service—but it did help create a momentum which has since, if anything, accelerated. Working increasingly closely with HMIC—to such an extent some senior police officers considered the two organizations to be treading on each other's territory, such that the distinctions between 'audit' and 'inspection' were becoming blurred (Savage, Charman, and Cope, 2000: 136–7; Cope and Goodship, 2002: 36)—the Audit Commission helped to forge a veritable revolution in police thinking along the lines of VFM and NPM. In this respect the combined efforts of HMIC and the Audit Commission were to further the cause of two other policy developments reflecting the ethos of NPM: on the one hand the proliferation of *performance indicators and targets* for policing; on the other the rise and rise of the *Basic Command Unit* as the geographical and decision-making bedrock of policing activity.

Performance Indicators for Policing

From its earliest studies, the Audit Commission had emphasized that *performance measurement* was an indispensable tool of effective management. Furthermore, the Commission also from those early days onwards considered it important to *compare performance* force-by-force. For example, the second Police Paper, *Improving the Performance of the Fingerprint Service* (Audit Commission, 1988b), presented data on variations across police forces on performance areas relating to the use of fingerprints, including performance indicators such as 'identifications made using fingerprint evidence as a proportion of notifiable offences' and 'identifications per fingerprint officer per year' (Audit Commission, 1988b:8). The rationale behind measurements and indicators such as these, with specified *targets* in many cases and the comparative use of data force-by-force, was both to enable managers to *know* how operations and activities are panning out in reality but more importantly, to *drive up* performance, particularly amongst those forces doing less well than others in those areas of activity.

After a number of years attempting to sell this message to the police service, the Audit Commission eventually published its first set of national performance indicators in 1995 (Audit Commission, 1995) which presented force-by-force 'performance' in a range of performance areas, including:

- speed of response to 999 calls;
- total amount of crime;
- rate of detection;
- number of officers available for operational duty; and
- cost of policing per head of population.

For the first time the public (and the media) could see how each force was performing in these areas and where each force stood in what were in effect *league tables*. What attracted most publicity to this report was the wide variation in performance across the police forces for England and Wales in these respects. For example, in terms of 'percentage of crimes detected by primary means per officer', performance ranged from a high of 14% in Nottinghamshire to 5.5% in the Metropolitan Police, and 'crimes recorded per 1,000 population' ranged from 156.8 in Humberside to 37.2 in Dyfed-Powes. The publicity such information attracted was not welcomed by ACPO, and in response ACPO issued a statement which challenged the legitimacy of these performance indicators as measures of policing activity, along the lines that 'The indicators only cover what is measurable. The qualitative element of policing is not addressed.' (*Police Review* 14 April 1995). The term 'qualitative' in this respect reflected ACPO's own work (discussed in Chapter 4) on the 'Quality of Service' initiative, which laid emphasis, amongst other things, on public satisfaction with policing standards (Waters, 1996).

Ever-sensitive to the need to cultivate support for their management philosophy within the police service, the Audit Commission duly responded (*Police Review* 15 December 1995) by adding a range of 'qualitative' indicators to their suite of performance indicators for the police service, which included:

- percentage of people satisfied with police actions in response to 999 calls;
- percentage of victims satisfied with the initial response to reports of burglary of a dwelling; and
- percentage of people satisfied with the level of foot and mobile patrol.

As Paul Vevers of the Audit Commission commented, 'There is widespread support for ACPO's qualitative measurements so we have decided to adopt those in our statutory indicators.' (*Police Review* 15 December 1995). This was significant in that although ACPO had challenged the specific range of measures used in the first set of national data by suggesting an *alternative* range of performance areas, they had exhibited an acceptance of the *principle* of performance measurement—they had effectively bought in to this particular expression of the philosophy of NPM. Since that point the whole gamut of performance indicators, targets, and league tables have become institutionalized features of the

British policing world. Over time, at the instigation of government, the Audit Commission moved to work ever more closely with HMIC (Hale, Heaton, and Uglow, 2004: 294), despite concerns expressed in some quarters about 'turf wars' and overlapping functions (Cope and Goodship, 2002: 36), and that has been reflected in the production of ever more detailed sets of performance indicators and tables, the results of which are published yearly in HMIC annual reports. The instruments for the comparisons of force-by-force performance have also become more sophisticated. For example, in 1997, HMIC created the framework of 'families of forces' across England and Wales, forces considered to be operating in similar geographical and social environments (Hale, Uglow, and Heaton, 2005: 4), in order to more effectively compare 'like with like'. Through the regime of inspection and audit, performance measurement, as a key element of the performance culture, had become deeply embedded in the mindset within and about policing.

The Basic Command Unit: The Hub of Police Management and Activity

Another major reform of policing to come out of the combined efforts of the Audit Commission and HMIC was the establishment of the Basic Command Unit as the accepted geographical and decision-making hub of British policing. It has been noted already that one expression of NPM is the notion of *devolved management*, that wherever possible decision-making, both in terms of policy and in terms of managing finances, should be undertaken as close as possible to the point of service delivery. The case for devolved management as a model for both private and public sector organizations is based on a number of considerations (see Bromwich and Lapsley, 1997). First, that it places decision-makers closer to 'consumers' (customers) and increases the responsiveness of the organization to consumer preferences and ties local planning and objective-setting to local conditions rather than on assumptions made 'on high' and remote from the consumer (ie at the level of organizational headquarters). Secondly, that it creates a management framework with a span of supervision and monitoring which is small enough to enable effective management to take place—managers are closer in every sense to their workforce and can consequently track individual performance and administer reward systems more accurately. Thirdly, that it serves to reduce on-costs attached to multiple tiers of management and allows for the reduction in the number of levels of management—creating the 'flatter', 'leaner' organizational model. Fourthly, that it increases the accountability of managers both up and down the organization: up the organization in terms of them having to live within their budgets and not spend unwisely because that will get 'lost' in a central budget; down because of that closer relationship that managers will have with their workforce, so as well as being more able to supervise staff, managers will also be able to listen to those staff and respond accordingly to the messages coming from those staff.

The message of the virtues of devolved management has coloured the work of the Audit Commission in all of its work (Cope and Goodship, 2002). In the policing context the earliest and most explicit expression of this came with Police Paper 9, *Reviewing the Organisation of Provincial Police Forces* (Audit Commission, 1991). This report criticized what it called the 'top-heavy' management structures of police forces and, in particular, the spread of command between police divisions—seen as often too far removed from the operational end of policing, sitting as they were between headquarters and operational police units—and the police sub-divisions, which were often to *small* to cover a sufficiently wide range of policing functions. The answer to this, it was proposed, was two-fold: on the one hand to 'de-tier' police management, by removing the divisional structure and thus 'flattening' the police hierarchy; on the other hand to merge existing sub-divisions, where they were deemed to be too small, into bigger management and operational units. The aim would be to create a unit at the 'lowest level in the command structure which can provide a 24-hour policing service, able to respond to all incidents and deal fully with most of them without frequent external support.' (Audit Commission, 1991). This was soon to be labelled the 'Basic Command Unit' (BCU) but the principle was also reflected in labels such as 'area policing' and 'geographic policing' (see Ashby, 2005). It did not take long for the Audit Commission's case to gain support. It came in political form from the then Home Secretary, Kenneth Baker, who, in a speech to the 1991 Police Federation Conference, praised 'area policing' where it had taken off and put the case for the BCU in populist terms:

> I want to see the re-emerging of the local police chief of police for towns like Rugby, Oxford, Stockton, Dorking, York. That implies the devolution of real responsibility to the *local commander*—responsibility for a local budget, responsibility for judging between competing priorities and real local accountability, as well as accountability to the force. (*Police Review* 28 June 1991—emphasis added)

The case for the BCU was later reiterated in another Audit Commission report, *Cheques and Balances* (Audit Commission, 1994), in this case in terms of the specific benefits of financial delegation to local areas, by which time the case for the BCU was already deeply imbedded across the police service. HMIC soon took up the cudgel and began to inspect forces with an eye to assessing their progress along the lines of establishing BCUs as the main level of the command structure below headquarters (Harper et al, 2002). In many ways the BCU notion has been the most resilient of the police reform measures to emerge in the early 1990s, as it has remained a cornerstone of the management of the police organization and of operational delivery of policing in Britain. Some measure of this is that in the police reform agenda which emerged under the Labour government in the early part of the twenty-first century (discussed at length in Chapter 5 and later in this chapter) the BCU was placed at the heart of the 'police modernization' programme. Furthermore, in a highly significant move in 2001, HMIC were given a mandate to have specific and direct inspections of force BCUs and become primary units for the provision of information on police performance indicators (Mawby and Wright, 2003: 177). This sent out a message that the BCUs were in some senses autonomous or at least semi-autonomous of force headquarters, an important part of the case for what was to become the 'force restructuring' agenda later in that decade (see later). The BCUs were to become pivotal to the case that forces could be merged at the level of headquarters in the direction of 'regionalism', because they could be presented as preserving 'localism' in terms of responsiveness to local priorities and locally-focused decision-making. The case for BCUs as emanating from the perspective of NPM could be used, conveniently, to support a much wider agenda for police reform.

Through the work of the Audit Commission and HMIC, as central regulatory agencies within the machinery of police governance, a change the mindset of and about British policing in the direction of NPM and VFM was taking place. The Commission and HMIC were not the only messengers of NPM principles visited on the police service in the early to mid-1990s. In Chapters 4 and 5 the Conservative police reform agenda which was launched around 1993 will be discussed. That involved three main pillars: the 'Sheehy' inquiry into police roles and responsibilities (Home Office, 1993a); the 'Posen Review' of 'core and ancillary' police functions (Home Office, 1994); and the reforms of police governance first outlined in the White Paper *Police Reform: A Police Service for the Twenty-First Century* (Home Office, 1993b). Without going into these initiatives in any detail at this stage, it is evident that, in each case, elements of NPM were at work in helping set out the approach adopted. The Sheehy Inquiry was an explicit attempt to apply *business sector models* of staff deployment, rewards, and appraisal to the police sector. Additionally, and symbolically, it was headed by the Chairman of a major business corporation, Sir Patrick Sheehy. The Posen Review was undertaken to determine whether areas of what was then 'police-work' could be *civilianized* (in a way far more radical than had then been the case) or *outsourced* to other bodies. Over twenty areas of 'police-work' were initially identified as potentially suitable for this treatment, ranging from dealing with stray dogs, through schools liaison work, to licensing of gaming (Fielding, 2005: 161–2). The rationale behind this initiative reflects some of the NPM notions outlined above, including: the division between 'steering' and 'rowing' in the delivery of services (the police could potentially steer but not row in some of these areas); 'quasi-markets' (the 'police monopoly in these areas could be opened up for competition between public and private sector providers); and what was referred to earlier as the *auxiliarization* of police-work (the separation between a highly trained core and a less well trained—and less expensive— 'lower tier' of providers). Finally, the White Paper *Police Reform* reflected NPM principles by introducing the notion of bringing people with *business backgrounds* into newly configured and more *business-like* police authorities, in place of some of the elected members on the police authorities. Again, the objective was to challenge the traditions of the public sector with management philosophies drawn from the commercial sector. Later chapters will document the only partial success of such initiatives; however, the deeper foundations of NPM were already being laid within the policing mindset by the work of the audit and inspection bodies.

From the issue of Circular 114/83 to the publication of the Audit Commission report *Streetwise* in 1996, the NPM agenda in general for the public sector and for the police sector itself had been forced through under *Conservative* governments. On the basis of what has been discussed earlier in terms of the rise of the 'new right' within Conservative politics, it is easy to identify NPM with Conservative regimes, even if, as will be examined in Chapter 5, policing was periodically treated as a special case by the Conservatives when it came to public sector reform. However, there was to be no slowing down of the push for VFM when New Labour took office in 1997; if anything, the emphasis on the '3Es' for the police service was to be even more pronounced under Labour.

New Labour Meets New Public Management: More in Store for the Police

Simon Jenkins, in his book (pointedly) named *Thatcher and Sons* (Jenkins, 2006), paints a not unconvincing picture of a line of continuity in ethos running from Margaret Thatcher, through her Conservative successor John Major, to his *Labour* successor as Prime Minister, Tony Blair. Blair's admiration for aspects of Thatcher's style of government was well known (Jenkins, 2006: 253). This included her sceptical view of the public sector and its traditions, and the need to continually challenge the status quo of state institutions and 'vested interest' groups such as the public sector trade unions (Thomas, 2001).

Blair's ideological stance embraced the notion of the 'Third Way' (Giddens, 1998), which Blair summarized as follows:

> The Third Way in essence seeks to combine economic dynamism with social justice. Indeed, it does more, it avows that the one depends crucially on the other. If a country generates no wealth, it cannot afford social justice. (Blair, 1999)

The Third Way, as the intellectual basis of Blair's 'New Labour' philosophy, was clearly distinct from 'Thatcherism' (as discussed earlier), in the sense that it places value on social cohesion and 'social justice'. However, the Third Way also advocated that governments support wealth creation—referred to above as 'economic dynamism'—and this entailed governments facilitating *markets* and encouraging enterprise. This was a shift away from the 'Old Labour' tendency of state intervention in the market economy and constraint of business activity. It also entailed a decisive movement away from the 'tax and spend' approach of Old Labour with a determination to rein in public spending wherever possible. A clear marker that this was to be the case was the announcement prior to the General Election of 1997 by Blair's then Shadow Chancellor, Gordon Brown, that Labour would live within the three-year spending targets set by the Conservative Chancellor, Kenneth Clarke. Public spending would abide by a 'golden rule' to balance revenue and spending (Jenkins, 2006: 253–4). This commitment to Conservative spending plans, whilst also designed to neutralize opposition claims that once in office Labour would revert to its old 'tax and spend' ways, was also a statement that there would be no significant departure from the VFM culture which had grown under the Conservatives. Indeed, a special label was to emerge as Labour's own particular version of VFM: *Best Value*.

Following the General Election of 1997 the new Labour Government made clear its intention to 'modernize' local government. The broader base of the modernization agenda is discussed in Chapter 5, but we can in this context consider one key element of that agenda: the introduction of the Best Value (BV). The rationale behind BV was spelt out in the White Paper *Modern Local Government: In Touch with the People* (DETR, 1998a):

> Best value will be a duty to deliver services to clear standards—covering both cost and quality—by the most effective, economic and efficient means available . . . Local authorities will set those standards . . . for all the services for which they are responsible . . . Under best value local people will be clear about the standards of services which they can expect to receive, and better able to hold their councils to account for their record in meeting them.

BV was Labour's alternative to the Conservative policy of *compulsory competitive tendering* (CCT). CCT was initially introduced as far back as 1980 under the *Local Government Act*, which required local authorities to put building and maintenance work out to competitive tender to drive up VFM. The scope of CCT was later widened under the *Local Government Act 1988* to include building and other cleaning, refuse collection, catering and vehicle maintenance (Pinch and Patterson, 2000). This had, for example, led the police sector to put the maintenance of police vehicles and police canteens out for CCT, a modest form of 'privatization' in many respects in the sense that such work in most cases went to outside commercial companies. The scope of BV, however, was to be much wider and 'deeper' than CCT (Leigh, Mundy, and Tuffin, 1999: 1–2). BV was to apply to *all* services provided by the sector (local authorities, police, and fire service), covering every activity associated with that service; a stronger focus on *quality* of the services in question; a focus on *partnership working*, particularly multi-agency partnerships (part of the 'joined up government' agenda—Long, 2002); and an emphasis on aiming high in terms of performance—services were to set performance targets to match the top 25% in the national leagues of performance measures in each sector. The overall ambition for BV was made clear in the legislation which introduced it, the *Local Government Act 1999*, where it placed a duty on BV authorities to 'make arrangements to secure *continuous improvement* in the way (their) functions are expressed, having regard to a combination of economy, efficiency and effectiveness' (Clause 3.1—emphasis added).

The machinery for BV, the 'continuous improvement' in service performance, was to have three dimensions (Boyne, 2000: 7). First, there would be *performance plans* which authorities must publish on an annual basis; in the policing context the plans would set out a strategy for local policing and examining police performance, identifying policing services (for example, police training) which seem to warrant further examination. A message from government was that the performance plans should be compatible with government targets on 'efficiency gains' for local authority expenditure of 2% per annum (Long, 2003: 633).

Secondly, in order to undertake such examination, there would be *Best Value reviews*, which were to be undertaken within a five-year period up to 2005. The reviews were to be based on what became known as the 'Four Cs' (DETR 1998a): the need to *challenge* why and how a service is being provided; the need to *compare* a service's performance with the performance of other services using a suite of performance indicators; the need to *consult* local taxpayers and service users (and the wider business community) in the setting of new performance targets; and the need to embrace the ethos of *competition* to secure efficient and effective services. The 'Four Cs' were rather like the 'Three Es' with heart—they coupled hard-edged NPM principles such as 'marketization' (competition) with softer notions of 'engagement' with the community (consultation), something that was to re-emerge in later reforms, as we shall see in Chapter 5. The Best Value reviews for the police were to come under the remit of HMIC as a special field of inspection (see HMIC, 2005: 56).

Thirdly, authorities would be required to produce *action plans* which reflect the BV reviews and which would include new performance targets for continuous improvement. Running through this machinery is the process of performance measurement, articulated through batches of performance indicators and built around *targets*—Jenkins (2006: 279–80) has referred to Blair/Brown's belief in the virtues of target-setting and the whole 'target-culture' under Labour as bordering on the 'maniacal', which ranged from the 'ruthless to the comical', forcing the police, for example, 'to balance more police crashes against improved 999-call answering'. Nevertheless, performance indicators and targets were the order of the day. As we have seen, the first suite of national performance indicators for the police was published by the Audit Commission in 1995. The BV regime was to move performance measurement to another level altogether. The *Local Government Act 1999* created a set of national Best Value Performance Indicators (BVPIs), including what were called 'corporate health indicators', designed to reflect the overall 'health' of the service in question. As Long makes clear (2003: 634–5; see also Boyne, 2000: 8) the BVPIs for the police fall into five main areas:

- *Strategic objectives*—which relate to public safety, level of crime and fear of crime and public safety and confidence in the police;

- *Cost and efficiency*—the levels of resources (for example numbers of officers) against outcomes of the deployment of those resources;
- *Service delivery outcomes*—information on how well the police service is doing in relation to its strategic objectives. These cover indicators on recorded crime, public disorder, number of files processed and traffic accidents;
- *Quality*—how the police service is experienced by users, based on users' (victims and witnesses) satisfaction levels, response times, summons, and cautions, etc;
- *Fair access*—focusing on ease and equality of access to policing services, including information on the use of stops of white and minority ethnic people, complaints against the police and information on racial incidents.

The BVPIs once collected helped form 'league tables' of police performance at a level of sophistication much higher than the first league tables referred to earlier. Furthermore, the tables were used more assertively and judgementally to *drive up performance*. As has been noted, under BV authorities are required to set performance targets which are in line with reaching the performance standards of the top 25%. Linked to this is the categorization of the remaining 75%, which in declining orders of 25% each, are 'striving', 'coasting' and, as the bottom 25% of the league, 'failing' (M. Long, 2003: 635), a label which the chief officers of the forces concerned might see as a sign that they might consider retirement. The whole panoply of audit and inspection, with the combined efforts of both the Audit Commission and the Inspectorate, later to be joined by the Police Standards Unit at the Home Office (see Chapter 5), was to be marshalled to support this machinery of driving up performance using the performance indicators and league tables. For example, HMIC moved to a force classification system whereby force performance in each of the main performance areas was classified along the two poles of 'poor-fair-good-excellent' and 'deteriorated-stable-improved' (HMIC, 2005: 32–3). At a glance the public could see whether their local police force was something to be proud or ashamed of. Furthermore, with the shift referred to earlier of presenting performance data from BCU-level policing, the league tables could offer interesting advice on whether to move house and where to move it. The BV agenda had raised the culture of performance management to another level altogether.

However, BV was only a part of the movement to drive up performance in the policing sector. Other reforms throughout the 1990s and since were designed to improve policing and drive up standards in various ways; ironically for a Labour Party anxious to ditch Old Labour commitments such as the nationalization of industry, they took the form of what has been called the *nationalization of policing* (Jones, 2003: 613–16; Johnston, 2000: 91–6). In this respect the primary driving force for reform was one of the Three Es: *effectiveness*.

The Nationalization of Policing: Improving Effectiveness through Centralization?

Successive governments have sought to improve performance in the British police service by centralizing aspects of and decision-making for policing. A service so steeped in the traditions of localism is bound to be faced periodically with attempts to bring in greater consistency and coordination, and the centralization of features of the service is a predictable response to that. The creation of national performance indicators, as has been seen, is one expression of that. However, the process of nationalization spreads much further than that. The rationale for nationalization, officially and otherwise, lies in the apparent virtues of national over local management and governance. First, that national frameworks enable the *coordination and consistency* across otherwise locally dispersed, diverse and fragmented policing units. Secondly, that national frameworks work to avoid *duplication of effort* amongst policing units, and in that sense, in principle, are likely to deliver efficiency gains compared with locally determined arrangements. Thirdly, that national frameworks enable *economies of scale* and can deliver services which dispersed and smaller policing units cannot. Fourthly, less overtly, that national frameworks facilitate *central control* of service provision and allow central government to force through centrally determined priorities and plans for policing—an issue which will be considered later. In these respects it is possible to categorize the 'nationalization of policing' process and the reforms associated with them in two forms: *national police agencies* on the one hand, and *national standards and policy frameworks* on the other.

National Police Agencies

Although typically viewed initially at least with suspicion, and even welcomed by some with talk of a drift to a 'police state', national police agencies have been appearing on the British scene periodically for a significant number of years (Mawby and Wright, 2003: 189–92; Savage, Charman, and Cope, 2000: 204–6), although interestingly more rapidly under Labour governments. The first clearly national, standing, policing body to be established was National Police Training, which was formed in 1993 as an attempt to better coordinate and standardize police training which, until then, was dispersed across a range of force-level and regional training centres, apart from the Police Staff College at Bramshill which was responsible for high-flyer and senior officer training. National Police Training soon developed its own national bodies when, in a form of emulation of universities, it formed the National Crime Faculty and the National Operational Faculty (Mawby and Wright, 2003: 191), which were set up to develop and disseminate best practice in criminal investigation and operational policing such as public order policing respectively. The Faculties also offered support to forces on a form of 'consultancy' basis, particularly when major criminal events took place, such as major murder inquiries. The rationale of centralizing police training was expressed even further when, under the *Criminal Justice and Police Act 2001*, NPT was rolled into a new body, the *Central Police Training and Development Authority*, 'Centrex'. Centrex embraced not just the old NPT but also scientific support for criminal investigation and the newly created *National Centre for Policing Excellence* (NCPE—discussed later). The brief for Centrex extended well beyond the predominantly training focus of National Police Training; however, as we shall see, Centrex, ironically, was itself later to be subsumed within an even wider process of nationalization.

Alongside the development of national police training bodies, parallel things were happening in the world of criminal intelligence work. Criminal intelligence and investigation had already, during the 1960s, broken through force boundaries, with the establishment of regional crime squads focused on cross-border crime. A move to a national framework for intelligence work, although relating to a specific area of crime, came in the 1980s with the formation of the National Drugs Intelligence Unit, based within the Metropolitan Police area (Mawby and Wright, 2003: 190–1). However, a broader national intelligence approach came with the creation of the *National Criminal Intelligence Service* (NCIS) in 1992, which included intelligence gathering and dissemination to local forces in both the drugs and football violence fields, although NCIS was not given a statutory basis—and an even wider brief—until the *Police Act 1997*. The work of NCIS covered four main areas of activity (Mawby and Wright, 2003: 190): strategic overviews of organized crime; intelligence on the most serious criminals; the coordination of intelligence and provision of specialist services; and 'knowledge products', such as the National Intelligence Model (see below).

The *Police Act 1997* also created the *National Crime Squad* (NCS), which was to work alongside NCIS in improving the policing response to serious and particularly organized, crime. NCS amalgamated what were the six regional crime squads in England and Wales. The main aim of NCS was to tackle Class A drug trafficking, organized immigration crime and other areas of crime identified by the authorities as priority crimes (Levi, 2003: 447–8). However, the scope of activity for NCS was to be far reaching, leading some to see its creation as a significant step along the way to a national police force itself (Uglow with Telford, 1997). As well being charged to prevent and detect serious crime covering more than one police area, NCS was also given the powers to provide support to any police force if the chief officer requested it, support the activities of NCIS if requested to do so by its Director General, institute criminal proceedings on its own behalf, and act in support of other law enforcement agencies other than the police, such as Customs and Excise (Johnston, 2000: 94–5).

As each of these national policing agencies has appeared on the scene concern has been raised about the loss of local autonomy their creation involves and the fear, as mentioned already, that they constitute steps towards the full nationalization of the British police (Uglow with Telford, 1997: 36; Jenkins, 2006: 292–6). More cautious criticism has been directed at the compromises which these developments entail in terms of accountabilities (Johnston, 2000: 93–5; N. Walker, 2000). British policing had traditionally been locally-based and locally-accountable, however fragile that accountability might have been. The formation of national policing bodies moves the processes of account- ability to other levels, allowing major decisions about policing to be made some distance away, both geographically and structurally, from localities. These new nationally-based accountability structures typically took the form of 'ser- vice authorities', oversight panels with membership comprising representatives from a range of stakeholder organizations—the Local Authority Association, ACPO, and so on—but which remain largely under the tutelage of the Home Office, because the Home Secretary has the responsibility to appoint the ser- vice authority chairs and set annual objectives and performance indicators for the body in question (Jones, 2003: 614–16). At the very least, the national policing bodies challenge the traditions of police accountability in the British context. However, they also become victim to the very processes which led to their creation. There is a form of inner logic within the nationalization process which means that the national bodies themselves get eaten up by even bigger fish, supra-national bodies. Just as Centrex was to be subsumed under a bigger national body (see below) so too were NCIS and the NCS.

In 2006, the Labour government announced the formation of the Serious Organised Crime Agency (SOCA). Labelled the 'British FBI' (*Guardian* 3 April 2006), SOCA was to amalgamate NCIS and NCS and also incorporate investiga- tors from the Customs and Immigration service. SOCA's creation was initially announced in 2004 by the then Home Secretary David Blunkett, as part of a wider government campaign to tackle organized crime head on. However, one rationale for rolling NCIS and NCS into a larger corporation was the desire to overcome the 'rivalry' and competition between them and the overlapping of their activities (Harfield, 2006: 745). The case for establishing SOCA was very much along the lines of the rationale for nationalization of policing itself, as outlined earlier. Commenting on NCIS and NCS, a statement in the House of Commons said: 'However good each of the bodies may be in its own right, the reality is that they are operating according to priorities and performance man- agement regimes that treat them as single bodies. They cannot be as *effective* as a single body which can focus its combined resources on a single strategy.' (Quot- ed in Harfield, 2006: 745–6—emphasis added.) The new single body was to start its first full year of operations with a budget of almost half a billion pounds and a staff of over 4,000 (SOCA, 2007: 7).

The stated aims of SOCA, as determined by the SOCA Board, (SOCA, 2007: 9–10) are:

1. To build knowledge and understanding of serious organized crime, the harm it causes, and the effectiveness of different responses
2. To increase the amount of criminal assets recovered and increase the propor- tion of cases in which the proceeds of crime are pursued

3. To increase the risk to serious organized crime operating in the UK, through proven investigation capabilities and in new ways
4. To collaborate with partners in the UK and internationally to maximize efforts to reduce harm
5. To provide agreed levels of high quality support to SOCA's operational partners and, as appropriate, seek their support in return.

In time-honoured NPM fashion, the SOCA Board also identified the types of performance measures SOCA would be assessed and monitored on (SOCA, 2007: 12): the quality of knowledge and understanding of serious organized crime; criminal asset performance (set against the government's wider asset recovery targets); dislocation of criminal markets (measured by the price and quality of criminal goods and services—the aim being to push prices up and quality down); and the quality of SOCA's relationships with others (measured by survey data). As shall be argued in Chapter 5, there is a deeper rationale for the suite of police reforms instigated by the Labour government from the beginning of the twentieth century, SOCA being one of them. However, there is little doubt that considerations of efficiency and effectiveness were key drivers of this, and other, shifts to national policing bodies such as SOCA.

A raft of other national policing bodies were to arrive on the scene during and since the late 1990s, but these more driven by a concern for raising and maintaining *standards* and the formation of and compliance with national *policies*.

National Police Standards and Policy Frameworks

The move towards national standards frameworks has already been considered in relation to national performance indicators and national league tables which, as has been noted, arrived in the policing world in the mid-1990s. However, as the Labour government embarked on its own comprehensive programme for police reform (discussed in Chapter 5) it was clear that there would be an accentuation of machineries for 'raising standards' in policing in addition to those already in place, such as HMIC. The White Paper *Policing a New Century: A Blueprint for Reform* (Home Office, 2001b) announced the setting up of the *National Centre for Policing Excellence* (NCPE) to be part of Centrex. NCPE would roll together two other national bodies (by now a familiar pattern), the National Crime Faculty and the National Operations Faculty, and was to become a 'centre of excellence for all aspects of operational policing, promoting evidence-based practices that have been professionally validated' (Home Office, 2001b: 41). NCPE would spread best practice, design training and development based upon that practice, and advise and support forces in its implementation. An example of this role was given in Chapter 1 in relation to criminal investigation—a major focus of the Labour government's attempt to drive up standards in policing—relating to the role of periodic 'review' of decision-making in investigative practice. The identification by the Macpherson Inquiry of the paucity of effective review of the initial and subsequent investigations in the Lawrence case, became in due course one of concerns of NCPE, which in due course drew up a 'doctrine' of best practice for forces to follow in this area of policing (National Centre for Policing Excellence, 2005). The establishment of NCPE was a further sign that the days of '43 different ways of policing' were numbered, and that the police service was to be under even more pressure to become more 'professional' in the way it went about its business (Neyroud, 2003: 586–9). Along with its parallel 'standards' body, the *Police Standards Unit*—also announced in the White Paper *Police Reform* and discussed in Chapter 5—the NCPE was to be a form of think-tank for the development of 'policing theory', or what was referred to as 'doctrine development', which could unify policing practice across the 43 forces of England and Wales and improve standards accordingly. One area of work which the NCPE addressed, and developed 'doctrine' on, was *intelligence-led policing*, and, in particular, the *National Intelligence Model* (NIM) (ACPO/Centrex, 2005). NIM was to become a national standards framework of its own.

As indicated, one area of policing where the Labour government was particularly anxious to standardize policing practice and drive up standards was in criminal investigation. NIM was seen as one way of doing this. NIM has a chequered history drawing as it does from a number of sources of influence, but its primary origin lies within *intelligence-led policing* (ILP), considered briefly earlier in this chapter in the context of the Audit Commission. ILP itself had some roots in policing initiatives in the 1970s in the United States, for example, the targeting of repeat and prolific offenders in police operations as a means of tackling crime (Heaton, 2000: 340–2). This was an approach which the Audit Commission, as has been seen, was to phrase in terms of 'targeting the offender rather than the crime'. However, ILP also had some roots in the work of the Metropolitan Police under Newman in the early 1980s, in particular, in relation to the 'planning cycle' as 'Management by Objectives' (discussed in Chapter 2) was rolled out in parts of the London area. A key element in the planning cycle was the systematic use of information and analysis as a basis for decision-making and actions in local area policing. ILP has been defined as 'developing and maintaining a detailed and up-to-date picture of patterns of crime and criminality in order to intervene in it most effectively to disrupt network and remove prolific offenders'. (Tilley, 2003: 321–3). ILP has various elements and dimensions, the core of which (Grieve, 2007) are:

- the development and employment of an *analytical capacity*; utilizing analytical systems to process information on crime and suspects and specialist personnel (now usually known as 'crime analysts') to undertake analysis of available information;
- the comprehensive use of *information technology* to store, process and produce reports on information on crime and suspects;

- the systematic use of *surveillance* and *informants* to gather information and develop intelligence; and
- the use of *coordinating and tasking groups* and *area intelligence* groups to respond to intelligence produced to ensure a managed and effective response—these groups hold regular meetings to gather intelligence, make assessments (tactical or strategic), allocate personnel to tasks and review progress.

Although ILP has a distinctively 'policing' feel about it—surveillance and use of informants are not practices common in other organizations—it does bear some of the marks of best practice in the commercial world. Product development in private corporations would normally be based on market research, which can provide 'intelligence' on the potential market a new product line might exploit. Once a product line has been developed, marketing activity would normally be 'intelligence-led' in the sense that marketing would be concentrated in areas where customers are more likely to be located. Indeed, it has been argued that the 'intelligence systems' generated by the commercial world—such as 'MOSAIC', used by large corporations to create geodemographic profiles for marketing purposes—can be applied directly to crime problems and policing solutions (Hayden, Williamson, and Webber, 2007). However, ILP also draws from sources closer to home, such as the practices in the security services, where intelligence, criminal and otherwise, is the life-blood of operational strategy.

Support for ILP grew steadily within the police service during the 1990s, and ILP was eventually adopted by HMIC as best practice and it become the subject of a thematic inspection in 1997 (HMIC, 1997), some measure of its wider acceptance. The full arrival of ILP on the national stage, however, came with the establishment of NIM. It was initially developed by NCIS on behalf of the ACPO Crime Committee (NCIS, 2000) and was even given a statutory footing in the *Police Reform Act 2002*, when the government required police forces to comply with minimum standards as set out in NIM (known as 'NIM compliance'); NIM was later to be described by the government as 'the single most nationally implemented change in policing since 1997' (Home Office, 2004b: 31). The NCPE developed the model further by producing extensive guidelines for forces on the full implementation of NIM and the creation of 'intelligence products' (ACPO/Centrex, 2005). NIM was presented explicitly as a 'business model for law enforcement' (ACPO/Centrex, 2005: 8) and the NIM 'business process' contained nine stages of the 'intelligence cycle':

1. *Assets*. The foundation for NIM was the set of assets the police have or need to have in order to operate 'intelligently'; these relate to resources such as specialist knowledge (eg forensics); systems assets in the form of infrastructure, support, and security; and 'people assets' in terms of skilled staff prepared to carry out intelligence functions and management (such as crime analysts).

2. *Information sources.* The main sources of information on which the intelligence function can operate and which come in by way of focused intelligence gathering, routine policing, or by way of volunteered information. This included information from victims, witnesses, prisoners, forensic examination, communities and members of the public, undercover operations, surveillance, and prisoners (the latter would require close cooperation between the police and prison services).

3. *Information and intelligence recording.* The recording and management of the information coming in to the police, involving the assessment of the information and decisions about disseminating it to other parts of the police organization or elsewhere (which could include international agencies).

4. *Research, Development and Analysis.* Once information is received and assessed, further information might be sought (eg from the sources above) and various analytical techniques would be used to interpret and interrogate the information; the latter could include crime pattern analysis, offender profiling, network analysis (who suspects network with and how), and market analysis (eg how guns are purchased for firearms offences or the pricing structures within drugs markets).

5. *Intelligence Products.* These are the assessments and profiles which emerge out of the intelligence analysis—for example, they might identify priority areas for further information gathering or identify intelligence gaps.

6. *Strategic and Tactical Tasking and Coordination.* The processes by which intelligence products are acted upon by managers at strategic levels (headquarters or national levels) or tactical levels (BCU level). This is the point at which individuals are identified as 'plan owners' and timescales for action are set out.

7. *Tactical Resolution.* The stage of planning actions and carrying them out—this might include targeted patrol, offender targeting, media campaigns, arrest, and so on. Before ILP became accepted, this was typically the *first* stage of policing! With NIM the emphasis is very much on the 'business processes' which are undertaken *prior* to policing activity in the operational sense.

8. *Operational Review.* A 'results analysis' which asks critical questions about the nature of intelligence underpinning the police operation, the impact of policing strategy and tactics on the problem addressed (eg the extent of crime reduction, disruption or displacement), and what lessons can be learned from the whole experience for future activity.

NIM reflects NPM in at least two senses. On the one hand, as has been seen, it is explicitly a *business model* for policing, employing business process models to the world of policing. On the other hand, it is another example of a national *standards framework*, frameworks which had emerged as a means of driving up performance in the policing sector and which have become very much part of the scenery of the performance culture within British policing. There was more to come on this front, with the establishment of the *National Policing Improvement Agency*.

Just as SOCA involved the formation of a 'supra-national' body to merge existing national agencies into a larger, more comprehensive, corporation in the field of intelligence and criminal investigation, the parallel formation of the *National Police Improvement Agency* (NPIA) was to do the same for policing bodies associated with police training and development, technological provision, and policing standards. NPIA was first presented as ACPOs response to the government's 2003 Green Paper *Policing: Building Safer Communities Together* (Home Office, 2003a). NPIA was ACPO's answer to the question of how to enhance central support for the police service (Home Office, 2003a: 27); ACPO proposed establishing an agency to support the implementation of national standards in policing which would eliminate the duplication it argued existed in the then current framework. The government announced the formation of NPIA in the White Paper *Building Communities, Beating Crime* (Home Office 2004b), and it was given statutory footing with the *Police and Justice Act 2006*. This supra-national standards body would roll together Centrex, including NCPE, and the Police Information Technology Organisation (PITO), the agency responsible for the development of police information and communication technologies (ICT). The NPIA would have three main functions (Home Office, 2004b: 112): good practice development; support to forces implementing change agendas; and providing operational support for police forces. It would not only take over the functions of Centrex, NCPE and PITO, it would 'rationalise the landscape of national organisations' (Home Office, 2004b: 113). This included, significantly, a *policy-making* role for the police service, presenting potential territorial overlap with the work of ACPO, which had worked hard over the years prior to this to standardize and harmonize police policy-making (see Savage, Charman, and Cope, 2000: 165–72). Indeed, as the White Paper expressed it: 'We also hope that many of ACPOs policy making functions will also become enshrined within the new body' (Home Office, 2004b: 113). The policy-making role was evident in NPIA's list of priorities for supporting the police service (NPIA, 2007), which included, as well as training and development and ICT work:

- identifying and planning for future challenges to face policing;
- finding and developing good practice in evidence-based policing;
- informing the priority and sequence of change programmes;
- playing a lead role in seeing that change programmes take place; and
- using research and analysis to improve policing.

The process of 'nationalizing policing' was by now highly advanced: the landscape was now dotted with the supra-national agencies, SOCA and NPIA, and the 'standards enforcement' agencies of the Police Standards Unit and HMIC—in 2002 yet another standards body was created, with a particular focus on occupational standards for police, the Police Skills and Standards

Organisation (later to be rolled into the broader Skills for Justice organization). When added to parallel development of *national plans* for the police service (see Chapter 5), the national frameworks of British policing were becoming major, if not dominant, features of the structure, governance, and functioning of the police service. However, there were still 43 police forces in England and Wales with organizational boundaries that had hardly changed in three decades. Sitting, increasingly uncomfortably, between the highly valued BCUs on the one hand and the plethora of national bodies and national standards frameworks on the other, the future of the police forces themselves could hardly fail to come under the microscope of the police reform process. This was indeed eventually to happen with the *force restructuring* debate.

Force Restructuring: Driving up Performance —Reducing Waste

In the discourse surrounding NIM a differentiation of 'levels of policing' emerged which took further some of the thinking associated with the formation of old Regional Crime Squads in the 1960s (Newburn, 2003: 92), the firming up of the key role of BCUs in the 1990s—as discussed earlier—and the emergence of the national crime agencies, NCIS and NCS. NIM was to apply to all levels of crime, and was to operate at three levels of policing (ACPO/Centrex, 2005: 12).

- *Level 1:* Local crime and disorder, including antisocial behaviour, capable of being managed by local resources, for example, crimes affecting a BCU or small force area.
- *Level 2:* Cross-border issues affecting more than one BCU within a force or affecting another force or regional crime activity, usually some level of organized criminality, such as Class A drugs problems, and major incidents and events.
- *Level 3:* Serious and organized crime usually operating on a national and international scale.

If 'Level 1' crime and disorder are the natural concern of BCUs, and 'Level 3' crime the natural concern of national policing agencies, the question is who or what should be responsible for 'Level 2' policing problems? This exposes the issue of whether the 43 police force structure is best equipped to handle the crime problems posed by cross-border crime and major incidents requiring extensive resources, such as major murder inquiries. Alongside the other reforms of the early twenty-first century, an old spectre was returning to the scene: *force amalgamation.*

The prospect of force amalgamation had hovered over the policing scene periodically during the 1990s. There were dark rumours in the early 1990s that HMIC had privately drawn up plans to reduce the number of forces in England and Wales to something like 25 forces, not helped by the refusal of the then Home Secretary, Kenneth Baker, to rule out amalgamations in the future. In a speech to the Police Federation Conference in 1991, interestingly praising 'area policing'—ie what became known as BCUs—Baker, whilst not at that stage openly advocating force amalgamations, said: 'I know there is concern is smaller forces about their future, and I cannot rule out the possibility that at some time I or my successors may want to review the position.' (*Police Review* 28 June 1991). The debate about amalgamations returned in the mid-1990s when the Police and Magistrates' Courts Act 1994 created new powers for the Home Secretary to order force amalgamations on the grounds of efficiency, an issue which was often looked over by critics of the Act who had focused on other concerns over the legislation (Jones and Newburn, 1997: 34–5; see Chapter 5). However, the question of force amalgamations really came to a head under New Labour's police reform programme.

It was perhaps inevitable that the amalgamation agenda would reappear under New Labour, not least because, as will be argued in Chapter 5, Labour was eventually to prioritize 'delivery' in its approach to the police sector, and force amalgamation is closely associated with notions of effective delivery of policing services—and of course with efficiency and economy, as shall be seen. The first stirrings of a re-visit to force amalgamations can with the White Paper, *Building Communities* (Home Office, 2004b), where a case was made that the response to 'Level 2' criminality (as defined above), was an area of concern and one needing review and reform. Expressing satisfaction that locally based policing is heading in the right direction (Level 1), and that national policing structures were falling into place (Level 3) the White Paper stated: 'The Government sees a need a highlight a particular level of criminality that falls somewhere between the two ends of the local/national spectrum—crime that crosses police borders...' (Home Office, 2004b: 114). One option outlined was the identification of 'lead forces' which develop particular specialisms which they could provide to other forces in the region (like the MPS role in counter-terrorism). However, there was clearly a wider agenda, even if the direction was not stated, not surprising given the sensitivities surrounding the issue, and the White Paper announced that HMIC were to be commissioned to examine the 'issue of force structures' further (Home Office, 2004b: 115). This set the scene for what was to be the controversial report, *Closing the Gap* (HMIC 2006), which did the government's dirty work by making a 'business case' for force restructuring on a large scale.

Closing the Gap was a review which from the outset had a particular 'offender' and 'offence' in its sights: the 'offender' was the 'small' police force, the 'offence' their failure to match up to the demands of Level 2 criminality. The area of police work in question was given the label of *protective services*—what needs to be provided beyond the level of neighbourhood and BCU policing (which deal with anti-social behaviour and volume crime) to *protect* the public, such as dealing with serious and organized crime the force, regional and national levels. The report reiterates the claim in *Building Communities* that the 'successes' of Level 1 and Level 3 policing compare all too favourably with the *lack* of success in responding at Level 2 (referred to as presenting an ad hoc approach to policing problems (HMIC, 2006: 17), particularly in the light of the growing challenges facing this level of criminality, in terms of:

- the threat posed by local and regional organized crime groups;
- the increasing challenges of dealing with major inquiries, particularly for the smaller forces, brought to a head most recently by the 'Soham' murders (See Chapter 1);
- the threat of terrorism; and
- concerns about the capacity for police forces to deliver on NIM in terms of interfacing with national level policing processes.

The question mark against the capacity of small forces to deliver was stated in blunt terms, raising the need 'to address the issues of whether or not some forces are simply too small to be able to provide a full range of protective services efficiently and effectively' (HMIC, 2006: 13). The report also doubted whether 'the new professionalism that has taken root at BCU level in delivering volume crime performance has . . . yet to make its mark in protective services' (HMIC, 2006: 13). Drawing on evidence from earlier HMIC work, the report then identified a range of areas of police work where 'performance gaps' were apparent as a result of the configuration of force structures and the policing approaches taken at force level (HMIC, 2006: 24–31), including counter-terrorism and domestic extremism, serious and organized crime, major public order events, major crime, critical incidents, civil contingencies and intelligence processes (along the lines of NIM). The picture presented was that larger forces were more able to live up to the challenges presented by these areas of policing than small forces. In addition to concerns about the effectiveness of the smaller forces to deliver protective services, *Closing the Gap* also questioned the *economics* of delivering those services and the financial resilience of the smaller forces to cope with large-scale demands on their resources (HMIC, 2006: 49–54). The conclusion was that the larger forces, because of their economies of scale, were much better situated when it came the question of financial robustness. The report labelled the forces better placed to deliver, and afford to deliver, protective services *strategic police forces*.

Closing the Gap did offer a range of options for addressing the problems it identified in terms of force restructuring (including the notion of 'lead forces' referred to earlier). However, it came down clearly in favour of consolidating existing forces, unless they were already at that stage (such as the large metropolitan forces), into *strategic forces*. Force restructuring along the lines of amalgamating forces into bigger operating units was now firmly on the agenda. HMIC could not resist the opportunity to declare that *size does matter*. It was now up to government to respond to the review it had ordered, one which had come up with the answer it clearly wished to hear.

The then Home Secretary, Charles Clarke, accepted the case constructed by *Closing the Gap* in full, and unlike his predecessor, David Blunkett, who saw force mergers as potentially damaging the wider reform agenda because they could distract attention, Clarke saw mergers as central to that agenda. This might have also had something to do with concerns about the quality of police leadership: a former Home Office civil servant revealed that Clarke had argued behind the scenes that there was an 'insufficient number of leaders with the right strategic leadership to go around' the 43 police forces (Rimmer, 2007). The issue of the quality of police leadership was a theme within other police reform programmes, as will be seen in Chapter 5. Nevertheless, the explicit rationale for restructuring was based on the issue of *effectiveness*. In a letter to the Association of Police Authorities (Clarke, 2005) Clarke stated 'I believe restructuring is essential and will make a major contribution to the improvement of our policing capacity in England and Wales ... the weaknesses and issues highlighted in *Closing the Gap* are serious and will not lessen with time, and I believe it is essential we tackle them quickly ...' The Home Office decided to progress the issue by inviting chief officers and their police authorities to come up with their own proposals for force mergers (and to do so within a very tight timetable). With the submissions in, the Home Office began work on assessing their viability.

However, following the series of crises to hit the Home Office in the spring of 2006, including the revelation that over 1000 foreign prisoners, including a number of sex offenders, had avoided deportation on release (*Guardian* 25 April 2006), Charles Clarke, the primary advocate of force restructuring, was relieved of his post. His successor, John Reid, came into office determined to overhaul the machinery of this most important department. Within a few months he was to make the startling announcement that the Home Office was not 'fit for purpose'—ironically the very term the Home Office, via HMIC, had used in relation to the configuration of police forces in England and Wales. The work of the Home Office was temporarily put on ice until a review (not unlike the review of force structures!) was undertaken. There were bound to be casualties in this exercise, and one of them was the force restructuring agenda. Perhaps stung by the loss of face Labour's law and order profile had suffered by the Home Office crises, Reid decided to shelve the restructuring agenda (*Guardian* 12 July 2006)—perhaps viewing it in the way Blunkett had previously, as an unnecessary distraction. Tony McNulty, then Policing Minister at the Home Office, later described how 'the argument about strategic forces went away over the Summer' (McNulty, 2007). He also stated that the Home Office would look at other ways of tackling the problems identified in *Closing the Gap* than restructuring (*Guardian* 12 July 2006). Force mergers were now an idea whose time had gone!

Despite the force restructuring agenda being unceremoniously dumped, Labour's wider police reform agenda was still very much on track. Another part of that agenda also exhibited a concern with effectiveness and efficiency, in this case targeted at the police *workforce*.

Workforce Modernization: 'More for the Same'

As has been seen, a core area of NPM is directed at reforming the configuration of the workforce. Both civilianization and the 'core–ancillary functions' review were driven by concerns to reconfigure the police workforce in order to achieve economies, and to increase the flexibility of employment practices in the police sector, not an easy task given the 'sacredness' principle outlined previously. However, as will be made clear in Chapter 5, New Labour became, over time, more and more determined to challenge, in fundamental ways, 'no go areas' in British policing. One key dimension of the police reform agenda that emerged in the early part of the twenty-first century was the '*Workforce Modernization*' programme. This programme re-opened many of the issues which had emerged in the civilianization and 'core–ancillary' debates and was to be the most radical attempt yet to drive NPM principles through the area of employment and deployment of staff within the police sector.

The Workforce Modernization Programme was first set out in the White Paper *Building Communities, Beating Crime* (Home Office, 2004b). In setting out plans for 'building a new workforce', the White Paper identified the aims behind the programme (Home Office, 2004b: 76):

- reinforcing neighbourhood policing and building a more 'citizen-focused' police service—in other words, a service more responsive to its 'customers';
- increasing the use of 'police staff'—the new term to emerge for what were previously called 'civilians' or 'support staff';
- enhancing the professionalism of police officers and police staff;
- opening the police service to 'new talent';
- strengthening police leadership at all levels, including at constable level; and
- making faster progress on diversity.

What was proposed was a widespread range of reforms to the 'workforce mix' to deliver a more flexible, effective, and efficient body of staff for the police service, later to be labelled, in classic NPM language, '*more for the same*' (Quick, 2006). At the heart of the of the programme was the notion of 'the central role of the constable' (Home Office, 2004b: 79). If the BCU was to be the core organizational unit of the police service, the constable was to be the core staff unit of the police service. The White Paper stated: 'we see constables increasingly working as *community leaders in delivering what the public sees as priorities in their area*' (Home Office: 2004b: 79—emphasis added). This notion, and its link with 'neighbourhood policing', is examined in more depth in Chapter 5. However, at this point what was significant in the notion of the constable-as-leader was the implication that the constable is to be seen increasingly as a *manager*. The constable was to play a key role in setting *priorities* for policing at the 'micro-local' level, and a key role in the *management of resources* at the local level ('team leader' of other staff such as PCSOs and volunteers). The constable was also to be pivotal in enabling a more consumer-responsive police service because she/he would be closer to the ground and closer to 'customers' of the police. In support of this vision, the White Paper and the subsequent reform programme included enhanced training for constables in the skills necessary for leadership and management, training previously restricted to supervisors and more senior officers.

The Workforce Modernization Programme also placed great emphasis on enhancing the role of PCSOs, as a means of furthering what has here been called the auxiliarization of policing through the extended policing family (discussed in detail in Chapter 2 and later in Chapter 5). The White Paper outlined a number of ways of doing this (Home Office, 2004b: 84–5). First, by increasing the *powers* available to PCSOs—for example, to allow forces to grant them the power of detention. Secondly, by developing more thorough role definitions and occupational standards for PCSOs in order to encourage more consistency and professionalism across this area of staffing. Thirdly, by enhancing the training of PCSOs through centrally produced training packages, improved supervision and other devices. Fourthly, by developing an enhanced rewards and career progression framework for PCSOs, including smoothing the way to move from PCSO to a sworn office. The message was that this tier of policing was here to stay and was not to be treated as the 'Cinderella' of the police service.

The Workforce Modernization Programme was to involve a number of measures for improving the quality and professionalism of police officers and police staff. These included:

- Allowing quicker progression through the ranks by ending requirements for officers to spend minimum lengths of time within rank before they could be promoted—this was a measure which would help bring the police more into line with other organizations and challenge the traditional rank-based hierarchy of policing.
- Developing a professional register and a formal qualifications framework for police officers to bring the police service 'in line with practice in other professions' (Home Office, 2004b: 89). For an occupation steeped in the traditions of a 'craft' rather than a profession as such, this was to be a significant shift. There was also to be a specialist qualification for BCU commanders as recognition of the critical role played in police management by this tier of managers.
- Allowing *direct entry* of suitably qualified people to various points within the rank structure. This again challenged British policing tradition, in this case the sacred principle that all police officers should start at the bottom as constables and move up each and every rank, over the years a hotly contested issue with claims being made of movement to an 'officer class' in policing whenever this issue arises (see Leishman and Savage, 1993: 227–30).
- Shifting the emphasis on police training away from in-service training to *pre-service* training, in order to bring policing more into line with other professions (Home Office, 2004b: 91). Again this is a challenge to the 'sacredness' principle, in the sense that it refutes the traditional view that only police officers can train police officers because of their unique experience as serving

officers. It also implies that the skills required of police officers are not *that* different from those required in other occupations. It also of course offers the benefit of offloading at least part of the costs of police training to the individuals who aspire to join the police service.

The Workforce Modernization programme also related to means of enhancing the diversity profile of the police service—on grounds both of principle and of tapping into pools of talent so far under-utilized. This included: restricting the right of police officers to join certain groups known for their racist tendencies; more representative recruitment selection panels; closer working with the National Black Police Association to strengthen support networks for minority ethnic officers; encouraging members of minority ethnic communities to apply for direct entry to more senior levels in the police organization (Home Office, 2004b: 94–6). In relation to enabling more women officers to progress through the police organization—the service still had to live with the legacies of the past when few female officers attained more senior posts—the programme entailed a number of measures: making police training and working patterns more 'family friendly' with more encouragement for part-time working; introducing targets for accelerated promotion for women officers; and review of stages in the promotion process to identify and tackle any barriers to progression for women officers.

The final area contained within the Workforce Modernization programme related to pay and conditions, revisiting some of the issues which arose with the debate around the Sheehy Inquiry in the previous decade (discussed in both Chapters 4 and 5), although by now it related to a police service (perhaps apart from the Police Federation!) more receptive to the sorts of private sector thinking Sheehy was associated with. The White Paper stated that 'Further pay reforms must support the operational requirements of the police service and deliver value for money in terms of improved performance' (Home Office, 2004b: 98). One of the reforms to emerge on this front was around the notion of the 'advanced constable'—a concept which had attracted media attention in previous years with talk about 'super bobbies' (*Guardian* 26 February 2001). Advanced constables would be in a more senior position within the constable rank and remunerated accordingly. This reform was also tied in with the leadership role of constables considered earlier. The White Paper also outlined plans to develop more flexible shift patterns for police officers and ways to enhance the *'right to manage'* police officers through more effective forms of staff appraisal and performance review (Home Office, 2004b: 88–9).

The police service responded quickly and comprehensively to the White Paper proposals—little evidence of the sorts of campaigns of resistance which had characterized earlier police reform programmes, as discussed in Chapter 4. Through ACPO (Quick, 2006), ten demonstration sites were set up across England and Wales to pilot the various dimensions of the Workforce Modernization programme, which were evaluated in due course (Home Office, 2006b). One initiative to emerge as a pilot was the creation of the equivalent of the PSCO for criminal investigation work: the *Investigative Support Officer* (ISO). This was a particularly significant application of NPM to policing because it opened up the sacred-within-the sacred world of policing, investigation, to 'auxiliarization'. ISOs were to be charged with undertaking low-level functions within investigative work, such as door-to-door enquiries and statement taking, in order to free up fully trained investigators to concentrate on the higher level functions, a task which appeared to be reaping benefits (Home Office, 2006b: 5). This added another dimension to the notion of the 'extended policing family', in this case, and a point made earlier, encroaching on territory close to the heart of policing: criminal investigation.

The Workforce Modernization programme, therefore, is a key component of the suite of reforms associated with Labour's attempt to deliver radical reform of the police—the deeper rationale for which will be examined in Chapter 5. It stood as another example of the impact of NPM and VFM principles of police reform in Britain. The fact that ACPO was more than comfortable with being given responsibility for its progress was testimony to the depth to which VFM thinking had penetrated the mindset of those concerned with policing policy, both within and without the police service itself. Effectiveness, efficiency, and economy were considerations which were now at the core of policing policy and major factors in shaping that policy. However, there were also other paradigms emerging within policing alongside the relentless growth of the VFM agenda, and these were more internally driven than imposed from above or outside of the police service. They relate to what can be called *forces from within*.

4

Forces from Within: Internal Drivers for Police Reform

Introduction

An impression which might have been given so far in this book is that the police have been dragged, kicking and screaming, into regimes of change and reform. Certainly, to a great extent the history of police reform has been of reforms being 'imposed' on the police, of change being 'forced' as a result of external or environmental pressures on the police. Of course, this is not uncommon in public sector organizations, as change, if left to the internal dynamics of such organizations, is something which, if it happens at all, tends to happen incrementally and piecemeal rather than radically, in the sense that much of the business of public organizations is concerned with 'muddling through' (Lindblom, 1979). In this context the exertion of pressures emanating from the external environment, or the occurrence of what were referred to in Chapter 1 as 'policy disasters', might be necessary if not sufficient forces to create the conditions for more fundamental reform and change. However, it would be dangerous to assume that police reform has only been a matter of the imposition of change agendas on a reluctant service. This can imply that the police have been only *passive subjects* in the game of police reform, whereas it is also important to acknowledge that the police are also *actors* and *agents* in the change process.

There are two primary senses in which the police may be seen as *active agents* in the police reform process. First, individual police actors may have been critical players in *initiating* or driving change. Key individuals within the police service, we might call them 'police visionaries', may have been proactive in police reform by identifying problematic features of the policing status quo, in proposing alternative policing approaches in order to respond to those features and in mobilizing support to carry those alternative approaches forward. Secondly, groupings within the police service may have had an active role in *agenda-shaping* in the police reform context. This is less about the initiation of change—although it may come to that in certain cases—than of intervening and mobilizing support to shape agendas for change as initiated from outside of the service. In that sense what is in question is the role of *police pressure groups* in shaping police reform agendas and indeed, in shaping reforms in areas outside of but related to policing, such as criminal justice policy and the criminal law. These two forms of active engagement of police actors in the police reform process, police visionaries and police pressure groups, constitute the two frameworks within which the 'forces from within' driving and shaping police reform will be considered in this chapter.

Policy Entrepreneurs and Police Entrepreneurs: Visionaries in Policing

Within the study of policy analysis there has been a concern to ensure that the understanding of the policy process—how policies change, how policies are made, how policies are implemented, and so on—must include an appreciation that *people* (actors and action) as well as 'structures' (systems and organizations), play a key part (Degeling and Colebatch, 1993: 351–4). In social and political theory this has been articulated in terms of the duality of *'structure'* and *'agency'* (Giddens, 1979; Sewell, 1992). Structure may be seen as the 'framework' which shapes people's actions and behaviours; human agency, provided by 'knowledgeable' actors, puts structures into practice and reproduces those structures (Giddens, 1976: 161). From the perspective of policy analysis, the classic example of the part played by 'agency' within the 'structures' provided by a policy framework, and one that has particular resonance for the police—although not to be examined here—is the role that 'street level bureaucrats' play in the shaping of public policies 'on the ground' (Lipsky, 1980). 'Street level bureaucrats' are the operatives who provide service delivery on the 'front line', typically lower down in the organization (such as police constables), who, so it is argued, can effectively govern how 'policies' are shaped because they may be able to dictate how policies are (or are not) translated into actions at the delivery end of the policy process (implementation). This is one way in which actors and action play a vibrant part in the policy process, whatever the systems and structures set in response to particular policy agendas. However, it is actors and action at the other end of the organizational hierarchy, leaders and opinion-formers, and the role they play in the policy process, which are of most interest in this context. In this respect the notion of *'policy entrepreneurs'* comes into play, as actors who can be critical players in the process of policy change and reform.

The concept of 'policy entrepreneurs' (Mintrom, 1997; Jones and Newburn, 2007: 148–9) is a development out of a wider policy analysis model known as the 'Advocacy Coalition Framework' (ACF) (Sabatier and Jenkins-Smith (eds), 1993). The ACF model is a conceptual framework for understanding policy change which considers the role of coalitions of actors, inside and outside of the policy sector, who share common belief systems and who seek to translate those belief systems into actual policies through coordinated action and the mobilization of political resources (Sato, 1999: 28–9). The ACF is a useful model for the analysis of 'pressure group' activity, as we shall see later in this chapter in relation to the role of the 'police lobby' in shaping the police reform agenda—in this respect a coalition was shaped around a shared belief in a model of policing steeped in notions of 'independence' and the 'special nature' of policing as a service activity. However, one limitation of the ACF is that, whilst it accounts for the processes of translating shared beliefs, through advocacy coalitions, into actual policies, it is less forthcoming about where those beliefs come from and as such where the *sources* for policy change lie (Mintrom and Vergari, 1996). The notion of 'policy entrepreneurs' was advanced to fill that gap. Mintrom (1997: 730) defines policy entrepreneurs as 'people who seek to initiate dynamic policy change... through attempting to win support for ideas for policy innovation'. Policy entrepreneurs, according to this view, use a range of activities to promote their ideas and beliefs, including identifying *problems* with the status quo of the policy sector, *networking* in the circles associated with that sector, *shaping* the terms of policy debates and, along the lines of the ACF, building *coalitions* of support (Mintrom, 1997: 739). In this way policy entrepreneurs can operate to shape policy agendas in certain directions.

The relevance of this for the present discussion is that areas of police reform may be seen as bearing the marks of 'policy entrepreneurs' or, more specifically, *police entrepreneurs*. One reason why it is dangerous to assume that police reform has been something 'imposed' on the police, often against their will, is that in a variety of ways, even if relatively limited, police reform, has been *internally* driven. This would not preclude external, environmental, or other forces for change. Indeed, policy entrepreneurs may come to the fore when 'windows of opportunity' for reform are opened by other forces, such as changing political climates (see Chapter 5), or system failure (as seen in Chapter 1). However, we should not underestimate the extent to which, as (relatively) independent variables, key individuals within the police service have created or at least furthered change agendas for policing. Those individuals have in some cases been *visionary* in their readings of problems within the status quo of policing and in their alternative scenarios for responding to those problems.

It could be argued that policing, at least in its British context, is a public service which is fertile territory for breeding visionary policy entrepreneurs, despite its more obvious tendency towards conservatism (Reiner, 2000: 95–7). There may be two related reasons for this. First, as has been made clear already and as will be reiterated later in this chapter, a core feature of chief officers' 'occupational culture' is the notion of the 'independence' of chief constables. Technically, this is to do with the (contested) constitutional position of chief officers as independent of any authority, other than the law, on policy or operational matters (Savage, Charman, and Cope, 2000: 122–4). However, the notion of independence, as it has been internalized within chief officers' cultural discourse, has been stretched to mean a form of 'professional autonomy' of chief officers over their domain of activity (Savage, Charman, and Cope, 2000: 196–8). This can be reflected in various ways, one of which is for chiefs to feel free—even 'duty-bound'—to be 'outspoken' on policing matters or even on matters some way removed from policing. Sir Robert Mark's highly public attack on the criminal justice system in 1973, whilst Commissioner of the Metropolitan Police, was one example of that (McLaughlin, 2007: 61), as was James Anderton's confrontational approach to his local police authority when he was Chief Constable of Greater Manchester Police in the 1980s (Reiner, 2000: 71; see also Chapter 5). However, another reflection of that sense of professional autonomy and independence, typically more constructive, is the encouragement it gives certain chief officers to feel free to develop and *express* their own 'vision' for policing, even if against the grain of the status quo. This is reinforced by the second relevant feature of British policing, the dispersal of policing into separate and often disparate police organizations—43 forces in England and Wales alone. Not only has British policing been steeped in the notion of the independence/autonomy of chiefs, but there are 43 of them all potentially seeking to express that independence. Of course, not all chiefs will be inclined or even able to develop a 'visionary' and individualistic approach to policing—as time has gone on chiefs have become increasingly more inclined to go with the 'corporate' voice of the Association of Chief Constables than go it alone (Loader and Mulcahy, 2003: 249–53; Savage, Charman, and Cope, 2000: 89–90). However, the ingredients for generating 'policing visionaries' lies there, in the combination of a culture of the professional independence of chiefs and the multiplicity of chiefs available to potentially express that independence. In the past at least, what Loader and Mulcahy (2003: 234) call 'police heroes', 'maverick' chiefs prepared to break the mould and state the case for change, were very much in evidence.

In this respect it may be useful to differentiate 'police visionaries' from 'police entrepreneurs' as such. The often fiercely defended notion of constabulary independence can actually militate against the sorts of *collective* action characteristic of the work of policy entrepreneurs. The 'maverick' stance of certain chief officers, almost by definition, is incompatible with the processes of mobilizing support, networking, and building of coalitions which, as we have seen, are the trade of policy entrepreneurs. On the contrary, the approach of some chiefs has been one of 'going it alone' and 'sticking your neck out' in the hope that others will, in due course, follow the same path. For this reason it is necessary to distinguish two types of policy actor in the policing context, both of which have been in evidence in terms of driving police reform from 'within'. On the one hand are the police 'mavericks' whose views on policing run against the grain, but who tend to let those ideas 'speak for themselves' and who do little to mobilize support for them. On the other hand are police leaders who both advocate new forms of thinking about policing and work strategically to bring those ideas into action—by employing the 'entrepreneurial' methods already referred to. John Alderson may be taken as the prime example of the former; Kenneth Newman and Peter Imbert are prime examples of the latter.

The Police Visionary: John Alderson and the Community Policing Paradigm

As we have seen (and as will be reiterated in Chapter 5), there has been no shortage of 'maverick' chief officers prepared to taken a stand on policing matters—and on matters some way removed from policing, such as James Anderton's notorious statements on homosexuality and AIDS (Stalker, 1988: 242–5). However, what matters from the perspective of this study are 'mavericks' who leave a longer term mark on the discourse of policing in terms of policing forms or policing philosophies. In this respect it is difficult to think of a police visionary more significant than John Alderson and his own take on the notion of 'community policing'. Reiner (2000: 110–12) has argued that Alderson's views on community policing (which, as we shall see, were 'out on a limb' when first articulated in the 1970s) were to become a key part of the 'post-Scarmanist orthodoxy' on policing, one accepted by most chief officers by the late 1980s. In other words, central features of the Aldersonian philosophy on policing had become *mainstream* in policing discourse by the end of that decade. Furthermore, given that the British adoption of community policing models has, as was made clear in Chapter 2, in a sense gone 'global', Alderson's influence may be seen to have international, as well as national, resonance.

John Alderson was Chief Constable of the Devon and Cornwall constabulary when his thoughts were first given exposure in the mid-1970s, although he had also previously held senior posts in the Metropolitan Police—a fact often ignored when he was being accused by fellow chiefs of not understanding the special demands of policing inner cities (*Police Review* 11 September 1981; Loader and Mulcahy, 2003: 236)—and was Commandant of the Police Staff College for two years, perhaps an opportunity to influence a new generation of police leaders in his line of thinking. What Alderson presented was a vision of and for policing which both rejected the status quo of policing in 1970s Britain and which articulated an alternative model for policing grounded in a number of fundamental principles—some of which, as we shall see in Chapter 5, were highly predictive of policing models which were to emerge even two decades later in the form of 'neighbourhood policing'. The essence of Alderson's case, presented most comprehensively in *Policing Freedom* (Alderson, 1979) and reinforced since (Alderson, 1984; 1998) was as follows.

First, Alderson challenged the post-1960s drift in British policing (Alderson, 1984: 122–3) towards 'reactive' policing methods based on such measures of 'efficiency' as rapid response to emergency calls. As Alderson reflected, 'I was determined to shift the accent from reactive to proactive policing' (Alderson, 1984: 135). In his submission to the Scarman Inquiry, Alderson lamented the extent to which reactive policing, whilst deemed 'efficient' and with a consequent orientation of policing to *mobile* rather than foot patrol, may actually be causing damage to police-community relations through the distancing of police officers from the community they police (Alderson, 1984: 222–3; this issue was also discussed in Chapter 2 in terms of the limitations of what in the USA is called '911 policing'); the pursuit of 'efficiency' may be at the expense of *effectiveness* in policing.

Secondly, Alderson restated the principle of nineteenth-century policing discourse, as expressed in Sir Robert Peel's instructions to the Metropolitan Police (Reiner, 2000: 56–7), that a primary objective of policing is the *prevention of crime*, but he argued that the 'art' of preventative policing is one that the police were now 'losing' in the wake of reactive policing methods (Alderson, 1984: 130). This reflected Alderson's view that the sources of crime lay in the deeper social conditions of the community and must be approached accordingly through a *social* strategy (Alderson, 1979: 199), rather than solely by means of a reactive law-enforcement strategy. The prevention of crime can come about, so he argued, only through the police working in close contact with their local communities, and with other *'services'*, with a common purpose. Crime reduction will come about with *proactive* policing, one which identifies the social problems which generate crime and which takes the necessary interventionist measures, with the agencies working together, to prevent those problems leading to crime. In turn a precondition of proactive policing, it was argued, was the establishment of dedicated community constables, dedicated not just in terms of commitment (something that would come about through specialist training (Alderson, 1984: 86–7), but also in terms of role and function—officers would need to be appointed to dedicated community policing roles (Alderson, 1984: 226).

Thirdly, Alderson called for a framework of *police-community consultation* in order to develop the two-way flow of sentiment seen to be critical to good police-community relations and, not least, to tap the *resource* that is 'people power' (Alderson, 1984: 205). Communities are to be seen as a resource for mobilizing the social changes needed to combat crime and as a resource for the prevention of crime; that resource will only be fully exploited if there are opportunities for regular contact between the police and local communities. For this reason Alderson rested great importance on the 'community forum', with representatives down to the level of a street or an apartment block, as a platform for such contact and consultation. As we saw in Chapter 1, this model was the basis of a key recommendation of the Scarman Inquiry.

Underpinning Alderson's vision for policing, however, were more fundamentalist notions. Drawing from another nineteenth-century notion, 'policing by consent' (Alderson, 1984: 224–5; see Reiner, 2000: 48–9), Alderson constructed the case for a *'social contract'* between the police and their communities (Alderson, 1984: 39–40; 1998: 26–9), a framework for working together in pursuit of the common goal of crime prevention and 'public tranquillity', or 'peace-keeping'. That social contract is one which would enshrine community *participation*, with the police, in tackling social problems, including crime, in terms of what Alderson himself called a form of *'communitarianism'* (Alderson, 1984: 216), or what would now be called 'active citizenship' or 'community engagement' (Marinetto, 2003). However, this social contract would be one in which the police would be expected to show *leadership* in mobilizing community action to achieve common goals (Alderson, 1979: 199), assisting the community to become active and engaged. Social leadership is something which Alderson believed was a core function of the police mandate.

Alderson moulded these notions of preventative policing, proactive policing, police-community consultation, dedicated community police officers, and a 'contract' between the police and community into his own model of 'community policing'. However, as a model it was one which may have been destined to remain a purely intellectual construct, with the exception of attempts to implement the model in Alderson's own organization in Devon and Cornwall (Reiner, 2000: 104–5). Indeed, as we have seen, some of Alderson's contemporaries were dismissive of what they considered to be the idealism behind Alderson's vision, more applicable to the rural village that the realities of the inner-cities (McNee, 1983). What enabled the vision to translate into more concrete policing forms however were the events in Brixton, as was seen in Chapter 1. Brixton and Scarman created the space and a platform within which Alderson's paradigm for policing could be aired and a climate in which that very different model for policing, one in stark contrast to the then dominant model of reactive policing, could be received positively, particularly given Scarman's own 'liberal' credentials. The 'window of opportunity' thrown open by the Brixton disorders was one which proved well timed for the Aldersonian agenda—with the sorts of policy outcomes which were mapped out in Chapter 1. However, the legacy of Alderson stretches much further than reforms which followed in the immediate aftermath of Scarman. As was argued earlier, Alderson's paradigm for policing has left a number of long-term imprints on British policing. As well as the most obvious legacy of the community policing model, two such imprints stand out.

Firstly, Alderson's policing paradigm helped to tilt the orientation of British policing in the direction of *service* rather than force (Stephens and Becker (eds), 1994). Having argued for a more appropriate 'balance' between the differing functions of the police in favour of the community-oriented role (Alderson,

1984: 218–19), Alderson signalled that a culture shift was necessary in the direction of the service function of policing. As we shall see later, this baton was picked up by other chief officers, particularly in the Metropolitan Police, who saw in the notion of 'police service' an opportunity to re-orient the police organization in fundamental ways. If anything, the service ethos has gathered pace since and found its most recent form in the shape of 'community engagement', part of the 'neighbourhood policing' agenda (McLaughlin, 2005: 482–3), discussed in Chapter 5. Given the choice of policing models in terms of 'force or service?' it would seem that the orthodoxy amongst senior police figures is now firmly in favour of the latter (Reiner, 2000: 109–10); that is due in no small measure to the Aldersonian vision for policing.

Secondly, Alderson's, admittedly philosophical, notion of a 'social contract' between the police and community and emphasis on close workings between the police and other agencies, laid the foundations for what would later become known as *partnership* policing (Crawford, 1998). As we shall see in the following chapter, the principle of partnership policing was most clearly enshrined in the *Crime and Disorder Act 1998*, which created a statutory requirement for police organizations to establish partnerships with local authorities and other agencies to reduce crime in local communities. Linked to an emphasis on crime prevention, partnership policing embodies such notions of multi-agency working (Hale, Uglow, and Heaton, 2005) early intervention, problem-orientation, and problem-solving, all within a framework of what under New Labour would be called 'joined-up government' (Long, 2002; see Chapter 5). What partnership policing also reflects was Alderson's attempt to *decentre* the police as a crime reduction agency. A constant message from Alderson was that the causes of crime lie in the social fabric of the community and as such the solutions to crime lie with the agencies most deeply connected with the community. The police are only one such agency:

> Crime is encouraged by factors which are clearly not the responsibility of the police, but of other agencies. As these other agencies become involved, the focus shifts from crime to other social problems such as housing, planning, welfare, education. (Alderson, 1984: 203).

In addition to the formal agencies, Alderson pointed to informal social controls (such as families) and voluntary agencies playing a key part in crime reduction (Alderson, 1984: 202). At the time the message was relayed police ideology was steeped in the notion of the police as the primary agency in crime 'fighting' and, as we shall see in Chapter 5, that was reflected in the policies of the Conservative governments of the day which prioritized expenditure on the police in the 'war on crime'. Alderson's alternative view, of the police as only *one* agency engaged in crime—and not even necessarily the key agency—went very much against the grain, both of government policy at the time and the stance of senior police figures, who, perhaps understandably, were content with being identified with the 'thin blue line' in the war on crime. Over time, that ideology was to be weakened in favour of Alderson's alternative scenario, one which eventually be reflected in the notion of partnership policing.

Alderson's legacy, if anything, was an alternative paradigm for policing, and operated mainly at the conceptual level—or at what one chief in Loader and Mulcahy's research referred to as the 'cerebral' level (Loader and Mulcahy, 2003: 235). His influence, spurred on by the Scarman agenda, was mainly about subtle changes in the 'mind-set' or ethos of policing, whether amongst senior police officers themselves or amongst policy-makers concerned with policing. In that sense Alderson's role was very much the police *visionary*. However, it is less evident that Alderson operated at the level of the policy *entrepreneur*. It is revealing that Alderson chose to submit evidence to the Scarman Inquiry independently of his professional colleagues in ACPO, something which led to him being rebuked by the then President of ACPO (*Police Review* 11 September 1981), perhaps not unconnected with the fact that Alderson's evidence offered thinly disguised criticism of other senior officers and their approach to policing (Loader and Mulcahy, 2003: 235). Alderson's 'campaign' was more a battle of ideas—he was quoted as describing it as an 'ideological struggle' (Loader and Mulcahy, 2003: 234)—than the sort of in-fighting typical of policy entrepreneurs, who, as we have seen, employ tactics such as networking and the mobilization of 'coalitions of support' for their cause. For Alderson, it was a matter of tabling ideas and principles whose 'time had come', although it took the stimulus of Brixton and Scarman to make others believe him. It was now left to others, more inclined to be entrepreneurial in the sense just outlined, to pick up the baton.

Policy Entrepreneurs and Reforming the Police Organization From Within—From Newman to Imbert

Reiner (1992: 253–61) draws a line of continuity connecting the Scarman agenda on the one hand and the stewardships of Kenneth Newman and Peter Imbert as Commissioners of the Metropolitan Police on the other. The basis of this connection is a growing re-orientation of policing along the lines outlined earlier—the partnership between the police and the community, the re-emphasis of preventative policing, multi-agency working, and the like. In other words, these individuals, as policy entrepreneurs and in responding to the messages coming out of Scarman, were to play key parts in realising the vision mapped out by Alderson at the organizational level. The Metropolitan Police organization provides rich and fertile territory for the policy entrepreneur. It is by far the largest police organization in the United Kingdom, with over 20% of the staff of the police service nationally, with responsibility for a one of the largest cities in the world. It is geographically and politically close to the heart of government, with a range of unique national functions such as counter terrorism and Royal Protection. Whoever leads the Metropolitan Police has a unique opportunity to shape policing nationally, not just because of its size but also because of its national profile and consequent political 'clout'. The 'Met' enjoys a degree of autonomy from the police service nationally, and from the professional police associations which represent the service, including ACPO (Savage, Charman, and Cope, 2000: 147–53), because of its profile. This leaves space for leaders of the Metropolitan Police to both 'experiment' and lead in directions which others will tend to follow, despite the cynicism abut the 'Met' out in the 'provinces' (Savage, Charman, and Cope, 2000: 150). Newman and Imbert were to take that opportunity and make their own mark on police reform. In doing so they were to 'work' the organization in order to achieve their goals and seek actively to create the outcomes they desired by means of organizational strategies.

Kenneth Newman became Commissioner of the Metropolitan Police in 1982, after a colourful career which began with colonial policing in Palestine and later took in such senior roles as Chief Constable of the Royal Ulster Constabulary, Her Majesty's Inspector of Constabulary and Commandant of the Police Staff College at Bramshill. By the time he became Commissioner he had earned the unusual reputation of being both a 'tough cop' (mainly because of his period with the Royal Ulster Constabulary) and a 'thinking cop', because of his work at HMIC and the Police College. On taking office he was confronted with the fallout of Scarman and the need to mobilize the Metropolitan Police organizational response to the Scarman recommendations. Newman, however, did not do so unenthusiastically. Indeed, on taking office he set out his own agenda for policing London, based on a notion not a million miles away from Alderson's vision of a 'social contract'. Under the heading 'Newman's contract', *Police Review* reported that 'Policing in London, according to the new Metropolitan Commissioner Sir Kenneth Newman will have its roots in a contract between the police and the public.' (*Police Review* 8 October 1982). This 'notional social contract' (Reiner, 1992: 259) was, from the police side, to prioritize:

- fairness and impartiality of police officers;
- respect for the dignity of the individual;
- the minimum use of force and the avoidance of inhuman or degrading treatment;
- professionalism in police conduct;
- the honesty and integrity of officers (*Police Review* 8 October 1982).

The contract also involved encouraging the community in 'joining the police in a constructive, problem-solving approach to neighbourhood trouble and disorder' and in 'co-operating in preventing crime' (*Police Review* 8 October 1982). Viewed from the present, these exaltations appear standard best practice for community-oriented policing within a human rights framework; at the time they were presented they seemed, and indeed were, about a fundamental re-orientation of policing (Reiner, 1992: 258), one which signalled a shift in the direction of 'service' (although that was not the term widely used) and away from the simple prioritization of law enforcement. Furthermore, given

Newman's role as 'top cop', it was clear that these were not to remain at the level of ideas and principles. In practical terms, Newman translated his priorities for policing London into a handbook of guidance for police officers in the form of a booklet, *'The Principles of Policing'* (Laugharne and Newman, 1985). Newman was also steeped in the management principles of 'policing by objectives' (Reiner, 1992: 260) and at the strategic level sought to disseminate those principles across his senior management, using two-day seminars (*Police Review* 12 November 1982), a method later to be used by his successor. In this way Newman could match the *vision*—the social contract between police and community—with the mobilization of 'coalitions of support' to seek to realize that vision. A change agenda was under way, even if up against some inevitable internal resistance, and that change was to come from within the organization and not just from without. The Alderson-Scarman agenda for policing was to be rolled out, aspirationally at least, in the largest police force in Britain.

The torch of the 'social contract' between the police and the community was to be picked up by Newman's successor as Commissioner, Peter Imbert. Imbert himself came with an interesting background. He was one of the senior investigating officers in the Surrey Police at the time of the 'Guildford Four' investigation (see Chapter 1). Later, then as Chief Constable of Thames Valley Police, he gave permission for the 'fly on the wall' documentary on the force, which became the subject of a huge controversy after it showed the hostile treatment by police investigators of a woman who had alleged rape (Reiner, 2000: 135; Mawby, 2002: 42). Imbert continued his commitment to 'openness' when appointed Commissioner with the courageous decision to open to Metropolitan Police to external scrutiny. In 1988 Imbert commissioned the public relations consultancy firm Wolff Olins, to undertake an internal and external audit of the organization in order to assess the 'identity' of the Met within and without the force (Mawby, 2002: 43; Wolff Olins, 1988).

The Wolff Olins Report identified a number of fundamental organizational issues at the time which signalled the need for change (*Police Review* 30 September 1988):

- The Met has no 'common sense of purpose'; officers interpret their role in different ways with little consensus between them on what 'policing' is about;
- There was exceptional inter-division rivalry, widespread misunderstanding amongst sworn officers of the role and value of civilian staff, and a low value placed on the work of beat officers by those in specialist departments;
- A 'minority' of officers damage the reputation of the Met because they are 'too free' with their language and adopt an 'aggressive' attitude in their relationships with people on the street;
- Corporate communications, both internal and external, were poor; Londoners were not given clear and simple information of how they can make contact with the Met; Met police stations were 'run down' and uncomfortable for both the public and the staff who worked in them;

- The morale of officers was low and many felt 'under siege' and lacked the confidence to admit fault when they were in the wrong.

On the basis of this damning judgement Wolff Olins made a number of recommendations, including that senior officers should spend more time on the street and that civilian staff receive more recognition and a more integrated into the organization. However, one set of recommendations was particularly significant in the context of this discussion because they related to the Met's 'mission'. The Report recommended that the Met's mission statement gives equal weight to the core functions of the police organization—crime prevention, crime investigation, and the provision of assistance to the public (the service role). The mission statement should, it was argued, make it evident that the organization is a *public service*. This was a message of major symbolic significance. Despite the efforts of Newman, clearly the re-orientation of the Met along the lines of a 'service ethos' had some way to go.

Although the Wolff Olins Report was a Met affair, there was little doubt that its observations on and recommendations for the Met had wider relevance. The Report in many ways could be taken as a status review of the police sector as a whole; it served as a 'wake up call' for senior police management across the sector, whether they saw it that way or not. A police organization had exposed itself to scrutiny in a way not seen before, and the overall message was of an organization drastically in need of reform. Imbert's own response to this message was the launch of the *Plus Programme* (PLUS) in 1989 (Rose, 1996: 255–9). Plus was a bold attempt at a form of cultural revolution within the Met with the overarching message that the organization was essentially a *service* to the community—and, symbolically, at around this time the organization formally changes its name to the Metropolitan Police Service (MPS)—and that the organization was committed to *quality of service*. Plus had a number of dimensions. First, it introduced a corporate mission statement, the *Statement of Common Purpose and Values*, which spelt out what was to be a re-emphasis of the service ethos of the organization (see Morgan and Newburn, 1997: 77–8). Secondly, it included a communications strategy which involved both police-public communication and police-media communications (Mawby, 2002: 23–4). Thirdly, Plus launched a challenging programme of seminars—the 'Plus Seminars'—which was to engage every single member of the organization (over 40,000 staff) in a corporate education exercise to win over the 'hearts and minds' of staff to the re-focused MPS. One important 'spin-off' of the Plus Seminars was the launch of what later became known as the 'Bristol Seminar'. In 1991 the MPS held a two-day event at Bristol Polytechnic for all of its minority ethnic officers—some 400 of whom attended. The aim of the Bristol Seminar was to give minority officers a 'voice' and an opportunity to share experiences. Subsequent to Bristol the network of minority ethnic officers it had facilitated was to spawn the Black Police Association, which was formed formally in 1994 (Brathwaite, 2005: 115–6; Holdaway, 1996: 153–4), the first of its kind and a precursor to the

Black Police Associations which would be formed in virtually all forces in the years ahead, culminating in the creation of the National Black Police Association in 1998 (Clements, 2006: 72–3). Black Police Associations have since developed key roles within the police organization in terms of providing support networks for minority ethnic officers, influencing policing policies in line with equality issues, supporting the development of positive strategies for minority ethnic recruitment to and retention within police forces, and working to support police relations with minority ethnic communities (Clements, 2006: 72–3). Their establishment across all forces in England and Wales was to be recommended in the Macpherson Report (Holdaway and O'Neill, 2007).

The more general Plus Seminars, however, were a different kettle of fish. As an attempt at a cultural revolution the Plus Seminars were on all accounts trying affairs, and in some cases were rather like mobilizing turkeys to vote for Christmas, such was the resistance to the messages contained in Plus from some more traditionalist quarters of the organization. However, the fact that Imbert was prepared not only to expose the Met to the initial review that was Wolff Olins, but also to take such concerted and determined action to respond to its recommendations through the Plus Seminars, was testimony to the entrepreneurial leadership Imbert exhibited. A policy entrepreneur in the police sector if ever there was one.

It was noted earlier that the messages contained in Wolff Olins were of significance to the police sector more widely. In what was almost certainly a partial acknowledgement of that, in 1989 the three main police staff associations, ACPO, the Police Federation, and the Police Superintendent's Association, mounted a large scale piece of research on the 'state of the service', the *Operational Policing Review* which included a survey of 2,000 police officers and a large-scale Harris poll to gather public opinion data. This was some measure of an enlightened concern to know more about internal and external perceptions of the state of policing and what could be done to improve policing. The most significant finding of the *Operational Policing Review* was that there was a dissonance between what the public seem to prefer in policing styles and orientation and what police officers themselves value in the role of officer. When officers were asked to grade differing policing strategies, 40% put 'strong, positive policing' as the best strategy, with only 8% favouring crime prevention and 6% favouring community liaison. In contrast, when asked on preference over two styles of policing, 'PC Smith' (the 'firm law enforcer') or 'PC Jones' (the 'caring constable with an ever-friendly approach'), 74% of the public favoured PC Jones's style. The *Review* also found that the public placed far more priority on officers working by foot patrol relative to car patrol than the police themselves (*Police Review* 16 March 1990).

The organizational response to the findings of the *Operational Policing Review* took the form of a policy statement issued by ACPO, *Setting the Standards for Policing: Meeting Community Expectations* (ACPO, 1990), which, mirroring the initiative within the MPS, included the Statement of Common Purpose and

Values, part of which was a mission statement around service-oriented policing:

> The purpose of the Police Service is to uphold the law fairly and firmly: to pre-
> vent crime; to pursue and bring to justice those who break the law; to keep the
> Queen's Peace; to protect, help and reassure the community; and to be seen to
> do this with integrity, common sense and sound judgement . . . we must strive
> to reduce the fears of the public and, so far as we can, to reflect *their* priorities
> in the action we take. (ACPO 1990—emphasis added)

A momentum was now gathering, moving the police sector ever more concert-
edly to a 'quality of service' orientation, something of a 'paradigm shift'
(Waters,1996). The core characteristics of this re-orientation were (and in many
respects still are) an emphasis on the service role of the police, responsiveness
to community priorities for policing, public reassurance, a willingness to accept
areas of weakness and to change accordingly, and a commitment to quality as
measured by a range of indicators (Waters, 1996: 209–10; see also Chapter 3).
Again, to reiterate a point made earlier, when viewed from the present these
principles seem standard best practice for policing, but when viewed from the
time they emerged they were seen as radical reforms of the police organization.
In this respect, the key role in driving the reforms were those 'insiders', as policy entrepreneurs, who took leading roles in turning the oil tanker that was
the police organization around and pointing it in the very opposite direction,
and before them the visionary who, at the ideological level, offered a different
paradigm for policing to the then dominant one.

The role of Alderson, Newman and Imbert as insiders driving the police sector
towards reform and re-orientation has been a focus for this discussion because
of the longer term impact their vision and activities had had on the shape of
the police organization. As visionaries or policy entrepreneurs they have been
key players in defining the ethos of British policing in late twentieth and even
early twenty-first century Britain. Other 'insiders' have of course also left their
mark. To begin with we should not forget those key players who have worked
'behind the scenes' to further police reforms and who have had more impact
than has been acknowledged in public. For example, as Reiner (1992: 264) has
noted, and as many of those involved will stress, the Plus programme owed
much to the drive and vision of Alex Marnoch, a Commander in the MPS at
the time (Rose, 1996: 256). Another example would be Tom Williamson, also at
one stage a Commander in the MPS, who worked tirelessly and often against the
odds to further the cause for ethical police investigations and in particular for
the now widely accepted principles of investigative interviewing (Williamson
(ed), 2006), a development discussed in Chapter 2. Furthermore, although
Loader and Mulcahy (2003: 234–8) are correct to identify that the days of the
'police heroes', maverick or individualist chiefs with a mission to change policing, are now gone, leaving in their place the more 'corporate' and pragmat-
ic chief (Loader and Mulcahy, 2003: 239–42), there is still some scope for

individual leaders to leave some imprint on the police sector for the longer term. In recent years, often in contrasting ways, we have witnessed the role of senior police figures in innovations which may have long-term significance for British policing. For example, Sir David Phillips, very much an 'enforcer' in policing ideology, has championed the notion of policing 'doctrine' (NCPE 2005), an attempt to lay down a body of principles and best practice for police operations along the lines of military doctrine. Coming from a different direction, Sir Ian Blair, at the time of writing Commissioner of the MPS, has been an outspoken advocate of the notion of the 'extended policing family'—as a more junior officer he had written in support of the notion of 'police auxiliaries', now called PCSO's (see Chapter 2), as far back as 1994 (*Police Review* 14 October 1994)—and, as the only senior police officer to deliver the Dimbleby Lecture since Sir Robert Mark in 1973 (Mawby, 2002: 75), chose the occasion to map out a vision for policing in the twenty-first century which prioritized neighbourhood policing, enhanced local police accountability and community leadership in policing policies (*Guardian* 17 November 2005). Future historians of policing may well identify these moments as watersheds in British police reform.

This chapter has sought to identify the ways 'insiders' within the police sector have played their part in the process of police reform, as a means of counterbalancing any assumption that police reform has always come about *despite* the police or that reform has always had to be *imposed* on a reluctant police sector. Police visionaries and policy entrepreneurs have had a significant impact on the shape and direction of British policing and on driving certain reforms within the sector. However, this should not be taken in the opposite direction, to exaggerate the enthusiasm within the police sector for reform and change. To begin with, those police visionaries themselves had to swim against the tide through much of their campaigns for alternative ways of doing policing; the battle was uphill for most of the way not downhill. Furthermore, there is (or at least was) an established tradition within the police sector, at all levels, of opposition and *resistance* to change and reform. That resistance is also important for the process of police reform because it may have, and indeed has, helped shape the forms which police reforms eventually take. This is about a rather different form of 'internal' activity to that of the police visionaries; it is about *agenda-shaping* and the role of *police pressure groups* in relation to police reform.

Police Reforms and Police Pressure Groups: Shaping Reform Agendas from Within

When we consider the role of 'police pressure groups' in relation to police reform we need to think in terms of *policy shaping* rather than reform proper. In other words, what police pressure groups have tended to do, with a few exceptions as we shall see, is seek to alter reform agendas, as set in motion from elsewhere, in the direction of their own perceived 'interests'. Police pressure groups have a role to play in police reform because in certain areas of policing policy they have influenced the outcome of reform processes, thus shaping the final forms which police reforms have taken. In a sense this is a *negative* contribution to police reform, concerned with seeking to inhibit change itself, in some areas almost as a matter of principle. This is most commonly the case with the Police Federation, which has often seen policy change as in conflict with its members' interests. A classic example of this was the Federation's unconditional opposition to the introduction of the police community officer scheme (discussed in Chapter 2), ostensibly on the grounds that it would create 'policing on the cheap', but most likely on the grounds that the scheme might in the long term lead to a decline in the numbers of officers at constable level, who comprise their own core membership.

However, it is possible to overstate the negativity of police pressure groups in relation to police reform, as there is something of a sliding scale in the role of such groups in shaping police reform. In another study (Savage, Charman, and Cope, 2000: 173–83) a distinction was made between three forms of engagement of police pressure groups (in this case ACPO) with police reform agendas. First, there is 'agenda-resistance', where the reform agenda is simply opposed and the aim of pressure group activity is to bury the proposed reforms altogether. Agenda-resistance involves denial, a refusal to accept either the case for reform or the particular configurations of reform which have been tabled. Secondly, there is 'agenda reshaping', where the tactic is to work actively on the proposed reforms in order to turn them in other directions, to neuter certain aspects of them (normally those most objectionable) and even to 'capture' the reform agenda and drive it in a way more compatible with the groups own perceived interests. Agenda-reshaping normally involves some acceptance that at least part of the case for reform is justified, but entails alternative configurations of reform to those originally presented. Thirdly, there is 'agenda-setting', where the strategy is to construct new policy forms and even new ways of thinking about crime and policing as a whole. This latter approach can actually be about the innovation of policy and in that sense at least be seen as 'positive' rather than negative in terms of policy change—although as the changes are police driven they may not be received as positive by other audiences. Agenda-setting can be proactive, involving both the identification of the need for change and the particular forms which change and reform might take.

The point of this sliding scale, from agenda-resistance through agenda-reshaping to agenda-setting, is that the activities of the police pressure groups have ranged from what in cricketing terms is a defensive block to hitting sixes, or in boxing terms from dodging punches to knocking the opposition flat. That range has been governed by historical development, in the sense that the tendency over time has been movement from the defensive to the more proactive. It has also been governed by the organizational ethos of the pressure groups concerned, what they see themselves as 'there for'. The capacity of a police pressure group to move from simple agenda-resistance to agenda-setting depends on various factors. The group may be oriented in history and design towards one approach rather than another in terms of its organizational ethos. In this respect the Police Federation tends towards maintaining the status quo of policing (McLaughlin and Murji, 1998), because its role, other than fighting for improvements in its members' pay and conditions of service, is essentially a trade unionist function of defending 'members interests', and this is typically associated with opposing change in policing—although the Federation might press for changes in the wider criminal justice system, such as with the rights of suspects (as will be seen later). Pressure groups however need more than political will to move from agenda-resistance to agenda-setting. The group also has to possess the resources necessary for effective pressure group activity, and this involves more than financial capacity, something of which the Federation for example has no shortage of. From the field of policy analysis, the conceptual models of the Advocacy Coalition Framework (ACF—as discussed earlier) and 'policy networks' are useful heuristic devices to account for police pressure group activity.

The ACF (Jenkins-Smith and Sabatier, 1994) assumes that policy actors can be assembled into 'advocacy coalitions' involving people who share sets of beliefs, whether normative—what should be—or causal—why things happen—and who take coordinated or concerted action from time to time. Those sets of beliefs are normally organized in a hierarchical structure, ranging from core beliefs to specific beliefs about the appropriateness of particular policies. In the British policing context, that hierarchy of beliefs might include core beliefs about the 'special' nature of policing—such as the principle of 'constabulary independence' (Savage, Charman, and Cope, 2000: 193–208; see also Chapter 5) or the notion of the police officer as 'not like any other employee', a notion employed by the Federation to defend itself during the 'Sheehy campaign' (McLaughlin and Murji, 1998—see below). Specific beliefs might include such issues as the appropriateness of the rank structure or entrance points into the service (both issues, as we shall see, which were matters of contention during the 1990s). Advocacy coalitions seek to translate their belief systems into policies—or 'non-policies' if the aim is to oppose or block policy proposals which conflict with the belief system—and they do this by mobilizing support around the belief system, support which might include political actors, standing bodies and associations, researchers and research institutions, the media, and so on. As we shall see, the ACF is a useful framework for capturing the activities of the Police Federation during the campaigns of the mid-1990s.

The *policy networks* framework is another model within policy analysis used to account for pressure group activity. The policy networks approach is an attempt to explain relations between central and local government and the various pressure groups which make up the governance of particular policy sectors (Rhodes, 2000: 54). It is based on a model of 'power dependence' whereby organizations are dependent on other organizations for resources and thus need to exchange resources in order to achieve their organizational aims; this creates a 'bargaining' of resources between and within those organizations (Rhodes, 1981: 97–133). The framework created by this process is a 'policy network', which can be defined as 'an entity consisting of public, quasi-public, or private actors who are dependent on each other and, as a consequence of this dependence, maintain relations with each other.' (de Bruijn and ten Heuvelhof, 1995: 163). Rhodes took the concept of policy networks further and developed a typology of different types of network, based upon a continuum of 'issue networks' through to 'policy communities' (Rhodes, 1988: 235–366). Issue networks are relatively unstable networks of policy actors, with open and fluid membership, degrees of conflict, and unequal distributions of resources and power between the organizations which make it up. In contrast, policy communities are highly integrated, with restricted 'membership', open only to a few privileged 'insider' groups who share a close relationship with one another, have a consensual view of the world, and who reach decisions in close consultation with one another.

The significance of this continuum from 'issue networks' to 'policy communities' is that it effectively captures the range of interventions by police pressure groups and the differing stances they adopt in the policing policy process. It also reflects the movement from 'agenda-resistance' to 'agenda-setting', in the sense that agenda-resistance campaigns have, as we shall see, been concerned with the defensive opposition to specific policy initiatives and have dissipated once those initiatives have been stifled, whereas agenda-setting has involved the longer term establishment of a *relationship* between the police and government. In that sense agenda-resistance tends to take the shape of an issue network which is transient and focused on specific outcomes—a set of policies deemed objectionable by those acting to oppose it. Alternatively, agenda-setting sits more comfortably with the workings of a policy community, whereby the police (or at least elements within the police) have managed to gain 'insider' status (Grant, 1989) in terms of access to the processes of policy-making and had, for a period of time, become an institutionalized component of the machinery for policy formation. If we consider the activities of the police pressure groups during the 1990s, particularly as they related to what was then a radical agenda for police reform launched by the Conservative government, it is possible to trace this shift from agenda-resistance to agenda-setting and the extent to which this involved a movement from an issue network to a policy community.

The Policy That Wasn't: Agenda-Resistance and the Demise of 'Sheehy'

The study of police reform, as has been noted at various points already, is about 'non-policies' as well as policies themselves. Indeed, as will have become clear, what has been distinctive about the police sector relative to other areas of the public sector is the extent to which it had *not* been reformed; the 'privileged' status of the police as a public sector agency (Loader and Mulcahy, 2003: 289; see also Chapter 5) had meant that the sorts of policy initiatives forced on other public services through the 1980s in particular did not find their way through to the police sector—they were in that sense 'non-policies'. However, the most notable example of a 'non-policy' in relation to the British police involved, ironically, an explicit attempt by government to positively initiate reform and change in policing: the 'Sheehy' agenda.

In Chapter 5 there is a detailed discussion of the police reform agenda launched by the Conservative government in the early to mid-1990s, an agenda which was both radical and bold. It signalled a shift in government sentiment from one intent on preserving the privileged status of the police as a public sector agency, to one concerned to challenge that status head on. As we shall see, the reform agenda had three pillars: first, to overhaul police governance arrangements; secondly, to consider ways of redefining police 'roles and responsibilities'; thirdly, to reform police pay and conditions of service. The police pressure groups were active in relation to all three pillars, but none more so than in relation to the third pillar, which became known as the 'Sheehy' agenda. The Conservative government launched a fundamental review of police pay and conditions in 1992 in the form of the Sheehy Inquiry, headed by Sir Patrick Sheehy, a prominent businessman. Hugely controversial from the start, Sheehy floated reforms ranging from fixed-term contracts for all police officers, through performance related pay, and local pay negotiations, to the abolition of overtime and a batch of special allowances then paid to officers. The recommendations of Sheehy are outlined in Chapter 5 (see also Chapter 3); what is of interest in the context of this particular discussion is the way in which the Sheehy agenda was handled by the police pressure groups and above all by the Police Federation.

Evidence of the extent to which that battle lines were being drawn between the Sheehy Inquiry team and the Police Federation in particular was to be found in a comment by Eric Caines, one of the more belligerent members of the Inquiry team and someone with a track record in public sector reform (in his case with the health sector), just after the Sheehy Inquiry reported in 1993. In an article for the *Guardian* called 'Stop money with menaces', Caines argued the case for 'taking on the boys and girls in blue' and targeted the Police Federation for specific comment:

> The Police Federation will object to most of the recommendations... in this it will be no different from the Prison Officers Association, the Royal College of Nursing and the British Medical Association, three of the most of the most *reactionary and arrogant staff interest groups in the public sector*. (Quoted in Judge, 1994: 486–7—emphasis added)

In making this comment Caines, who was the Sheehy team member given most public exposure, giving him an opportunity to exhibit his own blunt and abrasive style, was not only condemning the Federation as an unreconstructed 'trade union' determined to doggedly defend the status quo, he was also denying the central platform of what was to be the Federation's case against the Sheehy agenda—that the police were 'different' from other occupations, public and private sector, and were as such a *special case* (McLauglin and Murji, 1998). However, at least in part, it was this very discourse of the 'special' nature of policing which was to prove effective in the campaign against Sheehy launched by the police pressure groups and above all by the Federation. That campaign in effect began as soon as the Sheehy Inquiry started to call in evidence to assist in their deliberations. In response to the Home Office decision to commission the management consultants Ernst & Young to carry out the research for Sheehy into police roles and responsibilities, the Federation appointed its own major consultancy firm, Touche Ross, to conduct parallel studies on its behalf—interestingly, Touche Ross in an earlier piece of work for the police associations had concluded that performance related pay could not work for this sector (Judge, 1994: 473). The 'research' undertaken by Touche Ross provided useful counter-evidence to that coming from other sources into the Sheehy Inquiry, such as the hostility of rank-and-file officers to performance related pay, and constituted part of the Federation's own submissions to the Inquiry.

The wider campaign mounted during the deliberations of the Sheehy Inquiry and after the Inquiry report was published, one fought primarily by the Federation and to a lesser extent the other police pressure groups, has now become something of a feature of British policing history (Leishman, Cope, and Starie, 1996; McLaughlin and Murji, 1998; Mawby, 2002). Tactically, the anti-Sheehy campaign involved the police associations in forms and levels of public campaigning then relatively novel to those groupings. For the Federation, this including their newly acquired and emerging campaigning strategies, summarized by McLaughlin and Murji (1998: 371) as:

> (i) Protest meetings; (ii) issuing press releases; (iii) establishing a high media profile for their annual conferences and making them more 'media friendly'; (iv) vociferous campaigning against various 'anti-police' critics; (v) submitting evidence to public inquiries, commissions and committees; and (vi) placing advertisements in newspapers to appeal to the general public on particular issues.

Such strategies were employed for other campaigns than the 'stop Sheehy' campaign—they were also used for wider 'law and order' campaigns (Judge, 1994: 464–5; McLaughlin and Murji, 1998: 375–86)—but they proved most effective when directed at the Sheehy agenda. As one Federation leader expressed it in another research project on police pressure groups (Savage, Cope, and Charman, 2000: 159), with the Sheehy campaign 'we came of age in...[our] lobbying style'. The Federation, along with, as we shall see later, other police associations, had begun to employ the lobbying tactics long used by other pressure groups in seeking to further their ends; for the Federation, this included employing established lobbying firms such as Westminster Strategy (Judge,

1994: 488). However, in the case of the Federation, lobbying was backed up by public protest, the most notable event being the gathering at Wembley Arena, when 23,000 officers met to mark their opposition to the Sheehy recommendations—on all accounts something which caused ripples of consternation within government. What underpinned both the Federation's own lobbying activity and the public protest that was Wembley was a 'case' constructed around a discourse, one not just about the practical problems with the Sheehy agenda but about the *special* nature of policing.

The notion of the 'special' nature of policing, marking it out as different from other occupations, was a powerful weapon in the armoury of the 'stop Sheehy' campaign. As Judge (1994: 489–91) makes clear, according to the Federation's case a number of 'special' features of policing make the Sheehy agenda inappropriate. First, that the 'pay matrix' proposed by Sheehy, which was modelled on what were deemed to be parallel and equivalent occupational roles in other sectors (public and private), ignored the fundamental nature of the police role, which, particularly in the case of front-line policing, was variable, multi-skilled, and multi-faceted. It was not possible to reflect the richness of the police role in a 'bureaucratic' framework derived from other occupations. Secondly, that the quantitative measures of police activity required for the introduction of performance related pay would fail to capture the nuances of police performance and run counter to the need for officers to continue to use their discretion, discretion being a fundamental feature of policing. Thirdly, that the notion of fixed-term contracts for police officers ignores the fact that policing is a *vocation* and not 'just another job'—it is not something which is done for a few years before moving on to another 'job'. The Federation challenged Sheehy with the question: 'Is policing a job like any other, or a vocation which requires total commitment from men and women prepared to devote the greater part of their working lives to the service?' (quoted in Judge, 1994: 476).

Clearly, the case constructed by the Federation and supported by their colleagues in the other police pressure groups, ACPO and the Police Superintendents' Association (Savage, Charman, and Cope, 2000: 169–71), was that policing is indeed more than just a 'job', and different in key respects from other occupations, thus making it a 'special case' when it comes to issues of reform and reasons to maintain the status quo. Of course, it is also a case of 'they would say that, wouldn't they' in the sense that most occupationally-based interest groups will employ the rationale of 'special case' in order to defend incursions into their sphere of interests. The point about the police is that imageries about the 'British bobby' are deeply embedded within British culture (Mawby, 2002: 7–8; Emsley, 1992) and as such the language of 'special case' in relation to policing may find a very receptive audience within the public and across the media. This is not something politicians can easily ignore. The combination of tactical public campaigning and lobbying activity, strategic alliances between the police pressure groups and a sellable message of being a special case, was a powerful one which challenged government with force.

Whichever way, for reasons which will be examined in more depth in Chapter 5, Michael Howard, who inherited the Sheehy agenda from his predecessor Kenneth Clarke, announced within a few months of the publication of the Sheehy Inquiry that he would not be carrying forward key recommendations of the Inquiry (Judge, 1994: 482). With some exceptions (see Chapter 5) Sheehy had become a *non-policy* and that was due at least in part to the 'stop Sheehy' campaign in which the Federation played a central role. It had helped forge what was referred to earlier as an 'advocacy coalition' around opposition to the Sheehy agenda which marshalled support around a belief system which presented policing as a distinctive if not unique sphere of public service activity. The 'special' nature of policing as an occupation was portrayed as the main reason why the Sheehy agenda, one steeped in applying employment and remuneration principles found elsewhere in the public and private sectors to the police, could not and should not be allowed to survive. An organization which could all too easily be accused of simply defending its members' vested interests in maintaining the status quo of privilege had managed to appear to be appealing to the loftier principles of protecting all that is 'best' in British policing.

The extent of the Conservative government's eventual climbdown on Sheehy—and it was a climbdown in the sense that in selecting the Sheehy Inquiry team the Home Secretary of the day must have known what sorts of recommendations were going to be made—is evident by the response of the Federation to the final package of measures which followed in the wake of Sheehy. The lead 'negotiator' from the Federation side on the post-Sheehy 'deal', Lyn Williams declared:

> This agreement is *better than any of us could have anticipated*. It means that all the most objectionable features of Sheehy have been avoided. We have retained increments and avoided the damaging proposals for differentiation between officers in the same ranks in respect of posts. The pay scales will continue to be negotiated nationally, and we have held on to premium rates of payment for overtime. (Quoted in Judge, 1994: 496—emphasis added)

The content of the final package of actual reforms which followed Sheehy is examined in Chapter 5; suffice it to note here that the core features of the Sheehy agenda, including performance related pay, were abandoned by the Home Secretary. It was a policy agenda which did not see the full light of day, and the capacity of the Federation to lead a campaign of resistance to it was an important part in that 'non-policy'. However, if the Federation were the stars in the 'stop Sheehy' campaign, the other police associations were to come to the fore in other policy battles of the 1990s.

The Policies that Changed: Police Governance, Police Functions, and Agenda Reshaping

As has already been stated, the role and activities of the police pressure groups in relation to police reform can be situated on an axis from agenda-resistance at one end to agenda-setting at the other. Between these two poles is '*agenda-reshaping*', the process by which police pressure groups work to adapt and reshape reform agendas initiated by others in directions deemed more compatible with their members' interests and preferences. This is less about wholesale opposition to the reform agenda and more about active engagement with it as a means of influencing the eventual shape of the reforms. There are two prime examples of this (both discussed further in Chapter 5): the response to the Conservative plans for reforms of police governance, as set out originally in the White Paper *Police Reform: A Police Service for the Twenty-First Century* (Home Office, 1993b), and the response to the 'Posen' review of police 'core and ancillary tasks'.

The Conservative government, and in particular its Home Secretary Kenneth Clarke, was determined to reform the arrangements for police governance; there were two directions in which it wished to go. On the one hand it wanted central government to have a firmer hold on the ways in which policing 'priorities' were set and how policing plans were drawn up on the basis of those priorities. On the other hand it wanted to change the constitution of the local police authorities to make them more 'business-like' in terms of size (it was proposed to roughly halve the size of police authority membership), make-up (more involvement of people with experiences from the business world or other areas of expertise) and accountability (a closer link between the police authorities and local taxation). At the time, these objectives were hugely controversial, in particular, there was widespread concern that policing was about to become highly 'centralised', a movement which was seen to be against the grain of traditional British policing. Certainly there was anxiety across the police service itself that this new reform agenda was a threat to the localized nature of policing and even a threat to the 'independence' of the police from 'political interference'. Coming so soon on the heels of Sheehy, the police associations felt that it was once again necessary to challenge the government on key aspects of its plans to reform the police. However, by now they had been 'blooded' by the experience of fighting Sheehy and had become more adept at the dark arts of politics, and in this case ACPO was to take more of a lead role in the lobbying process.

As the proposals contained in the 1993 White Paper were drafted into legislative form as the *Police and Magistrates' Courts Bill 1993* the police associations opted to seek to unravel aspects of the proposed legislation as it passed through Parliament. This task was made somewhat easier by the decision by the government to start the legislative process in the House of Lords, one it might have regretted since within the ranks of their Lordships were many, Conservative peers included, who were uncomfortable with what they saw as the 'centralizing' ethos of the Bill and who were inclined to offer their ears to the concerns of the police associations. This was an opportunity not wasted upon the likes of ACPO, which set about nurturing support within the Lords for the blunting of at least some key elements of the Bill. In addition, ACPO, the Police Superintendents' Association (with its increasingly high-profile President, Brian McKenzie, much in evidence—destined to become a peer himself on retirement), and the Federation scrupulously cultivated support from leaders of the opposition parties, local Members of Parliament, the Local Authority Associations (which themselves felt threatened by the Bill), academics—Professor Robert Reiner made a keynote speech at the 1994 ACPO Summer Conference attacking the governance reforms (*Police Review* 15 July 1994)—and anyone else who would assist them in their campaign. Together with government critics in the Lords, this was a heavyweight force to challenge the reforms.

The formation of strategic alliances was a key feature of the campaign to reshape the reform agenda set in motion by the White Paper, as it is for pressure group activity in general (McRobbie, 1994). In this case there were both internal and external alliances. The three police associations, having started working together, as we saw earlier, with the *Operational Policing Review*, and having worked closely on the anti-Sheehy campaign, continued in that vein in response to the *Police and Magistrates' Courts Bill* and maintained an internal alliance within the police service in that response. That helped present more of a 'united front' in the face of a piece of legislation which could potentially have divided the police associations (after all, part of the Bill was concerned with the 'right to manage' in terms of amendments to police discipline procedures). The external alliances with politicians and other associations, such as the Association of County Councils (ACC) and the Association of Metropolitan Authorities (AMA)—which represented all of the local police authorities—were doubly useful. Not only would they add their not inconsiderable weight behind the campaign to reshape the Bill, they would also bring with them their own well-honed lobbying skills, skills still relatively novel to organizations like ACPO; as one past President of ACPO expressed it in another research project (Savage, Charman, and Cope, 2000: 170):

> We didn't have any experience in lobbying at all in the Houses of Parliament; the ACC and the AMA had considerable experience of that and so we worked well with them . . . which created an enormously powerful alliance of interests, *and that still exists.* (emphasis added)

This is an interesting comment in another sense: it refers to a *continuation* of an 'alliance' beyond the specific campaign around the *Police and Magistrates' Courts Bill*. This is some indication of what will later be discussed as the progression from an *issue network* to something closer to a *policy community* in relation to the police associations and ACPO in particular. Whichever way, as we shall see in Chapter 5, the outcome of the strategic alliances around the Bill was a climbdown by the government of key aspects of the Bill, including the proportion of locally elected members on the new, slimmed down, police authorities (the government was forced to accept more elected members than they had wished), and the process of appointment of police authority chairpersons (it would now be chosen locally rather than by the Home Secretary as in the original Bill).

The *Police and Magistrates' Courts Act 1994*, whilst still a major piece of police reform in terms of transforming the machineries of police governance (Jones and Newburn, 1997), had been reshaped in key respects by the activities of those determined to blunt it, including the police pressure groups.

The second case of agenda reshaping was if anything more evidence of a growing capacity within the police associations to alter the terms of police reform agendas. Alongside plans to reform police governance the government harboured ideas about challenging the status quo over what tasks and functions the regular public police should be responsible for and what might be handed over to other bodies or occupational groups. As the police had become a relatively well paid and more highly trained profession, and as demands on their resources had increased over time, the case for a scrutiny of what tasks only a warranted officer could undertake and, alternatively, what tasks currently undertaken by warranted officers could be undertaken by other, less expensive operatives, had grown. As a reflection of that in late 1993 Michael Howard set in motion a 'review of police core and ancillary tasks' under the direction of a senior Home Office civil servant, Ingrid Posen—the team was to be a small one of two other civil servants, an accountant and an economist, together with a seconded chief inspector (at least, unlike Sheehy, there was to be *some* police representation on the Review team!). The official purpose of the Review was: 'to examine the services provided by the police, to make recommendations about the most cost-effective way of delivering core police services and to assess the scope for relinquishing ancillary tasks' (Home Office, 1994: 1).

In a sense this agenda was merely was a more radical version of the 'civilianization' agenda of the 1980s, as discussed in Chapter 3. However, in the atmosphere of the mid-1990s and with the other reforms still in the air the announcement of what became known as the 'Posen Inquiry' was treated with a high degree of suspicion (Leishman, Cope, and Starie, 1996). The spectre loomed of a police service 'stripped down' to a crime fighting function, leaving the 'service' roles of the police to other bodies or groupings. ACPO, supported by the Federation and the Superintendents' Association, released a statement along these lines: 'We believe that the review is being driven by the desire to save money and that the police may be forced to withdraw their vital social service role.' (quoted in Leishman, Cope, and Starie, 1996: 16). This concern was reinforced when the review team set out an initial discussion paper commenting on the option of extending the Special Constabulary and of increasing the 'interface' with the private sector (see Judge, 1994: 505).

In this context any anxieties the police associations might have had about yet another fundamental challenge to the 'British way' of policing could now find expression in other ways than as 'outsiders looking in' to the policing policy process. As we shall see in Chapter 5, the mood within government for 'taking on' the police service in terms of police reform had changed to one much more inclined to be conciliatory with the police sector—Michael Howard was a very different beast to Kenneth Clarke. Furthermore, as we have seen, the police associations and ACPO in particular had sharpened up their act as lobbying bodies (an issue which shall be discussed later); they were already a more formidable force than they had been in working against reform agendas. The Posen Review provided an ideal opportunity capitalize on this new found strength and for ACPO to position itself more on the 'inside' of the policing policy process, as a means not just of blunting a reform agenda, as it had with the *Police and Magistrates' Courts Act 1994*, but in order to *capture* and redirect a policy initiative.

One effect of the change of climate coinciding with Howard taking over stewardship of the Home Office was a willingness to be decidedly more receptive to the 'police voice', not just on policing policy but on criminal justice in the wider sense. As we shall see later, this was to include old chestnuts such as the 'right to silence', a perennial concern of the police service and one stretching as far back as to debates around the Phillips Commission between 1979 and the publication of the RCCP Report in 1981 (see *Police Review* 4 May 1979 and Chapter 1). However, in the context of the Posen Review, this new receptiveness was to be reflected in a more inclusive approach of the Home Office to the workings of a scrutiny into policing, certainly in comparison to the way in which the Sheehy Inquiry was set up.

An early sign that the Review was not to be as threatening as the staff associations had feared was a statement made by Michael Howard to the Police Federation conference (*Police Review* 20 May 1994) that the review would not lead to reductions in the numbers of police officers: 'I do not want to see a reduction in the police service at all' he told the conference, rather it was about freeing officers from 'unnecessary burdens'. He also intimated that even those functions deemed 'not central' may not be lost to the service. He went further than that when speaking some months later at the ACPO Summer Conference, when he stressed that police officers' views would be 'taken into account' throughout the Review and that it was not 'inevitable' that police duties would be 'privatized' as a result of the Review (*Police Review* 15 July 1994)—although at the same conference the ACPO President expressed continuing concern that the Posen Review might damage the nature of British policing by moving it away from its 'service' ethos. That on-going concern was expressed in the decision of the then ACPO Vice-President, John Hoddinott, to participate in a 'counter-review' into policing in the form of the 'Cassels Inquiry' into the role of the police, an independent inquiry set up by the Police Foundation and the Policy Studies Institute (*Police Review* 5 August 1994; Morgan and Newburn, 1997: 176–8).

As the Review got under way, other more conciliatory signals were coming out of the Home Office. To begin with, the starting point of the Review was a survey of all chief officers to determine what *they* considered to be 'core' policing functions and what policing functions could be carried out by other bodies (*Police Review* 11 February 1994; see Morgan and Newburn, 1997: 7–8; Fielding, 2005: 162). A senior civil servant involved in the Review, interviewed as part of the research by Savage, Charman, and Cope (2000) emphasized the need to keep ACPO 'on board' and to a degree to 'own' the Review process if it was to make progress:

> we needed ACPO to own it in order to deliver ... we had to have that close agreement and therefore it was perfectly proper that they should have some influence over the agenda and that they should like and want to do what came out of it otherwise it would have been hopeless ... it had to become operationally viable, well who are the people who are going to tell us whether it is operationally viable but the police?

Having experienced the initially hostile reception to the Review from ACPO and the other police associations, the Review team found ACPO in particular were soon adopting a much more positive approach to the Review process, and ACPO in particular were prepared to enter into constructive dialogue over the core and ancillary functions of the police, as the same interviewee commented:

> ... from then on it became a much more positive and proactive thing and I think from then on in it was pretty plain sailing. We worked on the pieces of work, actually there was very little distance when they [ACPO] said what they wanted to highlight, it accorded pretty well with what we wanted to highlight.

Once the Review team had identified the various areas of policing which were to come under scrutiny, working groups were set up for each with the police associations as members. Additionally, ACPO undertook its own research and produced its own position papers to influence the debate, which clearly had some impact on the eventual outcome of the Review, as the same interviewee made clear in commenting how policy recommendations changed through the Review process:

> Things that did change were the policy papers because it didn't go from nowhere to being a report ... we had a series of police papers that looked at particular areas of policing and those were very thoroughly gone over and often other groups produced working papers [including ACPO], we would be sitting there with our working papers and their working papers and reaching some kind of accommodation between different papers so there was quite a lot of development that took place and change took place with the working papers.

The Review process was therefore one that allowed groups like ACPO to shape the debate on the recommendations which were eventually to come out of Posen. Alongside that, politicians at the Home Office were making ever more reassuring noises to the police service. In an article by the incoming Minister for policing, David MacLean, it was stated:

> There is nothing fundamentally wrong with the police service at all ... The core and ancillary review is a response to *calls from within the police service itself* which, over the last few years, has taken on a whole range of new responsibilities ... (*Police Review* 12 August 1994—emphasis added)

Suddenly, the Posen agenda was being defined as something the *police* would want to see raised, as addressing problems *they*, rather than government, had identified; a new narrative of both the case for and the direction of the review was beginning to emerge. MacLean also talked in the same article of the need for a period of 'stability' after the rush of reforms in the recent past, another nod very much in the direction of police concerns—in his 'Christmas message to police forces' later that year Howard reinforced that message when he promised that the coming year would witness a 'period of consolidation' for the police service (*Police Review* 23 December 1994). The omens were becoming more promising for the police associations.

By the time the Review team presented their first interim report in late 1994 (Home Office, 1994), it was clear that the definition of 'ancillary' police functions, clearly potentially the most contested area as these were to be functions which could, in principle, be 'outsourced' away from the police service, was largely what ACPO and the other police associations *themselves* saw as 'ancillary', which included missing person reports, schools liaison, dealing with stray dogs, lost property, complaints about noise and responding to automatic alarms, and the stewarding of football matches. In these respects the report not only embraced this 'self-definition' of 'ancillary' but also to a great extent the police view on what the police role in relation to them should be. For example, ACPO had argued, successfully, that the police should continue to have a role in the safety education in schools within the area of schools liaison, but that trained stewards could take over the public order roles at football and musical events (see *Police Review* 4 November 1994). The interim report also identified areas where a 'consensus' on how to respond to them had yet to be reached—these were left as still open to resolution (Home Office, 1994).

The final report of the Posen Review was presented in June 1995 (Home Office, 1995). Significantly, Howard was accompanied at the press conference on the release of the report by ACPO President John Hoddinott, who as has been seen, was initially so frustrated with the agenda of the Review that he supported an alternative inquiry into police roles and responsibilities to the one set up by government. Hoddinott's participation in the press conference would have had something to do with the fact that the review team concluded that 'there was little scope for the police service to withdraw completely from large areas of current police work'—in other words, the Review had turned its back on the very thing which seemed at one point to justify its creation, the out-sourcing of policing functions. The only areas it did recommend the police handing over responsibility for—dealing with stray dogs, licensing, stewardship at sports grounds, the transcription of interview tapes, and the escorting of wide vehicles—were all functions the *police* submissions had advocated could go to other bodies. At the press conference Hoddinott's comments (*Police Review* 30 June 1995) revealed something both about the process of the Review and its conclusions. In terms of process he indicated that ACPO had played a key role, mostly behind the scenes, in influencing the direction of the Review: 'It was right to mark up concerns but you don't settle important matters like this by decibel debate. I hope that what we brought to the table was coherent and sensible.' Perhaps by 'decibel debate' the ACPO President was comparing ACPO's own approach to the Review, working *with* the Review as 'insiders', shaping the course of the debate from within, to that of the Federation, which had taken a predominantly oppositionist stance. Whichever way, in terms of the Review's conclusions, it was clear that ACPO was very content with those:

> It was a useful debate which produced a useful report. It is a rational set of conclusions, a very comprehensive study. It very helpfully ends the speculation which has been going on about what might happen to the British police service. I'm very pleased to think the unique qualities of British policing are to be maintained. (*Police Review* 30 June 1995).

This level of satisfaction with the final outcomes of the Review may have been a reflection of the fact that the recommendations were as much statements of *ACPO's* preferences as those of the Home Office; the 'ACPO' line had been bought, something almost acknowledged by Howard, who at the same press conference declared, in almost the exact language to that used, as we have seen, by ACPO representatives in their initial response to the calling of the Review:

> I don't intend to turn our police into a hard-faced, narrowly-defined law enforcement agency. It would be pointless and counter-productive to try to do that. We must maintain the human and humane face of British policing. (*Police Review* 30 June 1995).

This seemed to be a case of 'mission accomplished'! The wider political background to this 'turnaround' is discussed in Chapter 5. In the context of this discussion what is at issue is the extent to which ACPO, almost by stealth, gained a form of *ownership* of the Posen agenda, one it had initially challenged. By working within the review process and by taking a positive and proactive stance on the core/ancillary debate—rather than simply opposing that there be one—ACPO were successful in *reshaping* the Posen agenda in directions it could feel comfortable with.

In this respect the positioning of ACPO within the Posen Review was very much a *stage* in a development process which took them from being in many ways *outside* of the processes of policy-making on police reform to one very much *inside* that process. One way of describing this movement, which mirrors in some respects the 'outsider/insider' framework within policy analysis (Grant, 1989), which differentiates pressure group activity between those groups which remain 'outsiders' in terms of influence over policy- and decision-making on the one hand, and on the other 'insiders' who wield high degrees of influence over policy-making. Of course, as key actors within police decision-making, ACPO, one would expect, would always have enjoyed 'insider' status within policing policy-making. However, the way in which ACPO (and the other police associations) were 'wrong-footed', initially at least, on Sheehy and the police governance reform agendas, indicates that perhaps they were then what might be called '*insider-outsiders*' in terms of policy influence—they were constitutionally on the 'inside' as policy actors, but in relative terms 'outside' in terms of influence over policy agendas as the police reform programme was launched. What then happened, step by step, was that ACPO repositioned itself (or perhaps was *allowed* to reposition itself—see Chapter 5) increasingly inside the policy-making process—more as '*insider-insiders*', insiders both as policy actors and as a body with growing influence within the policy-making community. The Posen experience was a step along this path; what was to emerge alongside of Posen was an even more obvious example of ACPO becoming 'insider-insiders'—its progression to *agenda-setting* on wider criminal justice policy.

Out of the Blue: Agenda-Setting and the 'Rebalancing' of Criminal Justice

The development of a greater degree of 'insider' status within the policy-making process requires internal as well as external or environmental changes. As we shall see in Chapter 5, part of the shift towards the greater influence of the 'police voice' in the mid-1990s was due to a changing political environment in the direction of one more conducive to being receptive to police wishes and priorities. However, there were also institutional factors, internal to the police pressure groups, which played a part. Savage, Charman, and Cope (2000: 156–72) have documented how each of the major police associations, the Federation, the Police Superintendents' Association and ACPO, began to 'professionalize' their organization and its operations during the early 1990s, stirred into action no doubt by the police reform agenda itself. Of those associations, however, it is ACPO's trajectory which is most significant in this context, given its role as representing the views and interests of police leaders and its more obvious involvement in the policing policy process.

The history and development of ACPO has been studied in depth elsewhere (Savage, Charman, and Cope 2000). For the purposes of this discussion the features of that development of most significance to police policy-making and police reform will be the main focus of attention. In that respect it can be argued that ACPO as an organization has developed from one little more than 'members' club' from its inception in 1948 right through to the end of the 1980s, to one, by the mid-1990s, decidedly more corporate in ethos and strategic in approach. Throughout most of its existence it would have been stretching it to describe ACPO as the 'voice of the police service', or even the 'voice of police leaders', because chief officers were reluctant to give up their individual freedom in running their forces in the way they wished to the collectivity that was ACPO. The 'individualistic' ethos of chief officers of police, discussed earlier in this chapter, militated against corporate decision-making and a collectivist mindset, and chiefs, particularly chiefs of the larger forces, refused to sacrifice their autonomy to the 'greater good' of their own professional association.

However, a number of factors drove a change in that ethos and drove ACPO to become a more corporate body, some of them longer term developments, others more recent to the period in question (Savage, Charman, and Cope, 2000: 70–80).

First, there were *political* pressures on ACPO to adopt a more corporate stance as an organization. Home Secretaries, and particularly Douglas Hurd during his term of office (1985–9), had expressed concern that it was not possible to easily find what the 'police view' was on any particular matter because ACPO could at that stage could only offer a range of views from across its 43 chiefs and was reluctant to impose any more collective voice on that. Hurd found himself at a disadvantage when dealing with his European equivalents because, unlike them, he had no single point of reference from his police service to deal with. More significantly, Hurd had encouraged ACPO to take a lead role in harmonizing policing policy across forces as a means of moving away from the highly fragmented policy framework then apparent across police organizations (Savage, Charman, and Cope, 2000: 70–3).

Secondly, ACPO was stimulated to 'get its act together' by the *police reform* agenda itself. There is no doubt that ACPO was, as we have seen, 'wrong-footed' by the launch of the Sheehy Inquiry, and the fact that such a fundamental inquiry could have been undertaken by a team which included not a single senior police officer was very much a 'slap in the face' for the organization supposedly representing senior police management and the police service as a whole. Sheehy was seen amongst some within the organization as a 'wake up call' that sent the message that a disunited ACPO was easier to bypass and be ignored by those outside seeking to impose change on the police (Savage, Charman, and Cope, 2000: 73–4).

Thirdly, changing *environmental* pressures on policing had created a situation in which the 'go it alone', individualistic chief was becoming increasingly, even in practical terms, a thing of the past (part of a transition traced carefully, as we have seen earlier, by Loader and Mulcahy (2003: 249–53)). As each area of police work continued to become more complicated it had become more and more difficult for individual chiefs and their forces to keep abreast of issues and developments and to develop policies accordingly. They were becoming more dependent on their colleagues in ACPO, who between them had begun to differentiate their work into specialist areas, aligned with the committees and sub-committees within ACPO, for guidance on best practice on specific policy areas. This was illustrated by one of the chiefs interviewed as part of the study by Savage, Charman, and Cope (2000: 75) in relation to traffic policing policy:

> the service itself has moved so quickly and has had so much change upon it since the early 1980s that nobody can afford the time and energy to maintain individualists . . . I couldn't begin to understand the deep intricacies of traffic committee. I have to rely on my colleagues who look after traffic to say . . . we at traffic think the best way to police a motorway is this way.

Fourthly, pressures for change within ACPO in the direction of a more corporate approach was coming from amongst ACPO's own ranks. One the one hand was the role of what was referred to earlier as the 'police visionaries', in reading the likely future of the police service and in recognizing that only a more corporate ACPO could rise to the challenge. A number of ACPO presidents played key leadership roles in gearing up the organization, often against the odds and in some cases ahead of their time, in this direction, including Peter Wright (President 1987–8), John Smith (1993–4) and John Hoddinott (1994–5) (Savage, Charman, and Cope, 2000: 82–4). On the other hand, the *general* make-up of ACPO members, the chief officers themselves, was changing; the ACPO ranks coming through were increasingly what Reiner's study of chief constables referred to as 'bureaucrats', with a leadership style which emphasized democratic decision-making and 'professionalism and diplomacy' (Reiner, 1991: 308). The 'barons', 'bobbies', and 'bosses' (Reiner, 1991: 306–8), chiefs who in different ways adopted a highly individualistic leadership style, were a dying breed (Long, 2003: 638). This newer breed were far more inclined, as a matter of their professional upbringing, to adopt a more consensual, corporate and collective approach in their role, one reflection of which was to be receptive to the work and ideas of their colleagues in the pursuit of best practice. This also meant that they could more readily appreciate the benefits of concerted over individualistic activity in achieving objectives, something often critical to effective pressure group strategy.

There were other factors driving ACPO in a more cohesive direction, including the sorts of periodic system failures discussed in Chapter 1 which, as well as driving police reform itself, served to sharpen awareness within ACPO of the need for a greater degree of collective response and greater harmonization of policing policies across the service (Savage, Charman, and Cope, 2000: 77–80). The organizational expression of these forces for change took three primary forms. First, as an earlier development in the late 1980s, ACPO adopted an organizational policy which ran along the lines that if its central Council had agreed a particular strategy or policing policy then it was *binding* on all members, unless a particular chief could not accept that policy in which case he or she would have to state that in writing to the ACPO President. This replaced the previous status quo whereby if a policy had been agreed by ACPO Council individual chiefs could simply ignore it if they wished. This shift has been called the 'presumption in favour of compliance' (Savage, Charman, and Cope, 2000: 82–3; see also Loader and Mulcahy, 2003: 251–3), an important corporate development which created the presumption that ACPO members, and in particular chiefs, were to respect collective decisions when forming their own force level policy-making.

Secondly, following a recommendation of the Home Affairs Select Committee to professionalize ACPO as a policy-advisory body for the Home Office (Home Affairs Select Committee, 1989), ACPO established a full-time professional Secretariat to administer its affairs, including servicing the administrative support to the main ACPO Committees ('Crime', 'Traffic', and so on), which were the primary policy-making bodies within the organization. The Secretariat also included a press office which could more effectively manage information flow and media relations than had been the case. Of course, such organizational resources are important elements of successful pressure group activity as well.

Thirdly, and strategically significant, ACPO decided in 1993 to split its organization into two wings; it separated its 'staff association' functions, concerned with negotiating the pay and conditions of its members, from its 'policy-making' and advisory functions as a 'professional body'. The rationale for this (Savage, Charman, and Cope, 2000: 83–5) was that it would allow a clearer distinction to be made between two different and confusing types of 'representation': on the one hand representation of 'members' interests (pay and conditions of service) and on the other representation of the *policing profession*, particularly on the policing policy front. One could be seen explicitly as a 'union function', not to be confused with the more 'detached' and 'professional' function of advising government on what is best for the police service—and criminal justice as a whole—as the *'voice of the police service'*. This organizational schism was eventually carried through in 1996, with the creation of the Chief Police Officers' Staff Association (CPOSA) alongside ACPO itself. In crude terms, the split could allow ACPO to deny that any stance it took on a policy matter could be dismissed as 'vested interests', because as an organization it was now more clearly speaking about what is best for the police service *as a whole* and even what is best for justice as a whole—'vested interests' would be what are represented by CPOSA.

With these developments, over time, ACPO could be seen to be taking an organizational form which would more effectively equip it to fight its corner. What is significant however was how it increasingly *defined* its 'corner': as *criminal justice* in the broader sense and not just policing and law-enforcement. What emerged from the early 1990s was a determination within ACPO to broaden its scope of activity and influence from a specific focus on policing policy to a wider focus on *criminal justice policy*. Even as ACPO was being 'wrong-footed' over Sheehy, it had begun to work actively and proactively lobbying for changes to the criminal justice process and, as it took on its more professionalized organizational machinery outlined above, pushed further in that direction as time went on. There were various phases of this process of engaging with the wider criminal justice agenda.

Firstly, ACPO responded to the establishment of the Royal Commission on Criminal Justice (RCCJ) in 1991, one set up, as we have seen, in the wake of miscarriages of justice for which the police were to held largely to blame, by challenging other features of the criminal justice process as well—something along the lines of 'if you thought we were bad, you want to see what the rest are like'! In its evidence to the RCCJ in 1991 (see ACPO, 1995) ACPO did indeed make the case for improvements in policing and argued the need for better quality police investigations and the videoing of police interviews with suspects. However, it also called for wider changes in the criminal justice process, including:

- greater 'openness' in trial procedures;
- advance disclosure of the defence case to the prosecution;
- allowing the courts to be able to draw adverse inferences from suspects' use of the right to silence;
- admitting previous convictions as evidence in court where the defendant denies intent; and
- making greater use of DNA evidence.

Not only did it present this wider 'wish list' of criminal justice reforms, it did so with dossiers of research-based literature, including its own survey evidence, to back up the case, taking their submission above that of simple statements of preference. As one past ACPO President expressed it in the research undertaken by Savage, Charman, and Cope (2000: 178):

> I think the Runciman Commission ... would say that they were impressed by the evidence that was prepared by the police because it was extremely well prepared, was based on good research and indeed there was marked absence of anecdotal evidence.

The reference to 'anecdotal evidence' relates to a criticism about the quality of the police case presented to the previous Royal Commission on Criminal Procedure (RCCP), as shall be seen shortly. Whichever way, what was revealing about the ACPO stance in relation to Runciman was its *proactive* and *agenda-setting* nature. It was seeking to change the terms of the debate on justice from one which focused initially on police shortcomings to one which turned the spotlight on the criminal justice process and, specifically, the *balance of justice*. This was more timely then ACPO might have realized at the time. To begin with the RCCJ had itself moved in ethos somewhat in the direction ACPO would have liked, in terms of proving to be as concerned with the *failure* to convict and with the 'injustices' involved with people escaping conviction, as it was with wrongful convictions, much to the disappointment of the civil liberties groups and liberal commentators (Sanders and Young 1995; Rozenberg, 1994: 321–4; see also Chapter 1). However, even more significantly, ACPO's 'wish list' fitted neatly into a new era of government thinking on crime associated with the arrival in office of Michael Howard as Home Secretary. This relates to the second phase of ACPO engagement with the criminal justice agenda.

As will be discussed in Chapter 5, in October 1993 Howard launched his '27 point plan' on crime which was in many ways a reversal back to the tough 'law and order' stance of the early Thatcher government of the late 1970s and early 1980s. This heralded a new climate for criminal justice (and, as we shall also see in Chapter 5, for the destiny of the police reform agenda), one in which 'justice' would be 're-balanced' in favour of 'victims' and in support of securing more convictions. ACPO could not miss this opportunity to push further its agenda as submitted to Runciman. As Howard contemplated how to respond to Runciman, ACPO chose to continue to push one particular policy, the amendment of the right to silence, and elaborated further its case for allowing the courts to draw adverse inferences for suspects' use of the right to silence. Of course, as we have seen in Chapter 1, senior police officers had long argued for changes to the right of silence, convinced that it allowed 'experienced criminals' to avoid conviction. As far back as 1979, submissions were made by the ACPO to the RCCP arguing for changes in the law to allow magistrates and juries to draw inferences from the refusal to answer questions. However, interestingly, the Chair of the RCCP went on record as being critical of the quality of the case presented by the police in this regard. Commenting on what he regarded as the lack of 'objectivity' of the police submissions to the RCCP, Sir Cyril Phillips argued that the police had failed to present their views 'in a form which shows that an attempt has been made objectively to observe, and analyse them. An essential component in the proof is therefore missing.' (*Police Review* 12 October 1979). This is another way of saying the police 'case' then submitted for the amendment to the right to silence amounted to little more than a statement of *preference* rather than an argument supported by evidence.

In stark contrast, and with considerable tactical acumen, the approach adopted by ACPO both during the RCCJ deliberations and in this 'window of opportunity' thrown open by Howard's new era on criminal justice, was to present argument which was supported by *research*, in this respect a survey carried out on the behaviour of over 3,500 suspects dealt with by the police over a two-week period in 1993 (*Police Review* 8 April 1994). The findings of the ACPO survey were presented as a means of challenging what were argued to be a number of 'fallacies' in the case in favour of retaining the right to silence in its then current form, 'fallacies' which were in fact core arguments recently employed by the RCCJ in 1993, backed up by its own research, in supporting the status quo. Each of these 'fallacies' were then debunked in turn by the ACPO research findings (*Police Review* 8 April 1994):

- *Fallacy 1*: 'that the right to silence is rarely exercised'—the ACPO survey found that over 20% of suspects refused to answer some or all questions put to them by the police
- *Fallacy 2*: 'that the right to silence is not related to types of offence'—the ACPO research found that certain types of offence were more likely than others to be associated with the use of the right to silence, particularly offences such as robbery
- *Fallacy 3*: 'that criminal experience of the suspect does not affect the exercise of the right to silence'—the ACPO survey found that suspects with five or more convictions were more than three times as likely as those with none to exercise the right to silence
- *Fallacy 4*: 'that access to legal advice makes little difference to the exercise of the right to silence'—the ACPO research found that 57% of suspects receiving

legal advice exercised the right, compared with only 13% of those not receiving legal advice.

The validity of the research conducted by ACPO is not of concern here, rather the fact that it was undertaken and employed as a means of constructing a case and rationale by ACPO to press for the policy changes it desired. With all of the heated controversy which surrounded the debate over the right to silence, ACPO could point to the 'evidence' which undermined the case against amending the right to silence in the directions it wished to see carried through. There was a quantum difference between this approach and strategy to that taken some 15 years earlier with the Phillips Commission. Of course, in some senses they were pushing at an open door, because, as shall be seen in Chapter 5, Howard was highly inclined to accept the case for amendment in any case. Nevertheless, in terms of pressure group activity and tactics, ACPO had moved onto a higher plane and in some way had contributed to the change in the law they desired, which duly followed with the *Criminal Justice and Public Order Act 1994*. It had also been successful, as we saw in Chapter 1, in making the case for the extension and use of DNA and the setting up of a DNA database and in changing the rules on disclosure of the defence case.

However, that was only the beginning. Having tasted the success of the campaign around the right to silence and sampled the receptive environment to criminal justice reform then around, ACPO took its campaigning through to another phase. In 1995 ACPO presented a position paper on the need for further reforms in the direction of 'rebalancing' justice because of 'public concern' with the 'failure of the [criminal justice] system to convict and treat victims and witnesses properly' (*Police Review* 27 October 1995). The paper, entitled *In Search of Criminal Justice* (ACPO, 1995), talked of ACPO's 'achievements' to date in the areas of the right to silence and DNA evidence, but then went on to identify other areas where reform of criminal justice were necessary, including further reforms of disclosure to limit defence 'tactics' of requesting all evidence available to the police and the prosecution, the admission of hearsay and co-accused evidence, along with improved treatment for victims and witnesses. Success in influencing the wider criminal justice agenda and in setting those agendas themselves had become an acquired taste.

What ACPO's approach to the RCCJ and subsequently to criminal justice reform exhibited, was the completion of the movement from what has been called here 'agenda-resistance' through 'agenda-reshaping' to 'agenda-setting'. That movement also entailed a shift in the policy network framework for police and criminal justice policy. The initial responses to the police reform agenda of the early 1990s took the form, as has been seen, of *issue networks* which operated around strategies of resistance and networks of representation which focused on the opposition to aspects of the reform agenda, most notably Sheehy. Aspects of that issue network were still in evidence with the campaign to neuter certain aspects of the police governance reforms reflected in the initial *Police and*

Magistrates' Courts Bill, although much of the network dissipated once that Bill had been duly amended and passed into law. By the time of the Posen agenda, ACPO in particular had begun to take a more participatory and engaging approach with the reform agenda (mirroring its already more active engagement with the criminal justice agenda in relation to the RCCJ and its aftermath); the network was progressing more into a *policy community,* as defined earlier, with ACPO becoming increasingly integral to the process of policy and criminal justice policy-making and more of a regular 'inside player'. ACPO had not just got its foot in the door, it had well and truly got its feet under the table. Its strategy of developing an internally corporate organization and its strategic approach to pressure group lobbying activity had earned it a place at the policy-making table. This was not just a matter of Howard's largesse for the police (see Chapter 5); by the time Labour took office in 1997, ACPO had become a central part of the policy-making scenery, so much so that one commentator could complain: 'Labour . . . increasingly appears to be listening to a few select voices. In the criminal justice area the tough-on-crime policy translated as hearing only the demands of the Association of Chief Officers.' (Donovan, 1997)

This might be an exaggeration—and as we shall see in Chapter 5, Labour had its own plans for police reform which were to come home to roost as the new century dawned. However, if, as has been argued here, the 'police view' as represented by ACPO has now become an institutionalized and integral part of the policing (and criminal justice) policy-making process in terms of participation in a form of 'policy community', then *police reform* itself takes on a different form. It is less and less something which tends to be *imposed* on the police service and more and more something of which the police service takes forms of *ownership,* or at least co-ownership. As we shall see in the case of Labour's subsequent police reform agenda in the following chapter, despite that agenda being radical in a range of ways, ACPO was actively engaged with that agenda throughout, notwithstanding the critical messages it contained for the police service. What this does is reinforce the central thesis of this chapter, that 'forces from within', whether 'police visionaries' or the police pressure groups, are important factors in driving or shaping police reform in Britain. However, *how* important is a matter influenced by the wider framework of the *politics of law and order,* the subject of the next discussion.

5

The Politics of Policing and the Politics of Police Reform: Too Hot to Handle or Too Hot to Leave Alone?

Introduction

At various points in previous chapters a caveat was made regarding the relative influence of the differing drivers for police reform considered so far. That caveat concerns the extent to which any drivers for change and reform in policing are constrained in terms of influence by the *politics of policing*. Whilst each of the drivers of police reform discussed earlier has its own particular forms of influence over police reform agendas, each in turn must pass what we might call the political test—that the *political climate* needs to be one which is receptive to the messages coming through. This is not just a matter of the preparedness of decision-makers to accept this or that particular policy, although that is of course important. It is also a matter of whether the general climate is one in which 'interfering' with the police *at all* is seen as desirable or not. For whatever reason, there are times when governments have an appetite for police reform and others when that appetite is simply not there. However compelling a case and whatever has happened to place the potential for reform on the political table, if the political will is not one steeled for change then reform is unlikely to follow, or if followed may be very much a muted affair. Alternatively, the political will for change may be so strong that governments proactively look for areas where reform might be possible, rather than simply respond to agendas set in motion from other sources. The history of police reform in recent years is one littered with undulating political climates in which the political will for police reform is sometimes present, sometimes not. This is some measure of the political sensitivities attached to the policing and, in particular, to the risky business of 'disturbing the police'.

Policing, however, need not necessarily be an object of political controversy. Reiner (2000: 8–9) makes the important point that policing is inherently *political* but may not be *politicized* as such. Policing is inherently 'political' because it entails power relationships between the police and the community, relationships which involve the imposition of order, controls and at some point force and coercion over citizens (Reiner, 2000: 8). For policing to be *politicized* however it needs to become an object of dispute or conflict, explicit or implicit, between political actors or political organizations. As Reiner (2000: 9) puts it, 'Policing may be inescapably political, but it need not be politicised, that is, the centre of overt political controversy over its manner, tactics, or mode of operation and organisation.' There is little doubt that British policing has become heavily politicized in this sense, although arguably the schisms along which political controversies and disputes have developed are not as deep in the current climate as they have been in the recent past. In so far as there are political divisions over the nature and future of policing in that current climate, they tend to be about the best ways to ensure 'effective' and 'efficient' policing rather than whether the police are seen as partisan, trustworthy, out of control, or moving in the direction of a paramilitary force. In that sense the issues around which policing has become politicized have changed over time, and the temperature of the debate over policing may have declined somewhat, but policing nevertheless remains a political 'hot potato'. Policing is a matter of mainstream political discourse and of political debate and political division; if the controversies surrounding it are less emotive than they were, say, in the 1980s, policing is still very much a politicized world.

The politicization of policing, however, has varying sources, sources which serve to dictate the nature of the policing issues around which there is political division. In particular, we can distinguish between the politicization of policing due to 'police-led' factors on the one hand and the politicization of policing which stems from the wider politics of *crime* on the other. In that sense we can distinguish between the *politicization of policing* itself and the *politicization of crime*, which indirectly impacts on the politicization of policing.

Reiner (2000: 50–80) documents the various 'police-led' factors which together served to further the politicization of British policing from the 1960s onwards, some of which have already been considered in earlier chapters of this book. These include:

- the introduction of Unit Beat Policing in the 1960s and the impact of that on police-community relations (Reiner, 2000: 60–1; see Chapter 2);

- corruption scandals involving the Metropolitan Police in the early 1970s (Reiner, 2000: 62–4; see Chapter 1);
- the policing of anti-Vietnam War demonstrations in the 1970s and the use of crowd control tactics (Reiner, 2000: 61);
- miscarriages of justice and the police role within them (Reiner, 2000: 64–7; see Chapter 1);
- the policing of the National Union of Mineworkers' strike 1984–5 (Reiner, 2000: 68; Fielding, 2005: 70–4; see later in this chapter); and
- the political lobbying activities of the police pressure groups (Reiner, 2000: 71–4; see Chapter 4).

What such 'police-led' factors served to do was politicize policing by polarizing sentiment and political discourse relating to policing, often along either defensive or critical/oppositional lines. Some political actors will respond by defending the policing status quo, laying the blame for any apparent problem on factors outside of policing—for example, blaming 'political activists' for public disorder rather than problems within policing. Others will respond by taking a critical stance on the police, laying the blame for policing problems at the feet of the police themselves, at least in part, and by demanding *reforms* of the policing status quo, perhaps in terms of strengthening police accountability. As we shall see later, this polarization of sentiment on policing is often associated with the relationships between the *political parties* and the police, such that supportive or oppositional stances on the police fall along party-political lines.

The politicization of the police however may come about by a different route from one 'police-led'. Policing may become politicized because *crime* itself has become politicized. If crime becomes a headline concern of political discourse and a major issue for political debate then policing normally follows in its wake. Policing may be politically sensitive because crime has become politically sensitive. The police occupy the unique status, justified or not, as the agency with front-line responsibility for fighting and controlling crime. If crime is important to a political agenda then policing will almost certainly be of great significance as well; it comes as part of the package. There seems little doubt that crime has indeed become politicized as political debate rotates more and more around the 'politics of law and order' (Ryan, 2003: 111–13). Garland for example (Garland, 2001: 163–5), has referred what he calls the 'crime complex', a cultural formation characteristic of Westerns states in 'late modernity' involving high levels of public insecurity about crime, the politicization of crime as an issue of political discourse and deep concern about the effectiveness (or not) of criminal justice agencies. In such a cultural complex the effectiveness or otherwise of policing becomes a focal political concern. The politicization of crime can mutate into the increased politicization of policing as a result.

However, as will become evident later in this chapter, the politicization of policing which follows the politicization of crime may express itself in at least two alternative ways and take policing—and police reform—in two alternative directions. On the one hand, the position of the police as the front-line agency in the war on crime may earn the police a *privileged* status, a body to be courted by political actors and political parties anxious to demonstrate their 'support' for the police and concerned to negate any accusations that they are 'anti-police' and therefore 'soft' on crime. On the other hand, the politicization of crime may mean that precisely *because* the police hold such a critical role in the fight against crime they are increasingly placed under the scrutiny of the political microscope; their 'performance' and effectiveness might become a focal concern of political analysis and activity. The implications for police reform follow. The former scenario might render the police 'too hot to handle' in terms of police reform; police reform might be avoided altogether or if pursued, might be modelled on what the police themselves would prefer to see introduced. The latter scenario might render the police 'too hot to leave alone' and very much a target for reform, whether the police desire it or not. We shall see examples of both scenarios and both sets of outcomes in the discussion which follows.

It is the changing status of the police within political discourse and the consequent changing relationship between the police and the political parties which is the central concern of this chapter. The politics of policing in Britain has been a field of changing political climates, sometimes supportive of the status quo of policing, sometimes openly challenging that status quo. In that respect we can begin with the political climate generated around the political individual many would think most instrumental in politicizing the police—Margaret Thatcher.

The Early Thatcher Years and the Politics of the Police: Backing the Boys (and Girls) in Blue

In the run up to the 1979 General Election Margaret Thatcher made an announcement which both captured the essence of 'Thatcherism' and spelt out clearly where she and the Conservative Party stood on the matter of policing: '. . . the demand in the country will be for two things: less tax and more law and order'—a blunt statement summarizing what Gamble, in his attempt to define the politics of Thatcherism, later called 'the free economy and the strong state' (Gamble, 1988). 'More law and order' would mean a range of things, including the expansion of the prison system and the introduction of the 'short, sharp shock' for young offenders (Savage, 1990: 90–2). However, it would also mean a commitment to 'supporting' and strengthening the police. In 1981, William Whitelaw, then Home Secretary in the Conservative government, in a speech to the to the Police Federation Annual Conference—for which, significantly, he received a standing ovation from officers present—looked back at the mood when the Conservatives came into office in 1979:

> It is an age in which there is less respect for the rule of law . . . That is why
> this Government came into office convinced of the need to strengthen law

and order and why were determined to build a strong police service with high morale. (*Police Review* 29 May 1981)

The Thatcher Government came into office in 1979 with a clear and unequivocal pledge to 'back' the police service. For example, they had promised to implement in full the pay award recommended by the 'Edmund-Davies' review of police pay and negotiating machinery (see Judge, 1994: 332–54). On taking office, they duly honoured that promise, making an award which constituted an average increase in police pay in the region of 40%, and also backdating the pay award some ten months, providing officers not just with a substantial increase in annual pay but a lump sum to boot (Reiner, 2000: 72). Furthermore, as triggered by Edmund-Davies, the police were given a further 21% pay rise in 1980 (*Police Review* 17 October 1980). These awards were totemic of a relationship between the police and the Thatcher government which Reiner (2000: 73) has called a 'love affair'. However, it was an affair which started prior to the 1979 General Election and which was in many respects an illicit one. Not only were the Conservatives 'courting' the police, the police were almost openly courting the Conservatives and engaging in some seriously questionable political tactics. Tony Judge, in his 'insider's' history of the Police Federation, talks about Federation leaders getting 'as close as they dared to outright intervention in party politics' (Judge, 1994: 355). Reiner (2000: 71–3) documents how the Police Federation, from a point in the mid-1970s, adopted a strategy to get their 'message' on law and order across to the 'silent majority', culminating in the notorious advertisement in the national press urging voters to make 'law and order' a priority in the coming election, an effective invitation to vote Conservative (Reiner, 2000: 72). In relation to this, the Federation, on the advice of the Conservative MP and Parliamentary Advisor to the Police Federation, Eldon Griffiths, retained the services of a well-known public relations company, to mount their own 'law and order' campaign. One outcome of this was a sort of 'manifesto' which went out to all candidates standing in the General Election with a letter demanding to know whether they supported it or not. As Judge bluntly puts it:

> Seeing that the 'manifesto' was principally the work of Eldon Griffiths, and was virtually a verbatim reproduction of the Tory policy statements and campaign promises on law and order, there was no doubt as to which party the Federation was backing on this issue. (Judge, 1994: 355–6—emphasis added)

The fact that the Federation broke with their own tradition—which was that their Parliamentary Advisors were selected from MPs from the main opposition party—and maintained Griffiths as Advisor even though his party had won the election, (Judge, 1994: 357; Reiner, 2000: 72) added to the growing impression that the police, or at least the rank and file of the police, were forming a cosy alliance with the Thatcher government and that both had a common vision of the way to deal with law and order. A coincidence of philosophy on law and order between the rank and file of the police and the political right had emerged. A reflection of this, if rather extreme, is that in October 1979 Jim Jardine, then Chair of the Police Federation, was invited to speak to the Monday Club, the far right Conservative grouping, on policing matters. He used the occasion to attack the left-wing critics of the police who had voiced concerns about the way the police had recent public demonstrations, stating 'My members are sick and tired of being used as the whipping boys of the Marxist fringe of British politics' (*Police Review* 15 October 1979)—from Jardine's world-view, this probably included the Labour Party, an interpretation later reinforced when Jardine, on retirement, joined the Conservative Party (*Police Review* 12 November 1982).

In this political environment the predominant message coming from government to the police was one of 'what can we do for you?'. Chris Patten, one time member of the Thatcher government, summed up nicely the ethos of Thatcherism in this respect:

> homeowners and small businesses were encouraged, taxes were cut and enterprise unleashed, public spending was slashed . . . and the armed forces and the police were held in the highest esteem . . . . (Patten, 2006: 69)

Simon Jenkins, a political commentator who has written extensively about the 'Thatcher revolution' expressed a similar view rather more bluntly:

> Under Thatcher the police had, like the armed forces, enjoyed immunity from [Thatcher's] revolution. Unlike teachers, lecturers and doctors police forces were assumed to know what they were about. The reason was Thatcher's gratitude for the Police Federation being the first trade union to campaign for the Tory party (in 1979). She duly raised its pay and left it alone. (Jenkins, 2006: 181)

These statements indicate the rationale behind the 'privileged' status of the police relative to the rest of the public sector during the early years of the Thatcher governments (Loader and Mulcahy, 2003: 289; Morris, 1994: 308). Other public services were at the receiving end of expenditure cuts and institutional reform; this contrasted sharply with the treatment of the police. The main desire for police 'reform' lay in the determination to provide the police with sufficient numbers, equipment and police powers to launch the 'war on crime'. Conveniently and almost coincidentally, the Royal Commission on Criminal Procedure, set up under the previous Labour government in 1978, was ready to report in 1981, thus offering the Conservative government early in its first term a rich menu of reforms, mainly in the area of police powers, from which to pick. What was particularly comforting for the government was that the RCCP set out a range of proposals that was very much welcomed by the police staff associations, ACPO, the Superintendents' Association, and the Police Federation (*Police Review* 16 January 81). In other words the government were not faced with the embarrassment of either ignoring the findings of a Royal Commission in order to please the police, or of incurring the wrath of their new friends, the police, by being forced to accept Commission proposals with which the police were unhappy—Phillips had done it for them. Although the RCCP did not endorse amending the right to silence, as the police had hoped and even predicted (*Police Review* 4 May 79; see also Chapter 4), it did offer a plethora of recommendations for reform with which the police service could feel very much at ease. Admittedly some of the shine, from the police perspective, was taken off the reforms as the RCCP recommendations went through the legislative mill, leading to PACE (Reiner, 2000: 168–9). Furthermore, as we have seen in Chapter 1, the shock of the Brixton riots and the gravitas of the Scarman Report forced the hand of government and led it into other areas of reform, less easily swallowed by the police (such as those relating to police complaints procedures). Perhaps these were early signs that the police could not always expect things always to go their way, even under a Conservative government (see later). However, in the political climate engendered by Thatcher in the early 1980s the police could expect to see most things go their way most of the time.

Thatcher's support for the police and the 'love affair' between the police and the Conservatives might not have been solely the result of the symmetry between 'law and order/tough on crime' politics and the police world-view. The desire to deliver what Thatcher called 'more law and order' and the supportive attitude to the police with which this was associated may have been only a part of the story. It is impossible to articulate the relationship between Thatcherism and the police without reference to the hugely controversial issue of the way in which the Thatcher government handled the National Union of Mineworkers' (NUM) strike in 1984–5 (Fielding, 2005: 70–3). Police operations, involving the use of large numbers of officers deployed from forces around the country, and controversial public order tactics (Bunyan, 1985) were seen to have played a critical role in inhibiting the effect of mass picketing during the dispute, and in turn enabling the government to 'buy time' to see the dispute out—but there was a history to this.

When Thatcher became leader of the Conservative Party in 1975 the wounds of the 1972 NUM strike were still evident. The Conservative government of 1970–4 was badly damaged by the success of the NUM strike action and in particular by the effectiveness of the mass picket (also known as the 'flying picket') in blocking supplies of coal to the power stations, helping to create the energy crisis which, in the end, forced the government to capitulate to NUM demands. The defeat of the Conservatives in the 1974 General Election was widely attributed to tribulations of industrial strife and in particular to the NUM strike and the energy crisis it created—bringing with it the infamous 'three-day week' whereby factories and businesses were forced to reduce their working hours to ration energy. Perhaps the nadir of the government's fortunes were the events at Saltley Gates (Bunyan, 1985), where the police decided to close down access to a power station for lorries carrying coal rather than confront the mass picket any further, effectively ensuring 'victory' to picketing miners. Events such as this provoked the Conservatives to go to the electorate in 1974 on the theme of 'who runs Britain?' (Butler and Kavanagh, 1974)—unfortunately for the Conservatives too many voters answered 'not you'! In the wake of the Conservative defeat there was a resolve within certain quarters of the Conservative Party, and particularly the right, that it should be a case of 'never again' and Nicholas Ridley (like Thatcher, on the right of the Party) agreed to put together a plan, to be kept secret, to outline measures to be taken by a future Conservative government to defeat a major strike in a nationalized industry. The 'Ridley Plan', as it became known, was however secretly leaked to The Economist and it was revealed that included in it were steps to 'buy time' in the event of a strike by building up coal stocks and, significantly, to train and equip a large mobile squad of police ready to take on the mass picket (*The Economist* 27 May 1978).

It seems highly likely that Thatcher's commitment to 'strengthen the police' had some element of the Ridley Plan within it. After all, Thatcher's pre-election narrative of a 'lawless Britain' was one which lumped together not just the problem of crime but also political protest and *industrial* unrest (Bunyan, 1985). It was also clear that Thatcher was expecting a confrontation with the NUM at some stage after taking office (Gilmour, 1992: 104). Without being too conspiratorial, 'winning the police over' and 'supporting' the police in numbers and equipment may well have been related in part to their possible role in any future industrial action by the NUM and the 'flying picket'. Ironically, when the police did clash *en masse* with picketing miners in the 1984–5 dispute, the equipment used for the police operations—riot shields and NATO helmets—was available because police equipment had been recently overhauled in the wake of the inner-city disorders of Brixton and Toxteth. The irony was not lost on Whitelaw, who was to say 'If we hadn't had the Toxteth riots I doubt if we could have dealt with Arthur Scargill [the NUM leader]' (quoted in Gilmour, 1992: 104).

The ironic association between Toxteth and the Miners' strike has a further dimension. The policing of the miners' strike had another 'benefit' as far as Thatcherism was concerned: it helped further polarize the relationship between the police and the Labour Party, a polarization in which the events at Toxteth and other inner-city disorders had a role to play, thus making it even easier for Conservatives to claim that the Labour Party was 'anti-police' and easier still for the police to remain suspicious of Labour on the issue of policing. It would be wrong to assume that in the early years of the Thatcher government there was little appetite for police reform: there was plenty of appetite, but it was one that belonged to the left, in particular to the left of the Labour Party and to the civil liberties lobby. For a number of years sections of the left and the civil liberties bodies had grown increasingly agitated about the state of policing, largely because of an accumulation of critical incidents and developments. They included:

- deaths in police custody, such as the Jimmy Kelly case (Ryan, 2003: 70);
- the policing of anti-Vietnam war protest and the use of specialist public order units such as the Special Patrol Group, and in particular deaths resulting from police actions, such as the death of Blair Peach (Reiner, 1992: 83);

- clashes between Labour-dominated local authorities, such as Merseyside and Greater Manchester, and local and vocal chief constables—Kenneth Oxford and James Anderton respectively (Reiner, 1992: 91)—and, linked to this, the fallout of the inner-city disorders of the early 1980s; and
- the policing of the miners' strike itself, including police tactics to control the mass picket and the apparent central (to some 'government') control of police operations through the National Reporting Centre (Fielding, 2005: 70–3); even ACPO expressed concern that the dispute had produced a kind of 'national police service' (*Police Review* 7 September 1984).

Such events and developments served to encourage sections of the left to call for greater accountability and 'democratic' control over the police, something destined to cause hostility within the police sector. For example, in an almost amusing episode in 1981, James Anderton, the scourge of the left in many ways, made a speech on police accountability which, amongst other things, made a blistering attack on Jack Straw MP's 1979 Parliamentary Bill seeking to extend local police authority control over policing policy, dropping in the fact that Jack Straw was at one time President of the National Union of Students! Of course, as we shall see, Jack Straw was to return to the policing scene some 15 years later. In that attack Anderton launched into 'those who . . . insidiously and ideologically see that to dominate the police politically is to secure an unassailable bridgehead from which to move towards a totally monolithic power base'. (*Police Review* 6 February 1981)

Admittedly Anderton's narrative was extreme, even within police circles at the time (and it seems unlikely that the MP for Blackburn really was seeking to forge a monolithic state in the north-west of England), but it is no exaggeration to say that the Labour Party had, from the beginning of the 1980s, moved to a position essentially critical of and hostile to the status quo of policing. The police sector in turn had moved to a position of hostility to them. Yet this uncomfortable relationship was largely speaking irrelevant to the status quo of policing and most certainly has negligible relevance to police reform during the period. However strong the desire within the Labour Party for the reform of police accountability, the political impotence of Labour politics during most of the Thatcher years almost literally meant that such desires remained academic.

However, returning to the policing of the 1984–5 NUM strike, there is another political significance in that series of events: as Reiner (2000: 73) has argued, it was to be the zenith of the 'love affair' between the Conservatives and the police. Not only was there a growing sense within the police service that they were 'used' during the strike to deliver Thatcher's goal of defeating the NUM and with it the labour movement as a whole (Judge, 1994: 405; Gilmour, 1992: 110), but the affections of the other half of the 'affair' were beginning to cool. The political climate was beginning to shift away from the 'open cheque' for policing towards one more inclined to be critical of the police and what they had been delivering. The mood was beginning to shift to one more inclined to look for change within policing.

The Party's Over: Turning the Screws

We saw in Chapter 3 that from 1983 onwards attempts were made by government to impose more control over police expenditure through efficiency drives and the application of the Financial Management Initiative (FMI) for the first time to the police sector. This was an early sign that the privileged status of the police within the public sector was not to be taken totally for granted, even under Thatcher. However, the imposition of some form of efficiency regime on the police sector could hardly be avoided given the logic of the FMI and its implications for the public sector. More worrying for the police was a discernible shift, as the 1980s wore on, in the political mood within the Conservative Party over the police and what to do about them. This shift had two dimensions. On the one hand was a growing concern about the effectiveness and quality of policing in the light of year-on-year preferential funding and investment. On the other hand was the wider political climate within which the Conservatives could *afford* to think more critically about the police than they had previously.

Concerns about the effectiveness and quality of policing began to grow towards the end of the 1980s, because of what seemed to some senior Conservative ministers as the failure of the police to deliver appropriate returns on the levels of expenditure which had been directed at the police sector, particularly in the light of steadily rising crime rates at the time (Jenkins, 2006: 181–3). Kenneth Baker, at one point Home Secretary during this period, reflected on this in his political memoirs:

> there was impatience, if not anger [amongst ministerial colleagues], that although we had spent 87 per cent more in real terms since 1979 and had increased police numbers by 27,000, there had still been a substantial rise in crime. 'Where is the value for money?' asked my colleagues. (Baker, 1993: 450)

Thatcher herself came at it from a different direction. She was known to have reservations about the quality of police leadership and to be interested in the notion of an 'officer class', along the military model of an officer cadre, for the police service (*Police Review* 9 February 1990; Judge, 1994: 447). This might have been due in part to the prospect of the down-sizing of the military with the collapse of the Soviet Union and the demise of the cold war, freeing up highly trained military commanders for work elsewhere—after all, Margaret Thatcher was indebted to the military for delivering victory in the Falklands War. Whichever way, it was clear that Thatcher had in mind some form of scheme for introducing 'new blood' into police leadership from outside of the ranks of career police officers:

> It is essential to ensure that police leadership is of the highest calibre. All organisations need to consider how best to recruit talent and subsequently to develop it. All organisations stand to benefit from 'an injection of new blood and new ideas. (Quoted in Judge, 1994: 448)

The idea that a chief police officer might come from a route other than the 'single-entry' system, whereby all officers start as constables and move up through every rank, was like a red rag to a bull as far as the Federation was concerned (Judge, 1994: 447–8), despite the fact that most police forces worldwide operate with some form of 'direct-entry' system to police management positions. This notwithstanding, it is what the debate symbolized which was most significant: the Conservatives were beginning to challenge the status quo of policing in Britain and to move way from the sentiment of unconditional support for the police. These were the early signs of the fundamentalist approach to police reform which was to follow before very long.

The cooling of the affair between the police and the Conservatives was however not the only source of the changing climate for policing. The wider political environment in the mid- to late 1980s was one in which thinking more critically about traditional Conservative law and order policies—stronger police, more prisons—was made possible. It should not be forgotten that this period was also one in which the effectiveness of custodial penalties was challenged and 'community-based' penalties were prioritized as the alternative (Nash and Savage, 1994: 143–4)—some very 'un-Tory' things were happening. Alongside this the Government was warming to the idea that crime should be seen as a *community* responsibility and not just something to be left with the police—hence the interest in schemes such as 'neighbourhood watch' (Downes and Morgan, 1997: 94–5). It appeared that the Conservatives were now prepared to embrace approaches to crime control which were closer to liberal and academic thinking on crime policy than traditional Conservativism. So we saw both a growing dissatisfaction with the police themselves and also support for the expansion of community-based sentences and crime prevention strategies. This new tone of Conservative policy did not escape the attention of some within the Police Federation. Dick Coyles, Vice Chair of the Federation, spoke to an audience at a fringe group meeting at the Conservative Party 1991 Conference in the bluntest of terms:

> No government in history was elected on a more explicit or stronger law and order platform than was this one. Do you remember the conference where Willie Whitelaw talked about the 'short, sharp shock'? What have we got now? Punishment in the community, community service orders, yet more 'radical alternatives to custody'. Gone are the detention centres and the approved schools. Gone, in fact, is any kind of sanction that will really deter young villains. (Quoted in Judge, 1994: 466)

The irony was that the new emerging climate was not just about the demise of the beloved 'short, sharp shock' but also about fundamental changes to the way in which policing was organized. What the Federation was not aware of at the time was that, behind the scenes, it was the police, not just the penal system, that was in the firing line.

The explanation for the changing political climate on crime policy within the Conservative government, one which would ultimately have significant consequences for police reform, lies in more than the fact that the Home Secretary through much of this transformative period, Douglas Hurd, was of the 'one nation', centre-left school of Conservatism (Seldon, 1994: 43), less inclined to embrace the tough, law and order ethos of Thatcherism. Perhaps more important was the fact that this was a time when the Conservatives could *afford* to adopt a more arms-length relationship with the police and to take risks with more 'experimental' crime control schemes, such as new community-based sentences and community-based crime prevention programmes. Two related factors account for this environment. First, that the Conservatives were enjoying a period of serious political dominance, having had two consecutive landslide victories in the general elections of 1983 and 1987 (Kavanagh, 1994: 6–8). They had no need to feel threatened by the opposition, whatever stance they chose to adopt on crime policy. Linked to this, the Conservatives were streets ahead on the specific issue of law and order itself. A poll in March 1988, which tested public opinion on the question of 'which party has the best policies on law and order?', revealed that 50% of those polled said the Conservatives, and only 15% said Labour; Labour's standing had actually declined from their position in 1979, when 19% of those polled thought Labour had the best policies on law and order (IPSOS/MORI, 2006). What better time to risk 'taking on' the police sector and to challenge the wisdom of tackling crime by imprisoning people?

If this was what was referred to in Chapter 1 as a 'window of opportunity' for police reform—in this case a political window—the Conservative government certainly did not balk at taking advantage of it. The simmering dissatisfaction with the police sector and talk of a 'crisis of police leadership' during the late 1980s transmuted into the police reform agenda of the early 1990s. What emerged was a root and branch police reform agenda more radical than perhaps any seen since the formation of the public police in the nineteenth century. It is significant that the Home Secretary who launched the reform agenda was Kenneth Clark, who took office in 1992 after a ministerial career which had seen him confront not only the teaching unions but also the health professions, in parallel attempts to push through reforms in those public sectors. Clarke had something of a 'taste' for challenging the traditional vested interests in the public services and was known to be much more of a 'reformer' than a 'consolidator' (Seldon, 1994: 43). His strategy was to attack the police service on all fronts.

The framework of this police reform agenda was discussed in Chapter 4, but to reiterate for the purposes of this chapter, it entailed three main dimensions. Firstly, the government established an 'independent' inquiry into the police roles, rank structure, and pay and conditions of the police service, to be known as the 'Sheehy Inquiry' (Home Office, 1993a). Clarke announced the setting up of the inquiry to the Federation Annual Conference in 1992 and what he was to say came as a surprise not only to Federation delegates but also to the Chief Inspector of Constabulary and the President of ACPO, who were also in attendance. One part of Clarke's speech, explaining the rationale behind the inquiry, captured the moment best:

> Is a blanket increase in pay for every rank and every officer, irrespective of type of work or competence really the best way of reimbursing the police for the huge spectrum of work they do? (Quoted in Judge, 1994: 469)

After over a decade of preferential treatment within the public sector, the police were now being told that serious questions were being asked about the appropriateness of their rewards system, and, worse, the spectre of *performance related pay* was introduced. To add insult, it was to become clear that the team of experts who were to conduct the inquiry would not include anyone with direct experience of policing and was to be chaired by someone—Patrick Sheehy—from the *private sector*. This was some measure of the political will to turn the tables on the police service, and this from a Conservative Home Secretary. The fact that Clarke chose to announce the inquiry, one that would potentially target where it hurt most—police officers' pockets—to the Federation's own conference, was symbolic of the political mood within government regarding the police service. The Sheehy Report made a number of recommendations, most of which were like a red rag to a bull for this or that part of the police service:

- reduction of the number of police ranks, including the abolition of the ranks of chief inspector and chief superintendent (Home Office, 1993a: 189);
- reduction of police officers' starting salaries (Home Office, 1993a: 69);
- limiting the time officers could take as sick leave on full pay (Home Office, 1993a: 81);
- abolition of overtime payments for inspectors and restriction of overtime payments for other officers (Home Office, 1993a: 82; 83);
- relating the police pay to roles, responsibilities and performance of officers rather simply to rank and years of service (Home Office, 1993a: 40–1); and
- the introduction of fixed term appointments for all officers, including ten-year fixed appointments for new constables (Home Office, 1993a: 118–22).

The reception of this package of proposals across the police service was something discussed in Chapter 4. Suffice it to say here that the Sheehy agenda did not balk at challenging some of the most entrenched traditions of police pay and police roles; it was a bombshell of a document as far as officers were concerned. If Sheehy was radical in terms of its implications for police pay, roles, and conditions, the second dimension of the police reform agenda, that was spelt out in the White Paper, *Police Reform: A Police Service for the Twenty-First Century* (Home Office, 1993b), was radical as regards police *governance*. Furthermore, whilst much of the hostility to Sheehy came from inside the police service, the White Paper caused consternation in much wider circles.

The political background to the 1993 White Paper is not absolutely clear. Certainly the continuing rise in crime through the late 1980s and into the 1990s would have had some part to play. A feature of the White Paper was an emphasis on more central direction and influence over local police decisions and this might reflect a determination to ensure that the police 'stand and deliver' on the crime front. The White Paper may be seen as the first step in ensuring that the police start to get their own house in order and get on with the business of *delivering* what government wants them to do. As we shall see later, this ethos of 'delivery' was to re-emerge in the following decade. Furthermore, there is an element within the White Paper of facilitating more external involvement in policing (outside of central government) which was reminiscent of Thatcher's desire, mentioned earlier, to 'bring in outsiders' to improve the quality of police leadership. Above all, however, there was a political will to expose the police service more fully to the regimes of *performance management* which had been applied to other parts of the public sector some time before (see Chapter 3). This inevitably clashed with traditional notions of 'police independence' (Savage, Charman, and Cope, 2000: 193), so deeply imbedded in the British police mindset and so seemingly out of kilter with the messages contained in the White Paper. Taken together, these driving forces behind the White Paper *Police Reform* constituted a political determination to 'take on' the police service despite the risks in doing so.

The main proposals in *Police Reform* were:

- the introduction of new powers for the Home Secretary to set out 'national policing priorities' for the police service as a 'strategic framework' within which chief officers and their police authorities will operate (Home Office, 1993b: 24);
- the reform of the constitution of the police authorities (Home Office, 1993b: 17–23) involving:
  - giving police authorities more autonomy in setting their own budgets;
  - requiring police authorities to work with their chief officers in setting out local policing priorities, reflecting the national policing priorities set out by central government;
  - reducing the size of the police authorities, particularly the locally elected element, and changing membership of them to include people with specialist knowledge and experience outside of policing, such as those with expertise in business and finance; such members were to be appointed directly by the Home Secretary;
- the expansion of compulsory competitive tendering within the police service to include a range of corporate and construction services (Home Office, 1993b: 16);
- the strengthening of HMIC, including the introduction of 'lay' Inspectors of Constabulary with specialist expertise, in particular management skills (Home Office, 1993b: 36–7), and the opening up of the Metropolitan Police Service to HMIC inspection;

- increased monitoring of police performance at both local and national levels (Home Office, 1993b: 18–19) and, in effect, the introduction of performance *league tables* for police forces;
- provision for future police force amalgamations to reduce the number of police forces in England and Wales (Home Office, 1993b: 42–3).

Viewed from a twenty-first century perspective many of these reform proposals might seem mundane and even benign; from the perspective of the early 1990s, in some quarters, they were viewed as highly subversive, threatening the very heart of British policing and what it stood for. As the proposals of the White Paper were translated into legislative form, initially in terms of the *Police and Magistrates' Courts Bill*, the hotly contested political battle began (Newburn, 2003: 93–4; Reiner, 2000: 193–5). The consequences of that battle were discussed in Chapter 4; suffice to note here again that there was a degree of 'backing down' before the legislation was given Royal Assent as the *Police and Magistrates' Court Act 1994*. In particular, the Government was forced to withdraw the clause giving the Home Secretary the power to directly appoint the new 'independent' members of police authorities and the chair of police authorities. None of this however takes away the fundamentalist nature of the police reforms around police governance embodied in the *Police Reform* White Paper.

The third dimension of the police reform agenda of the early 1990s related to police *functions*. As was seen in Chapter 3, during the 1980s a number of 'policing' functions were subject to 'civilianization', taking them out of the direct remit of warranted officers. However, there was still a view in government circles that other spheres of policing activity could be undertaken by operatives other than regular police officers. To this end in 1993 the Government set up a review of 'police core and ancillary tasks' (Home Office, 1995), known as the 'Posen Inquiry'—Posen being the head of the small team of civil servants appointed to conduct the review. The agenda for the review was to identify which policing tasks are 'core' and as such can only be undertaken by the regular police, and which tasks may be defined as 'ancillary' and might potentially be undertaken by others, be they civilian staff in the employ of the police service, or other public service employees of private companies. It was the latter which the police staff associations most feared, as was seen in Chapter 4 the spectre of the further 'privatization' of policing functions haunted the police representative bodies. This was further evidence of what was referred to in Chapter 3 as the 'marketization' of policing, the exposure of policing services to the workings of public and private sector marketing mechanisms. Although, as we have already seen in Chapter 4 (see also Savage, Charman, and Cope, 2000: 176–8), the bark of Posen was in the end much worse than its bite, there was no doubting the intent of government to put policing functions and roles under scrutiny and test whether they really need to be undertaken by fully trained, and it must be said, well paid, police officers. Posen, at least potentially, squared the circle of a fundamental police reform agenda for which nothing, it seemed, was sacred.

It is striking how much of the ethos of the early 1990s police reform agenda was to re-emerge in the even more radical reform agenda during the early years of the twentieth century, as will be seen later in this chapter. However, much of the sting of the 1990s reform agenda was taken out as concessions were made and other factors came into play. Although Clarke had been the driving force for many of the reform initiatives it was left to Michael Howard, the new Home Secretary, to see them through as Clarke moved to the Treasury. By the time Howard had taken over, a very different political climate on crime, and ultimately policing, had already begun to take shape.

The Second Honeymoon: Police Back in Favour

In a speech in 2004, then as Leader of the Conservative Party in opposition, Michael Howard reflected on his record as Home Secretary. He stated: 'As I showed when I was Home Secretary...if you are resolute, if you are determined, if you have the will, you can cut crime.' He also claimed to be the one who 'ended the 1960s consensus' on law and order when he became Home Secretary in 1993, a consensus which had assumed that crime was an illness to be cured and that society was to blame for crime:

> My approach was simple: to give the police the powers they needed to catch criminals; to give the courts the powers they needed to convict criminals; and to give our prisons the space to take persistent, serious and dangerous offenders out of circulation altogether. (Howard, 2004)

If Howard was the one who 'ended the consensus', the implication was that his immediate predecessors in his own party were part of that consensus. In other words, they had failed to get it right in their approach to crime, with their concerns for alternatives to imprisonment and a leaner and more efficient police service, whereas Howard's way was *more* imprisonment, *more* police and *more* powers for the police. The claim to have ended the 1960s consensus is a revealing one which is some measure of the transformation of the political climate on crime at around the time Howard took office as Home Secretary. When Howard took over from Clarke he inherited a reform agenda he was not at all comfortable with; he was in the anomalous position of having to see through an agenda which was critical of, not sympathetic to, the status quo of policing. This did not sit easily with the wider approach Howard was to take on crime, which had 'supporting' and' standing by' the police at its core. The message he would have preferred to give to the police was not 'you've got to change' but 'how can we help you?'.

Howard launched his alternative to the '1960s consensus' at the 1993 Conservative Party Conference in his notorious '27 point plan' for crime speech in which he also famously announced 'prison works'. The plan covered a wide range of criminal justice processes and related to activities as esoteric as squatting, anti-hunt demonstrations and even 'rave' parties (Savage and Nash, 2001: 104–5). It also, significantly in this context, referred to changes in *police powers*. As was made clear in Chapter 4, Howard accepted the police case in relation to the right to silence, going against the majority recommendations of the RCCJ to leave the right to silence regulations intact. His decision to adopt the amendments to the right to silence proposed by the police—which were eventually enshrined in the *Criminal Justice and Public Order Act 1994*—was highly symbolic of his political direction on crime and policing at that time. It was indeed very much in the mould of 'how can we help you?' as far as the police were concerned. Like the extension of police powers to take intimate samples and extend the DNA database (provisions also contained in the *Criminal Justice and Public Order Act*), as argued in Chapter 4, Howard seemed to be highly receptive to police preferences on crime and policing. As Howard expressed it: 'I will never do anything to undermine the police' (*Police Review* 8 October 1993). So where did this leave the police reform programme?

Each of the three agenda for reform, the Sheehy Inquiry, the White Paper *Police Reform*, and the Posen Review, for differing reasons, eventually lost or ran out of steam. As the reform proposals made their way through to implementation, they became much paler versions of their original forms. The demise of the Sheehy agenda was perhaps the most dramatic. Despite the fact that the report was published in July 1993, by October 1993 Howard was announcing to the House of Commons that he was rejecting some of the major recommendations of Sheehy (*Police Review* 3 November 1993), including fixed term contracts—only ACPO ranks would be subject to these—the model for performance related pay put forward by Sheehy, the abolition of housing allowances and the abolition of the rank of chief inspector. Furthermore, even those recommendations which were to survive through to implementation, such as the abolition of the rank of chief superintendent and deputy chief constable, were overturned with the passage of time.

As regards the White Paper proposals, it was a case of the government being forced, reluctantly, to stand down on certain key areas of reform of governance arrangements. The final version of the *Police and Magistrates' Courts Act 1984* did embody a number of major reforms proposed in the White Paper. For example, it provided for the reconstitution of the police authorities, with the reduction in membership by almost a half, the reduction in the proportion of elected members, and the establishment of police authorities as semi-autonomous revenue-raising bodies. The Act also created new powers for the Home Secretary to issue National Policing Objectives and mechanisms to ensure these were being adopted as policing priorities at the local level. These were substantial and controversial reforms very much along the lines proposed in the White Paper. However, the government did not get all that it sought to achieve in the wake of the White Paper (as discussed in Chapter 4). A revolt by Conservative members within the House of Lords, involving figures such as Lord Whitelaw, helped force a number of concessions, some of which were explicit proposals in the White Paper, some of which had emerged as the White Paper was translated into legislative form (Fielding, 2005: 164–5). The concessions included:

- the Home Secretary would not have the power to appoint police authority chairs, as stipulated in the original Bill, they would be elected by the authority members instead.
- the 'independent' members of the police authorities would be drawn from a local listing *approved* by the Home Office but not directly appointed by the Home Secretary, as originally proposed.
- there would be one more seat for the locally elected members of police authorities (nine) than magistrate members and independent members combined (three + five respectively); the original proposal was an equal measure of elected members on the one hand and magistrates/independent members on the other—for the local police authorities this was a vital matter of principle.

These concessions rebalanced the final Act somewhat in favour of the local authorities and at the expense of Home Office control and influence over policing, even if at a marginal level. The Posen Review was also blunted along the way. As was argued in Chapter 4, the radical potential of Posen was undermined by a strategic approach by ACPO to 'capture' the agenda, for example, in terms of taking responsibility for parts of the research which was to inform the review and other forms of what here has been called 'agenda re-shaping' (Savage, Charman, and Cope, 2000: 176–8). It was rather like inviting guests for dinner and allowing them to take over the cooking. There was little surprise that the final conclusions of the review were far less threatening to the status quo than many had anticipated at the outset.

The reason why the radical promise of the early 1990s police reform agenda failed to materialize in the form clearly intended under Clarke is open to conjecture. One obvious factor, as has already been noted, was that Howard did not share Clarke's scepticism about the quality of British policing or the need to 'take them on'. After all, Howard was more on the traditionalist right-wing of Conservatism where law and order was concerned. However, it would seem that factors more fundamental that this were at work. These factors conspired to diminish the appetite within government for a police reform agenda which might place the government in vulnerable light as 'anti-police' at a time when law and order was moving to the centre of a political storm.

As Rose (1996: 323–5) has argued, the murder of Jamie Bulger in 1992 was a turning point in crime policy in Britain. It triggered a moral panic about youth crime and a surge in public anxieties and insecurities associated with crime. The murder was treated in media and political discourse as not just about a matter of the actions of the two young boys responsible, but, in Rose's words 'a signifier of national depravity' (Rose, 1996: 323). It is significant that the murder followed some months after other events involving 'troublesome youth'—'joyriding' stolen cars and clashes between gangs of young men and the police—in the housing estates of Blackbird Leys in Oxford and Meadow Well in North Shields

(Allen and Cooper, 1995), further fuelling a growing sense of national 'decline' (Loader, Girling, and Sparks, 1998). The problem for the Conservatives was that this shift in the national mood had taken place under their watch, and this the 'party of law and order'. It was this mood, at least in part, that Howard's 27 point plan on crime was seeking to assuage. The record of the government in the crime policy area in the years before—one of reducing the use of custody and the other 'liberal' measures we have seen—hardly seemed the right example to set. Furthermore, in this context, to spend time attempting to strip the police of roles and responsibilities, limit them to fixed term contracts, subject them to performance related pay, and to make it easier to fire them seemed perverse to some more inclined to be supportive of the police, and Howard was one of those.

In addition to the changing public sentiment on crime, and perhaps related to that change, was the striking shift in the reputation of the Conservatives in public opinion on the issue which they had been so dominant—law and order. Whereas in March 1993 the Conservatives were ahead of Labour in the opinion polls on the question of 'which party has the best policies on law and order?' by 40% to 26% respectively, by September 1993 they had begun to actually trail Labour by 23% to 26% (IPSOS/MORI, 2006). This would not matter as much were it not for the fact that law and order had, for a number of years, moved up the list of issues which the electorate saw an major factors determining their own voting intentions; it was now firmly established as in the top three issues influencing voting behaviour, behind health and education (IPSOS/MORI, 2006). The irony was that the process of turning law and order into a central concern of voters began with the end of the 'post-war consensus' on crime which Thatcher herself had done so much to undermine (Downes and Morgan 1977). The Conservatives were facing a crisis of public confidence over what had been one of their electoral trump cards, and this was showing in their overall standing in the opinion polls on voting intentions (Crewe, 1994: 108). In this context pursuit of the full police reform programme could have potentially reinforced a view that the Conservatives were 'soft' on crime, because they had sought to 'rein in' the police. This is exactly the sort of narrative which the revived Labour Party, now as 'New Labour', were beginning to apply, as we shall see shortly.

Of course, loss of ground on the issue of law and order was not the only problem for the Conservatives. Its record of economic management had taken a battering in the wake of 'Black Wednesday', when the government were forced in September 1992 to withdraw from the Exchange Rate Mechanism and interest rates rocketed as a result (Jay, 1994: 185–6). Furthermore, the government, as well as the Conservative Party out in the country, was deeply divided over the question of Europe (Forster, 2002: 106–29). Faced with a crisis of public confidence and internal strife, 'getting tough' on crime seemed to be something of a comfort blanket for the Conservatives, something on which they could unite and hopefully face up to Labour. Indeed, Rose (1996: 323–4) has documented how even for the Prime Minister, then John Major, crime had become the 'dominant issue of the hour'. Crime had been lifted into a position of centre-stage for policy-making as the Conservatives sought to respond to the political crisis which confronted them in the early to mid-1990s. In that sense making up ground on law and order had become a priority. In this respect evidencing their 'support' for the police fitted more neatly with this political agenda than pursuing police reform as such. This stance was evident in statements made by the Home Office Minister with responsibility for the police, David MacLean, which amounted almost to a confession about how the Home Office had 'overdone' its police reforms. Writing in 1995 in *Police Review*, MacLean referred to his role as 'changing the culture of the Home Office, which perhaps dealt rather arrogantly with the police force, regarding it as something we control. That's all changed.' (7 April 1995). A little later he continued in the same confessional vein, further distancing the Home Office from the police reform agenda. To repeat a quote made earlier, 'perhaps we have tended to see the police as an organisation to be regulated and told what to do. ACPO has shown it is certainly capable of *managing its own affairs*' (*Police Review* 21 July 1995—emphasis added).

Not only does this statement further testify to the role of ACPO in 'capturing' the reform agenda, as discussed in the previous chapter, it stands as some measure of the extent to which the Conservatives were keen to keep the police on board as they pursued the law and order agenda. However, they were not the only party seeking to make up ground on law and order and to demonstrate their 'support' for the police. A new politics of law and order was beginning to emerge in many ways far more surprising than the tribulations of law and order politics under the Conservatives. New Labour was on the rise and its stance on crime and policing was to an extent totemic of the new politics associated with it.

New Labour and New Friends: A Labour 'Concordat' with the Police

If public opinion failed to respond to Howard's 'ending the 1960s consensus' on crime, in the sense of gaining confidence in the Conservative's policies on law and order, the approach certainly seemed to go down well with representatives of the rank and file of the police service. The Chair of the Police Federation stated in October 1993 that Howard 'is the best Home Secretary the police had ever had' (*Guardian* 16 October 1993). The tense relations between the police rank and file and the Conservative government which had emerged in the years before had begun to mellow. However, ironically, just a few months earlier a young Tony Blair, as Shadow Home Secretary, was given a standing ovation at an ACPO Conference. This was a hugely symbolic and well as highly political moment. As we saw in earlier in this chapter, the history of the Labour Party's relationship with the police had been one characterized by confrontation. The battles in the

1980s between local Labour councils and their chief officers, and left/Labour concerns about abuses of police powers and the policing of public order events, both coupled with demands for more 'accountability' of the police, had served to create a relationship of at best mutual suspicion between Labour and the police service. However, the coincidence of two political shifts created the conditions of a more fruitful relationship. On the one hand, as we have seen earlier, was the Conservative determination in the early 1990s to reform the police and in particular the concern to provide central government more direct control of policing priorities and policies. On the other hand was New Labour's strategy of burying the image of the Labour Party as 'soft on crime', more concerned with tying the hands of the police than with tackling crime itself. New Labour's new slogan of 'tough on crime, tough on the causes of crime' (*The Independent* 4 December 1993) was the clearest reflection of this (Savage and Nash, 2001: 106–7); this was the political version of a 'left realist' approach to crime (Matthews and Young (eds), 1992), the acceptance that crime 'really is a problem' in itself and that the police have a key role to play in tackling that problem. New Labour was determined to have a positive engagement with the police as a means of both neutralizing its past image as 'anti-police' and of preparing for a constructive relationship with the police in tackling crime when they gained office.

Labour's adoption of the slogan 'tough on crime, tough on the causes of crime' signalled a new chapter in the politics of crime and law and order in Britain and captured a number of dimensions of a new political agenda. First, it seemed to be an acceptance that no major political party could now go to the electorate seeking office without a headline stance on law and order; furthermore it seemed to be resigned to the fact that electoral success would not come about without some image of the party in question being 'resolute' or 'tough' on crime—meaning in effect to come down hard on *offenders*. In the Labour context, as we shall see in more detail later, the chosen target in this respect was 'anti-social behaviours' and low level disorders—loutish behaviour, begging on the streets, and so on (as discussed in Chapter 2). Being 'tough on crime and tough on the causes of crime; was a statement about Labour now being *electable*. Secondly, the slogan carved out New Labour's own distinctive take on being 'tough' which was a form of what would later be called a 'Third Way' (Giddens, 1998: 28–33) approach to the issue. It stood somewhere between traditional left/Labour approaches to crime on the one hand, with a focus on social causes of crime and the role of *social* policy in crime reduction, and traditional right-wing approaches to crime on the other, which emphasizes notions of blame, responsibility, choice, and the role of the state in ensuring that crime has its costs as well as its rewards. The slogan seemed an attempt to marry notions of blame, choice and responsibility with sentiments of social justice and social change. Thirdly, and related to these points, the slogan was a statement of intent that New Labour was prepared to challenge the Conservative veritable 'monopoly' on crime and law and order, to take on the Conservatives on what was their 'home' ground.

Whichever way, the coincidence of a Conservative determination to reform the police and Labour's 'new realism' on crime helped create an environment in which Labour could hold out a hand to the police and offer support at a time when the service appeared under threat. The stage for this new-found friendship was the passage through Parliament of the *Police and Magistrates' Courts Act* which, as was seen in Chapter 4, involved an alliance between, amongst others, the opposition Labour Party and ACPO. New Labour could score two hits with this alliance. First, to demonstrate that the Conservatives were 'undermining the police' by taking discretion of policing policy away from the police themselves. The National Policing Objectives could be portrayed as diminishing the independence of chief officers. Second, in doing this, to demonstrate to the police, particularly at senior level, that they were now to be trusted as 'safe hands' when it came to policing matters. That warm reception at an ACPO Conference to a Labour Shadow Home Secretary seemed to indicate success on that front. Blair had been making noises that were well received by chiefs before that point—for example, he had come out against force amalgamations earlier in 1993 (*Police Review* 5 March 1993). In the years leading up to the 1997 General Election the relationship between New Labour and the police, at least at senior level, continued to develop.

It was clear that, in the end, Howard's attempt to reinvigorate Conservative fortunes through a beefed-up law and order politics failed; Labour's landslide victory in the 1997 general election put paid to that. Interestingly, the Labour Party 1997 Election Manifesto declared 'The police have our strong support', something which seemed to be stating the obvious from a prospective government, but with Labour's past record perhaps not so. Labour came into office with little by way of any explicit agenda for policing or for police reform, and for much of the first Labour administration it was a case of 'softly, softly' in relation to the police service (Savage, 2003), building on the pre-election 'concordat' struck up between Labour and the police. This entailed, for the time being at least, a high degree of acceptance of the status quo of policing but with some 'tweaking' here and there. For example, Labour accepted the governance arrangements within the *Police and Magistrates Court Act*, but saw within the Act the potential, perhaps underestimated by its critics (see Savage 1998), for *increasing* local influence over policing. In this respect the Home Office began to encourage local police authorities to engage in extensive local consultation in drawing up the 'local policing plan' for their area—early signs of what would later be called 'community engagement' as we shall see later. There were, however, a number of initiatives for policing which did emerge in the early years of the Labour government which were of significance in shaping policing in a more New Labour direction.

Two of those initiatives were governed more by wider Labour agendas, embracing the public sector as a whole, than by specific concerns with the organization of policing. One of these was the policy of *'joined up government'*, the other the *best value* agenda. The form which 'joined up government' (Long, 2002) took in the area of crime policy was primarily in terms of *crime partnerships*. The *Crime and Disorder Act 1998* heralded the first statutory framework for partnerships between the police, local authorities, health and educational authorities and other bodies aimed at reducing crime at the local level. The principles of audit, strategy, and planning were to be applied to tackling crime through formal partnerships at various levels of governance, the core of which was to be the *local authority* as the body given the primary responsibility for crime reduction. This framework has many ramifications (Crawford, 1998). However, from the point of view of the police service it was significant in two ways, at least potentially. First, it signalled that the police were to be seen more as only *one* 'crime-fighting' agency amongst others and no longer as necessarily the 'front-line' in the crime reduction process. In a very real sense it questioned the police 'monopoly' over law enforcement and opened up the prospect of serious *power sharing* in this area of policy and delivery. Secondly, it enabled consideration of the extent to which *alternative providers* of 'policing services' other than the 'public police' might be employed to deliver some at least of those services. For example, if a local authority, having conducted a 'crime audit' in their area, identifies a particular locality as requiring intensive and visible street patrols, it may, as the body with the statutory responsibility for crime in that area, decide that 'municipal' (local authority employed) patrol officers might be used, or even *private security* patrols, rather than (or as well as) regular police officers. The new forms of governance of the 'crime problem' inaugurated by the crime and disorder agenda have opened up the Pandora's Box of the police role, and enables forms of 'post-modern' responses to crime to unfold (Johnston, 2000: 18–27; see also the Conclusion to this volume).

The *best value* agenda if anything extended this process even further, as was made clear in Chapter 3. As has been seen, best value was Labour's equivalent of the 'value-for-money' agenda enforced by the Conservatives, although arguably involving a much more assertive and demanding framework of 'new public management'. Best value, to reiterate, is signalled by the 'four Cs': it emphasized *consultation* with communities for services they required; it required *challenge* of the need for existing services; it required *comparison* of services across sectors to obtain best practice; and it required *competition* to obtain value for taxpayers in delivery of service (DETR, 1998b). Each of these requirements presents new forms of challenges for the police service, but perhaps the demand for *competition* was potentially the most fundamental. Again, the public police had enjoyed a veritable monopoly over the provision of core policing services; this new agenda put the consideration of *alternative service providers* very much in the frame. The public police were being tasked more and more with the requirement to demonstrate that they and they alone are best equipped to deliver policing services, yet the case for this was not always apparent, even with apparently key activities such as street patrol (see later in relation to police community support officers). Best value invited local authorities to ask difficult questions about policing, such as 'do we need fully trained (and highly paid) regular officers to undertake street patrols?' Whilst this was not at the time a wholesale assault on the 'public police monopoly' over policing, a culture of challenge to some of the hitherto unchallenged traditions of British policing was emerging as a consequence.

Pressure for police reform also came from more specific directions. First, as we saw in Chapter 1, the police response to the murder of Stephen Lawrence led eventually to the *Macpherson Inquiry*. Macpherson put forward a plethora of recommendations for police reform, most of which were acted upon in earnest. Whilst much of the attention paid to Macpherson focused on the issue of 'institutionalized racism', it should not be forgotten that the Inquiry also raised fundamental questions about police competence and police management and ultimately of the quality of *police leadership* and *police training*. This helped set the stage for what, as will be seen shortly, was to become the police 'modernization' agenda. Secondly, as was discussed in Chapter 2, Labour adopted the recommendations of the Patten Commission on policing in Northern Ireland. Clearly this had direct significance for the policing of that particular part of Britain and major organizational reforms ensued as a result for what was to become the Police Service of Northern Ireland. However, *Patten* also raised generic questions about policing which provided material for police reform beyond Northern Ireland. As was argued in Chapter 2, as the nearest thing in recent decades to a 'Royal Commission' on British policing, Patten undertook a root and branch review of policing, including the 'police mandate', police accountability and governance, police culture and policing styles. Through its review and recommendations it offered as such a 'menu' for police reform per se. As we shall see further, some elements of *Patten* were to find their way into the wider police reform agenda which was to begin to emerge at the turn of the century.

The political climate relating to policing for Labour's first term of office can be described as a mixture of a conciliatory and supportive approach to the police sector on the one hand and, with the passage of time, a more questioning and challenging approach on the other. Labour sought to consolidate the constructive relationship with the police it had established whilst in opposition, but at the same time grew in determination not to let that relationship allow the police sector to escape the sorts of reforms going on elsewhere in the public sector. What was also undoubtedly significant is that Labour's own power base seemed fully secure; it had no reason to fear being outflanked by the opposition on crime or any indeed any other issue because it seemed highly likely, as the century neared its end, that the Conservatives were facing a long period out of office. In many ways, the situation was parallel to that facing the Conservatives in the mid- to late 1980s; political security had created an environment in which challenging the status quo was less risky than would otherwise be the case—'taking on' the police was one example of this. The great untouchable was once again coming into the firing line.

Into the New Century: The Gloves Come Off

It has been argued that governments often need substantial periods of time before embarking on some areas of more radical reform (Sabatier and Jenkins-Smith (eds), 1993); governments sometimes need some years in office under their belts before they are prepared to undertake major reform, particularly in sensitive areas—an area as politically charged and sensitive as policing may be one. The commencement of Labour's second term of office was perhaps the point at which police reform, and radical reform at that, could safely be placed on the political agenda. The early signs of what was in store, in this case relating to the adequacy of police performance, were presented in the White Paper *Criminal Justice: The Way Ahead* (Home Office, 2001a), which made play of the Audit Commission's statement that:

> There remain . . . significant variations in performance between police forces. These variations cannot simply be explained by differences in workload or by the varying circumstances forces face. (Quoted in Home Office, 2001a: 79)

This was backed up by a veiled threat that where 'gaps' in police performance were evident there would need to be consideration of how that gap might be filled by bodies and professionals other than the regular police:

> Where there are gaps which cannot be filled by experience or potential within the service, then there should be opportunities to recruit people with relevant specialist skills whether from the *private* or public sector. (Home Office, 2001a: 79—emphasis added)

Perhaps the most ominous element of Labour's emerging police reform agenda lay within what would later known, innocuously, as the 'extended policing family' (Johnston, 2005; see also Chapter 2). The White Paper went on to state:

> There has always been a wide range of people contributing to community safety in various forms. These include park keepers (some with constabulary powers), security guards in shopping centres, car park attendants, neighbourhood wardens, night club bouncers and the private security industry. The issue for policing is how these various activities can be co-ordinated to make the most effective contribution to making safer communities. (Home Office, 2001b: 83)

The full significance of such statements was to become more evident in two other documents, which focused specifically on police reform: the White Paper *Policing A New Century: A Blueprint for Reform* (Home Office 2001b) and the Green Paper *Policing: Building Safer Communities Together* (Home Office, 2003a). These documents formally launched a programme for police reform which the government explicitly heralded as 'radical', in its scope and intensity (Home Office, 2001b: 1). At least in relative terms and in comparison with British police reform agendas in the recent past (Savage, 2003), it was difficult to deny that claim. There were few areas of policing which the reform agenda did not touch, and the reforms themselves ranged from the strategic to the operational, from the cultural to the structural, and stretched from such seemingly mundane issues as pay structures to the fundamentals of governance and accountability. The reform programme itself was to unfold in two phases, coinciding in substance with the messages contained in the two White Papers. The first phase was to focus on governance and regulation, the formal introduction of the police community support officer scheme (see Chapter 2) and the reform of the police complaints system. The second phase was to focus on 'community engagement', neighbourhood policing, strengthening local police accountability, force restructuring (discussed in Chapter 3), and the reduction of the number of forces, and 'service modernization' in terms of rewards for good performance, 'enhanced leadership' and improved 'skills mix' of police officers and police staff (discussed in Chapter 3). Broadly speaking, the first phase was characterized by *centralism*, the second by an ethos of *localism*. Before considering some of the key reforms in more detail it is useful to consider the Labour government's own explicit rationale for this radical reform agenda.

To begin with it is important to stress that the British police reform agenda was part of wider agenda for public sector reform as a whole. In 1999, the Labour government launched a programme of public sector reform under the banner of 'modernising government' (HMSO, 1999). This programme focused around developments such as:

- 'joined-up' public services (better inter-agency working);
- the removal of 'unnecessary regulation' hindering front-line working;
- the introduction or expansion of performance related pay;
- a strengthened focus on 'delivery' (results) and a more 'flexible' workforce to deliver results;
- encouraging public services to be more 'responsive' to citizen's needs;
- closer monitoring of public services and greater use of performance management.

Elements of this broader 'modernization' agenda were to find their way into the police reform agenda itself. The Labour government's more specific justifications for *police* reform related, officially at least, to a number of 'problem' areas. As stated in *Policing a New Century* (Home Office, 2001b), the case for reform rested on a range of concerns:

- that levels of crime remain 'too high', particularly crimes of violence and 'anti-social behaviour';
- that fear of crime remains too high and that the gap between actual and perceived levels of crime remains too great;
- that police detection rates are unacceptably 'low';
- that police performance varies too much between individual police forces (ie between the 43 police forces of England and Wales)—a reiteration of the claim made in *Criminal Justice: The Way Ahead*;

- that police resources need to be better managed; and
- that public confidence in the police is falling and is particularly low within some minority ethnic communities (Home Office, 2001: 102).

This official discourse on the rationale for police reform, as we shall see, masks more fundamental forces for change, but as official discourse it has its own significance, not least because it is the case presented by government to the police themselves as the rationale for the reforms that are to follow. It is also interesting to note that despite the Labour government's own earlier strategy, considered above, of broadening the locus of responsibility of crime beyond policing to include local government authorities under the ethos of 'community safety' and 'partnership' (Crawford, 1998), the new rationale for police reform chose to maintain the ideology of the police as the central agency for crime reduction. Police reform was justified because of perceived failures on the crime control front for which the police are to take primary blame. Indeed, some of the underpinning arguments used by Labour for police reform were remarkably similar to those adopted by the Conservatives in the early 1990s. A former senior civil servant at the Home Office later revealed how Labour ministers, particularly those attached to the Treasury, viewed the police as the last major 'unreformed sector' in public services; ministers were also asking 'where is the return' for all of the money put into the police service (Rimmer, 2007). The similarity of these sentiments to those expressed by Conservative ministers in the late 1980s and early 1990s was uncanny.

Adding to the government's case, HMIC subsequently presented a number of more fundamental grounds for police reform, which included the changing global challenges to policing—terrorism, migration of peoples and organized crime—the growth of the night-time economy, concerns about the 'resilience' of existing geographical governance of policing (force structures), and the growth of wage and pensions costs (HMIC, 2004).

On these bases the Government officially laid down the grounds for 'radical' reform. One way of classifying the range of reforms which followed, as stated earlier, was between 'centralizing' measures on the one hand and 'localizing' measures on the other (McLaughlin, 2005). However, there is also virtue in differentiating the core reforms which were to emerge in terms of the seemingly contradictory forces of the *disempowerment* and *empowerment* of the police.

Radical Police Reform Under Labour I: Disempowerment

Police reforms by their very nature involve forms of 'disempowerment' of the police. As we saw in Chapter 1, reform often comes about because of system failure and the response to that failure may be to introduce forms of inhibition of police conduct or regulation (limitation) of police decision-making. In the context of the reforms introduced by Labour the process of disempowerment took two primary forms, one set relating to police policy-making, the other set to 'regulatory governance'.

Police Policy-Making

As we have seen at various points in this study, the ability of the British police to set their own priorities and develop their own policing policies had already been constrained over previous years, as the field of policing policy became more and more subject to *centralization*—the central state increasingly influencing the direction of policing at the expense of localized police decision-making. The government-appointed police inspectorate, HMIC, had become more interventionist and directive since the 1980s (Savage, Charman, and Cope, 2000: 27–8; see Chapter 3), and governments had used legislative changes, such as the *Police and Magistrates' Courts Act 1994* (as we saw earlier) to allow themselves more scope to influence policies, through such devices as the setting of 'national objectives' for policing (Jones, 2003). However, Labour's 'radical' agenda for police reform was to involve a quantum leap in terms of centralized control over police priority-setting and policy-making, and as such moved the disempowerment process significantly further.

New legislation, in the form of the *Police Reform Act 2002*, introduced new measures to tighten the grip of central government over local police forces. A central feature of this was the introduction of new powers for governments to produce annual 'National Policing Plans' which local forces were obliged to implement. For example, the National Policing Plan for 2005–8 included prioritizing violent and drug-related crime and the targeting of prolific offenders (Home Office 2004a: 5). The Plans were *directive* and not, as had previously been the case with government statements of priorities for policing, advisory. Senior officers could no longer, under this arrangement, choose not to follow the central state's preferences for policing. Local policing plans, drawn up by local police managers and their local police authorities, would now have to comply with and support the National Plans. In Chapter 3, the broader process of the 'nationalization of policing' was discussed, within which the development of National Policing Plans sits comfortably. In this regard, commentators have seen the National Policing Plans and other linked developments as evidence of a more fundamental shift towards the centralisation of British policing and the demise of localism in policing (Jones, 2003: 592; Newburn, 2003; Loveday and Reid, 2003). However, it is the role of such measures in *disempowering the police* which is of most significance in the context of this discussion. The power and authority of the police to set priorities for the policing of their locality, and determine their own policing policies, is transferred in large measure upwards and outwards to bodies external to those local police organizations—and in particular to central government. The tradition of local permissiveness in British policing, whereby central governments allow local chief officers of police forces to determine the policing policies for their force areas within a loosely defined and imposed central framework of regulation, had been dealt a fatal blow by the introduction of National Plans (Newburn, 2003: 95).

This process had been supported, subsequently, by an explicit challenge by the government to the doctrine of the 'operational independence' of chief police officers. A consultation document presented in 2003 by the Government entitled *Policing: Building Safer Communities Together* (Home Office: 2003a) questioned the appropriateness of the doctrine for policing in the twenty-first century. It suggested that the principle of operational independence of chief officers be replaced by the principle of the *'operational responsibility'* of chief officers, a proposal originally made in the Patten Report on the reform of policing in Northern Ireland (Patten, 1999; see also Kempa and Johnston, 2005; see also Chapter 2). This was a particularly significant shift in emphasis; 'independence' implies a high degree of autonomy, whereas 'responsibility' implies both a level of freedom to act and a degree of accountability for actions taken. 'Responsibility' is a status designation which can potentially open the doors to forms of *delegation* whereby chief officers can be delegated to carry out actions dictated by authorities over and above them. At the very least, were this redefinition of the chief officer's constitutional position from being 'independent' to 'being responsible for' transpire—at the time of writing this was not clear—it would amount to a significant loss of power and authority for those operating at this level of policing and for the organizations they lead.

'Radical' reform in these contexts means a radical shift in the locus of power and authority *away* from senior police officers, and the police organization as a whole, towards external authorities, and above all to the central state. This process was been supported by parallel shifts in the *regulatory* framework of British policing.

The Regulatory Framework

Braithwaite (2000: 49–54) has argued that the concept of the 'new regulatory state' has become a central criminological tool for understanding contemporary forms of law enforcement, justice and punishment. With the fragmentation and increasing pluralization of forms of social control and security in 'post-modern' societies (Rose, 2000: 186–7), the governance of control processes and agencies has shifted from direct state engagement with systems of control to regulatory governance, or forms of 'government at a distance'. This has been reflected in the proliferation of regulatory agencies which oversee, monitor, and review the activities and 'performance' of those responsible for the delivery of justice and security (Shearing, 1993). In the context of British policing, this process has been expressed both in the strengthening of existing regulatory agencies (for example, as stated earlier and as discussed in Chapter 3, in the increasing interventionizm of the police inspectorate) and in the creation of new bodies with regulatory responsibilities and authority. The 'radical' reform agenda offered us examples of both, and in each case forms of *disempowerment* of the police were evident.

First, as we saw in earlier chapters, the *Police Reform Act 2002* established the Independent Police Complaints Commission (IPCC), which for the first time introduced a fully independent system for the investigation of serious complaints against the police. The history of the machineries for dealing with complaints against the police in Britain, as was also seen in Chapter 1, is one dominated by the periodic and staged enhancement of the 'independent' or 'external' element in the oversight process (Smith, 2004), as it has been in other countries such as Australia (Prenzler, 2002b). The role of independent oversight in Britain is one which has moved from the largely peripheral engagement of 'lay' members on complaints panels, through to the more substantial independent oversight of investigations into complaints made against the police (Smith, 2004; Maguire, 1991). The establishment of the IPCC, in that sense, might be seen as a logical extension of a process that has been under way for some considerable time (Smith, 2004). The creation of a machinery for the independent *investigation* of complaints, as distinct from independent oversight of investigations undertaken by the police themselves, could be considered the next logical stage in the process of enhancing accountability by extending the external/independent element. However, the emergence of the IPCC was much more than an evolutionary development, and it is important not to underestimate the *symbolic* significance of the transfer of investigative responsibility for complaints against the police away from the police and over to a fully independent external body, making that process very much a watershed in police reform. This related to the fact, as discussed in Chapter 1, that the immediate spur for the formation of the IPCC was the *Macpherson Report* and the failings of the police in relation to the murder of Stephen Lawrence (Macpherson, 1999). The IPCC was born against a backcloth of official concerns not only that the police had failed, but that the existing machinery for exposing such failures was inadequate, at least in terms of generating public confidence. The police, as the agency most readily identified as technically equipped to undertake investigations, were therefore to be relieved of the right to conduct them where serious complaints against the police themselves were involved. This was a hugely symbolic statement in terms of official trust (or lack of it) in the police to conduct such affairs with full propriety. In comparison with the machinery which the IPCC replaced—the Police Complaints Authority (Smith, 2004)—the establishment of a fully independent system for the investigation of serious complaints against the police acts as a very significant form of *disempowerment* of the police. It involves a loss of control and influence over some of the core processes which can call them to account.

The second reform involving regulatory agencies also appeared within the *Police Reform Act 2002*. The Act established a body within the Home Office known as the 'Police Standards Unit' (PSU; discussed briefly in Chapter 3), a new component in the network of regulatory bodies associated with British policing

(Hale, Uglow and Heaton, 2005). The role of the PSU is essentially to regulate the 'performance' of individual police forces and sub-force level operational command units, which it does through various processes (Home Office, 2005a). First the PSU profiles performance using comparative data (gathered by HMIC) of police force and sub-force (Basic Command Unit BCU) levels—for example, of detection levels across police units. This allows the identification of 'poor performing' police units. Secondly, it has the power to conduct investigations into units performing 'below their best' and determine 'remedial actions' as required. This means in effect that the PSU, as a central agency, has the authority to intervene in the management of poor performing or 'failing' police units, which can include sending in teams of external specialists to 'support' managers of those units. Thirdly, related to the power of intervention, the PSU can identify 'best practice' in strategic and operational policing and disseminate such best practice across forces and units within forces. This assumes forms of 'core doctrine' for policing which are to apply irrespective of local variations in policing problems and the policing solutions which are to address them.

The establishment of the PSU sent out clear messages about the centre-local balance in British policing and as such about the police reform agenda more generally, messages which are as symbolic as they are practical. Regulation in terms of the PSU operates at three levels, each of which underwrites central authority over local police discretion. Firstly, the work of the PSU is focused on the extent to which police forces and police units within forces achieve centrally determined performance *targets* (Home Office, 2005a: 8; see also Chapter 3). These targets indicate the value which central government places upon particular policing functions and particular 'outcomes' of policing—such as detection rates, 'public reassurance', and so on. Secondly, the PSU is charged to guide police units on the *policing methods* which are best employed in achieving these targets. Known revealingly as 'Knowledge Management' (Home Office, 2005a: 9), this role of identifying and spreading best practice as a form of doctrinal dissemination contains an assumption the 'centre knows best' when it comes to models and approaches to policing; locally derived approaches should succumb where necessary to that principle. Thirdly, the PSU has in effect the power of *enforcement* over local police units deemed to be 'under-performing', in the sense that officers of the PSU can decide to 'engage' directly with police units where they are thought to be persistently failing in performance terms. Once the PSU has engaged with such units it will only 'disengage' when it is thought that the 'performance gap' has been breached.

The creation of the PSU stands as a classic example of the new regulatory state as defined earlier and as a measure of the tensions between central and local governance of British policing. On the one hand successive British governments have, since the early 1990s, maintained that policing should become more flexible and responsive to local conditions and have referred to BCUs at local levels as the core or 'backbone' of policing services (Mawby and Wright, 2003: 176–7; also discussed in Chapter 3). The critical role of the BCU was reiterated in the

Labour government's rationale for police reform (Home Office, 2001b: 9). The prioritization of BCUs points to *devolved decision-making* to the local level and increased variation in policing forms across policing units. On the other hand, the BCU acts as a source of localized and focused *performance data* which central governments, through the PSU (and also HMIC), can use as a basis for measuring the extent to which centrally-drawn targets are being reflected at the local level. As such the BCUs provide the site for what Newburn has labelled government 'micro-management' of policing (Newburn, 2003: 95) and the increasing *standardization* of policing. If the new regulatory state enables 'government at a distance', agencies such as the PSU demonstrate how 'distance' is no obstacle to the detailed management of local policing services by the centre.

The regulatory framework emerging out of the police reform agenda thus constituted forms of *disempowerment* of the police and the transfer of power and authority from police leaders and police organizations to external regulatory agencies. Coupled with the more direct loss of authority associated with police policy-making considered earlier, the outward drift of power seemed integral to the radical agenda for British police reform. However, as the case of the BCU illustrates, there is a *tension* between centralism and localism in contemporary arrangements for policing. That tension is compounded in the police reform agenda by a parallel tension between the measures which, as we have seen, involve disempowerment of the police on the one hand, and other measures which point in the opposite direction, one of *empowerment*.

Radical Police Reform Under Labour II: Empowerment

If the police reforms involving disempowerment of the police have impact most directly at the strategic levels and entail reduced discretion for police leaders, the reforms which involve empowerment relate primarily to operational levels and entail widening the discretion for front-line officers. They involve 'power' in both the specific and diffuse senses: specific in terms of technical *police powers* and diffuse in the sense of power in terms of social and political relations. The former relate to what can be called powers of *summary justice*, the latter to forms of *community engagement*.

Empowerment as Summary Justice

Since before it came into power in 1997 New Labour had chosen to make a political issue of 'anti-social behaviour' as a central part of its platform to be 'tough on crime; tough on the causes of crime' (McLaughlin, Muncie, and Hughes, 2001; Savage and Nash, 2001). The control of 'low level disorder' in the form of 'noisy neighbours', graffiti, public drinking, rowdy group behaviour, litter, begging, and so on, was one of New Labour's main objectives in pursuing the 'community safety' agenda on an inter-agency, 'partnership' basis (McLaughlin, 2002: 93–5). The emphasis on anti-social behaviour has had many expressions in legislative and policy terms, from 'Anti-Social Behaviour Orders' (civil court orders prohibiting individuals from certain behaviours, such as visiting certain areas of a town—known publicly as 'ASBOs'—see also Chapter 2), to campaigns to tackle truancy in schools, a sweeping and highly contentious range of measures (Brown, 2004). In the context of this discussion one reflection of the anti-social behaviour agenda is of particular significance: the creation of new powers for the police to administer forms of *summary justice* to members of their local communities.

Summary justice has of course been in effect for many years in Britain and elsewhere in the form of *fixed penalty notices*, which the police and/or local authority officers can issue for such acts as illegal parking, dog fouling, or dropping litter. Issuing officers have the discretion to impose specific forms of punishment, directly administered financial penalties, without recourse to charging, prosecution, and trial. The anti-social behaviour agenda encouraged the widening of the use and scope of summary justice, in terms of *what* can be punished, *who* can be punished, and *who* can do the punishing.

First, the anti-social behaviour agendas involved the widening of the range of activities where a fixed penalty notice, known revealingly as 'Penalty Notices for Disorder', can be issued <http://www.homeoffice.gov.uk/anti-social-behaviour/penalties/penalty-notices/> (accessed May 2007). The roll-call of such anti-social behaviours is very broad, and includes:

- wasting police time;
- sending false (hoax) messages;
- knowingly giving a false alarm to the fire brigade;
- causing harassment, alarm; or distress,
- drunk and disorderly behaviour in a public place;
- being drunk on a highway;
- throwing fireworks; and
- drinking in a designated public area (Home Office, 2003b: 76).

Furthermore, the government stated its intention to widen the range of behaviours for penalty notices beyond these activities, subject, significantly, to 'consultations with the police' (Home Office, 2003b: 84). Summary justice was seen, quite clearly, as a way ahead.

Secondly, the scope of fixed penalty notices for disorder was been widened in terms of those who can be issued with penalties. The minimum age at which 'offenders' can be issued such notices was originally set at 18, but was subsequently moved downwards to 16 years of age (Home Office, 2003b: 75). This form of 'net-widening' (Brown, 2004) opened up new sectors of youth for the imposition of summary justice. It also created new forms of police interaction with young people.

Thirdly, the anti-social behaviour agenda extended the range of officials who have the power to issue penalty notices. This range was broadened to include not just police and local authority officials but also police community support officers, non-sworn auxiliaries operating under the authority of the chief police officer, who provide a uniformed presence as patrol officers but who do not have the powers of regular officers. It has also been broadened to include 'accredited officers', staff who, under a community safety accreditation programme are, in effect, 'licensed' to provide local community safety services by the regular police force. This could include local authority community safety staff, staff employed by housing associations and, significantly, private security employees (Crawford and Lister, 2006: 170–1). Under the accreditation arrangement, such staff can be granted limited powers, including the issue of some fixed penalty notices, particularly those targeting 'environmental' problems such as graffiti and dog fouling (Home Office, 2003b: 84). Summary justice had not only been extended in terms of the scope of behaviours which come under its remit; it had been extended in terms of the agents who can administer it.

The rise of summary justice constitutes specific forms of *empowerment* of the police. Above all, summary justice extends the *discretion* available to the police to act in certain ways and reach particular decisions; it does so both horizontally and vertically. Summary justice, in terms of the powers to issue fixed penalties to the range of activities listed above, extends police discretion horizontally, in the sense of the range of behaviours now to fall under the policing remit. Policing has always been concerned with a wider remit than law enforcement, and is better associated with the more nebulous role of 'order maintenance' (Reiner, 2000: 112–5). The extension of summary justice within the police role almost institutionalizes this wider function, opening up space for more by way of 'policing order' as compared with 'policing crime'. In this respect it should be noted that the offending behaviours now encompassed by fixed penalties necessarily involve greater subjectivity of judgement on behalf of the police over what constitutes an 'offence'. For example, the 'offence' of causing 'distress or alarm' requires a judgement both of the feelings of 'victims' and on the behaviour of potential 'offenders'. The issue of fixed penalties in these areas of behaviour carries with it none of the (relative) certainty of traditional fixed penalties, such as those attached to speeding, illegal parking, or dropping litter, all of which involve little by way of subjective judgement (they either did, or did not, take place). It has been argued that the antisocial disorder agenda more generally is inherently at risk of allowing (or even requiring) arbitrary judgement on behalf of enforcement officers (Brown, 2004). In relation to ASBOs, for example, Reiner has argued: 'The Anti-Social Behaviour Orders . . . constitute indirect criminalisation of amorphous and ill-defined behaviour perceived by complainants and the police as nuisances.' (Reiner: 2000: 169).

The expansion of summary justice in this context embodies a broadening of police discretion to embrace a wider remit and horizon of 'unacceptable behaviours'. However, that expansion also involves enhancing police discretion in vertical directions in terms of decisions at the disposal of the police. Put bluntly, the police officer can now combine the function of policing with those of prosecutor, judge, and jury. The police would now be empowered to decide not just *who* should potentially be sanctioned, but *whether* they should be sanctioned and *how* they are to be sanctioned. Fixed penalties allow the circumvention of processes that traditionally inhibit police decision-making, such as the independent prosecution service and the courts, and avoid the checks and balances that come with those processes. Almost literally, summary justice enables the police to become a law unto themselves.

However, the rise of summary justice has empowered the police in another way. As we have seen, the reforms under the antisocial behaviour agenda have also enabled a range of 'accredited persons' to issue fixed penalty notices. Although in one sense this could be seen as a dilution of the authority of the police, in the sense of the 'pluralization' and 'fragmentation' of policing functions across a range of service providers other than the public police (Bayley and Shearing, 2001), it should not be ignored that 'accreditation' now placed the public police in a position of *control*. The power to approve and licence other public and private providers of policing services belongs to the public police. As Crawford and Lister (2006) have argued, accreditation involves a reconfiguration of governance rather than a loss of authority:

> Accreditation schemes represent a form of 'arms length' governance through which the police may seek to govern at a distance—or steer—the policing work of others. In this respect, accreditation facilitates the 'responsibilisation' of private organisations . . . It also aims to allow *greater police control* over certain elements of the private security industry. (Crawford and Lister, 2006: 170—emphasis added)

In this sense the rise of summary justice entails both direct and indirect empowerment of the police: direct in terms of the power of the police to apply summary justice through fixed penalties for a specific range of behaviours; indirect in terms of the power to control other agencies and groups which possess the power to issue fixed penalties, such as police community support officers and other local authority personnel. This, however, relates to and can be understood by a wider form of empowerment of the police, one which has come through *community engagement*.

Empowerment as Community Engagement

In addition to the 'technical' empowerment associated with the rise of summary justice, the police reform agenda involved a more diffuse form of empowerment by means of the redefining of policing styles and the police role. Mention has already been made of the pivotal role of what has been called *'neighbourhood policing'* in the radical reform agenda (Kempa and Johnston, 2005). Neighbourhood policing is a specific form of community policing which prioritizes 'community engagement', police intervention at the 'micro-local' level with neighbourhood communities using dedicated policing teams (McLaughlin, 2005: 482–3). The teams, known as Neighbourhood Policing Teams (NPTs), act as a nucleus of policing services and are typically made up of a small group of officers representing the 'mixed economy' of the 'extended police family' (Kempa and Johnston, 2005)—several regular uniformed officers, together with various mixes of police community support officers, special constables (volunteers), neighbourhood wardens, park rangers, and private security guards (Home Office, 2005b). In what has been called the 'new localism' (McLaughlin, 2005), neighbourhood policing was to become the central vehicle for community engagement, the articulation of policing with local communities. The Labour government committed police forces to the roll-out of neighbourhood policing in each and every locality in their force-area by 2008 (Home Office, 2005b)—by any standards, a revolution in policing.

The explicit rationale by government, and one largely accepted by the police (ACPO, 2001), was that neighbourhood policing and community engagement are necessary measures to tackle the 'reassurance gap', the gap in perception between actual rates of crime, which have been falling since the mid-1990s, and the level of public anxiety about, and fear of, crime, which has risen rather than fallen over this period (Millie and Herrington, 2005; Fielding and Innes, 2006). What neighbourhood policing offers above all is *visible* policing, even if what is visible is a uniformed presence largely attached to auxiliary and voluntary personnel rather than the regular force. Such visibility is associated with *accessibility*, whereby local communities can more easily make contact with locally-based officers. Increased visibility and accessibility, so this rationale went, will improve senses of security and safety and, it was hoped, bring levels of fear of crime more in tandem with actual rates of crime. In this respect a central target for neighbourhood policing was antisocial behaviour rather than crime as such, for it is people's experiences of incivilities and antisocial conduct which are, so it is argued, most to blame for the reassurance gap (Millie and Herrington, 2005: 43). Neighbourhood policing, therefore, is from this perspective essentially *reassurance policing*.

It has been argued convincingly that the 'new localism' may be seen as strengthening the accountability of and controls over the police at the local level (McLaughlin, 2005). In that sense, the 'new localism', at least potentially, empowers local communities and orients policing in directions which the community, rather than the police, prefer. There is no doubt that the introduction of more effective forms of police accountability and the development of more 'responsive' police organizations are core features of the government's strategy for local policing (Home Office, 2004b: 20). However, if we interrogate the reforms further it is apparent that 'community engagement' is also in large part about *police leadership* of the anti-crime and antisocial behaviour agendas, and in that sense involves empowerment as well as the enhanced accountability of the police.

The 'vision' behind the push for neighbourhood policing is more fundamental than the rationale for other models of 'community-based' policing. It is more than advocacy of a 'partnership' approach to crime reduction (Crawford, 1999) and the simple 'visibility' of the police in localities; it is both of these things but more besides. This is evident from official comments such as the following, on the new roles of constables within the neighbourhood policing framework:

> Constables are taking on increasingly skilled roles within neighbourhood policing teams, *managing* a diverse range of staff and acting as *community leaders*. (Home Office, 2004b: 9—emphasis added)

The vision in question was one in which the regular police were to adopt the role of *leaders* in the process of 'building safer communities'. It is significant that a key part of the police reform programme was called 'workforce modernization' (see Chapter 3), a programme of professional development for officers (through improved recruitment strategies, training and staff development) to prepare them more effectively to undertake *leadership* roles. The rationale for workforce modernization was spelt out as follows:

> At the heart of the Government's strategy is effective leadership throughout the service ... we want to support, in particular, the *leadership role of the constable in the community*. (Home Office, 2004b: 78—emphasis added)

There is a remarkable symmetry between this notion of the role of the constable as community-leader and John Alderson's model of the community constable as a form of 'social diagnostician', an agent for identifying and solving social problems (see Chapter 1), apparent in his attempt to define the objectives of an ideal police system, one of which was: 'To provide leadership and participate in dispelling criminogenic social conditions through co-operative social action.' (Alderson, 1979: 199)

In Alderson's view, the police officer should aspire to exhibit 'social leadership' in the process of strengthening communities (Alderson, 1979: 40) as a means of proactively tackling social problems, including crime. The role of the front-line regular officer in the neighbourhood policing programme seemed very similar. Neighbourhood policing is about the police taking the lead role in *mobilizing communities*:

> We want such teams [NPTs] to develop a sense of being responsible for and *'owning'* their local areas. This means involving communities in negotiating priorities for action, finding lasting solutions to local problems. (Home Office, 2004b: 48–9—emphasis added)

This interpretation is reinforced when it is made clear that neighbourhood policing is to be built along the lines of *intelligence-led* policing:

> [NPTs] will take an intelligence-led, proactive, problem-solving approach to enable them to focus on and tackle specific local issues. They will involve their local community in establishing and negotiating priorities for action and identifying and implementing solutions. (Home Office, 2004b: 7)

Intelligence-led policing is a model of policing which, following on closely from the principles of *problem-solving policing* (Tilley, 2003: 321–4; see also Chapter 3) prioritizes policing based on problem-identification, information gathering, action planning and the mobilization of resources to carry those actions out. The point here is that if policing is to be 'intelligence-led', intelligence-led policing is *police-led*. Neighbourhood policing, designed to embody intelligence-led policing, is therefore concerned with police leadership of a community safety agenda. 'Community engagement' in this respect is not about a passive partnership between the police and the community; it is about the regular police taking the lead role in mobilizing community resources to achieve goals of public safety and senses of security. The Aldersonian ideal would seem to be moving closer to reality in the government's police reform agenda.

For this reason it is possible to view the neighbourhood policing/community engagement agenda as one which involves forms of *empowerment* of the police, in this respect in terms of enhancing the authority of the police in general, and front-line regular officers in particular, to lead the process of 'building safer communities'. In partnership terms, the police are to be given the pivotal role in community regeneration. On top of the empowerments considered earlier associated with the rise of summary justice and the levels of control concomitant with 'accreditation', neighbourhood policing, at least potentially, strengthens the status and authority of the public police as a social agency.

At this point it is useful to summarize the twin forces of disempowerment and empowerment of the police in tabular form.

Table 5.1 The Bifurcation of Police Reform in Britain

Trajectory of reforms	*Disempowerment*	*Empowerment*
Type of police reforms	Strengthened central controls over policing policy-making Enhanced regulatory governance	Rise of summary justice Neighbourhood policing and community engagement
Direction of police discretion	Narrowing	Widening (horizontally and vertically)
Decision-making level	Strategic Managerial	Operational Front-line
Drift of governance	Centralism	Localism
Locus of governance	National/regional	Micro-local
Police leadership model	Performance management	Community leadership
Core rationale	Achievement of government objectives—delivery	Public reassurance
Focus of policing	Volume crime; organized crime	Anti-social behaviour and low level crime

Given the apparent paradox between these two movements in the police reform agenda, two overlapping sets of question present themselves. First, why did police reform in Britain take a *radical* turn in the way it did at this point in the Labour government. Secondly, why did police reform involve a process of *bifurcation* along the lines of the simultaneous disempowerment and empowerment of the police? It will be argued here that the answers to both sets of questions lie with the logic and consequences of the politicization of law and order.

Labour, Police Reform, and the Politics of Law and Order: Too Hot to Leave Alone

The argument here is here that that the politicization of law and order, which began in earnest in Britain in the late 1970s and which has intensified ever since (Downes and Morgan, 2007), contains within it contradictory forces as far as policing is concerned, and those contradictory forces can shape whether or not governments will be prepared to open up the Pandora's Box of police reform. On the one hand, given the pivotal role of the police in the *imagery* of the politicization of crime and law and order, as the front-line in the 'war on crime', the police may be courted by government, given a privileged status as a public service, support for whom can be paraded as evidence of the determination of government to confront the issue of law and order. Even if reform of policing is considered necessary, the dangers of reform appearing to be 'anti-police', an image easily exploited by the opposition—and indeed by the police themselves—may prove fatal to those beliefs. Here the spectre of the police being, what was referred to earlier as 'too hot to handle', presents itself. However, there is another side to this scenario. Garland (2001) has referred to the emergence in late modernity of what he calls a 'crime complex', a cultural formation characterized by sets of attitudes and beliefs about crime which, amongst others, contains the characteristics whereby: 'crime issues are politicized and regularly represented in emotive terms . . . . [and] the criminal justice state is viewed as *inadequate or ineffective* . . .' (Garland, 2001: 163—emphasis added)

As the politicization of crime and law and order intensifies, the anxieties and insecurities about crime on which it feeds can, according to Garland, have the effect of calling into question the effectiveness of those charged with dealing with crime. As the 'front-line' agency in this regard, the police may be particularly challenged. Whilst the police may be perceived as potential saviours in the war on crime, they are also potentially a target for blame, should crime continue to be seen as a threat. This is the point at which governments may shift their stance on the police from one of them being 'too hot to handle' to one of the being *too hot to leave alone*. In this respect the political approach to the police sector may shift to one focused on ensuring *delivery* according to government goals.

The case presented here is that such a shift is indeed what underlies the development of Labour's radical police reform agenda in Britain. The vortex created by the politicization of crime and law and order creates an insatiable public demand for 'more' law and order, what Downes (2001) has called the 'upward spiral' of 'governing through crime'. States and societies get locked into a vicious circle of ever increasing levels of public anxiety about crime, in which the politicization of law and order both feeds off but also fuels those anxieties, leading to ever more punitive and excessive law and order solutions. Furthermore, as Downes expresses it: 'once embarked on a course of 'governing through crime' ... with the heightened emotionalism and bidding-up of punitive measures that this entails, no society has managed to find a way of extricating itself from that upwards spiral.' (Downes, 2001: 68)

Whilst Downes documents the impact of this 'upward spiral' on penal policy, it has a parallel effect on policing, creating ever increasing demands for 'more' and 'better' policing. In this context a 'hands off' or permissive approach to the police sector becomes increasingly untenable as a political strategy, however attractive it might have been in the short term. On the contrary, the priority shifts to one concerned with *guaranteeing the delivery* of policing services as crime fighting resources. The emergence of the radical agenda for police reform, with its emphasis on centrally directed policing policies and a strengthened regulatory state, may be understood in exactly these terms. Highly centralized controls on what the police are to do and how effectively they are to do it are a concomitant of this ever increasing demand for 'more' law and order. This accounts for what has been called the process of *disempowerment* of the police within the police reform agenda. Disempowerment of the police is necessary in order to exert central control over policing priorities and the means of achieving them. In that sense the roots of Labour's radical agenda for police reform, and in particular radical measures which serve to disempower the police, lie within the inner rationale of the politicization of law and order and the 'upward spiral' it generates.

However, we also have to explain the process of what has here been called the other dimension of the *bifurcation* of police reform within Labour's radical agenda. This also lies with the politicization of law and order and its consequences. It has been noted that the driving force for the 'empowerment' of the police through neighbourhood policing is the desire to bridge the 'reassurance gap' between actual levels of crime and the publicly perceived extent of the threat of crime. What is not made clear, however, is why such a reassurance gap exists in the first place. Neighbourhood policing is seen as a solution to a problem whose causes are not fully understood. This takes us back to the 'upward spiral' of the politicization of law and order. The constant 'reminder' in political discourse surrounding crime is that people *should* be fearful of crime and be concerned to protect themselves from criminals. This can only serve to reinforce and exacerbate any existing unease about crime and feelings of insecurity.

The message here is that the politicization of law and order feeds off public anxieties about crime and security but in doing so fuels the process by which such anxieties are regenerated and reproduced. In Garland's words again, the 'crime complex' is one in which the 'emotional investment in crime is wide-spread and intense' (Garland, 2001: 163). Governments, by their actions and stances, can help exacerbate this. For example, the propensity of governments, under the regime of 'governing through crime', to constantly present new, ever more punitive and populist 'solutions' to crime cannot help but generate a public sentiment that things were not secure to begin with. In this respect the 'reassurance gap' is not some mysterious failure of the public to realize that crime is not as bad as they think; it is an inherent feature of the 'crime complex' which the politicization of crime and security has helped to cultivate. People continue to be fearful, or even more fearful, of crime, despite crime falling, because fear and insecurity are part and parcel of the anxieties associated with 'governing through crime'.

This is the context for the 'empowerment' of the police through extended summary justice and neighbourhood policing. That process of empowerment is a means of addressing the public insecurities associated with the politicization of law and order. More visible policing, more accessible policing, more evidently effective policing, are all sought as means of confronting public anxieties fuelled by the politicization of crime and the fear of crime—assisted of course by the media (Garland: 2001: 157–8). 'Reassurance' is necessary because such anxieties refuse to dissipate in the face of 'the facts' about falling crime. The empowerment of the police at the operational, front-line, 'micro-local' level is a means of repairing, or attempting to repair, the damage done by the populist politics associated with 'law and order politics'. There is a saying that justice should not just be done, but *seen* to be done. The empowerment of the police to become a visibly active presence in localities is about policing not just being done but *seen* to be done.

Labour's twin track approach to police reform and its 'radical' reform agenda overall was the latest chapter of a history of policing and police reform which really began in the late 1970s. The pivotal status of the police in the vortex of law and order politics has had mixed message for the police themselves. According to the political climate and environment of the day, the police were to be in or out of favour, protected from the blast of reform or exposed to it accordingly. We have considered a range of drivers for police reform in this book so far, but each in turn must pay homage to the dominance of the politics of law and the politicization of policing which comes with that. It is only if the pressures for reform from those other sources—system failures, the 'Three Es', overseas influences and so on—fit the particular bill of political timing that they may lead police reform in this or that way.

In this respect there was to be yet another twist. Although Labour had already put in place some of the main pillars of its police reform programme, during 2006 signs were emerging that the appetite for police reform was, once again, diminishing. As was made clear in Chapter 3, one key part of the police reform programme, *force restructuring*, was shelved. Although, as has been seen, one factor behind this shift were the crises which hit the Home Office at around that time, in terms of 'lost prisoners' and the like, it could also have been linked to another change in the political climate surrounding policing in Britain. The apparent extent to which the restructuring agenda, as was stated in Chapter 2, mysteriously 'went away' over the summer of 2006—and, significantly, that the area of 'police reform' suddenly disappeared from the front page of the Home Office website, having been prominent for a number of years before—may have had something to do changing party fortunes at the time. With the decline in support for the Labour Party in the opinion polls following the war in Iraq, and the converse rise in support for the Conservatives under the 'modernizer' David Cameron, a scene parallel to Michael Howard taking over as Home Secretary in 1992, as discussed earlier, seemed to be emerging. The new Home Secretary, John Reid, who replaced Charles Clarke (a strong advocate of force restructuring) in the spring of 2006, may just have taken the same line as Howard—'Do I need to be seen to taking on the police in these circumstances?' Perhaps once again there was a partial shift back to 'courting the police', in a climate in which political insecurities, coupled with the ever heightening tensions around law and order politics, were making 'taking on' the police increasingly unattractive. The remarkable interplay between the politics of law and order and policing on the one hand, and police reform on the other, may just have been entering yet another new phase.

Conclusion

This study has attempted to illuminate the forces which have laid behind change in policing and police reform in the British policing context. As has been seen throughout, change and reform can be about specific policies, such as the creation of the police community officer scheme or, more fundamentally, about shifts in *ways of thinking about policing*, in terms of 'mind-sets', 'policing paradigms' and the like, such as the move towards community-oriented policing or the VFM agenda. Fundamental changes in 'ways of thinking about policing' can create the cultural conditions or climate within which particular policy forms can emerge or which are more or less receptive to policy innovations in particular directions. In the period covered by this book, from the late 1970s onwards, policing in Britain has changed or been 'reformed' in variety of ways, some of them essentially involving 'paradigm shifts' in the way policing is thought about, organized and delivered.

Five main sources of influence over policing policy or 'policy drivers' have been identified and their impact on policing policy assessed: *system failure; influences from abroad; new public management; 'internal' forces for change*; and the *politics of policing*. In considering these sources of influence a range of policy processes have been discussed and related to policy forms and outcomes, including: *policy windows; policy transfer* and *policy convergence; managerialism*; and *policy visionaries, policy entrepreneurs* and *policy networks*. In these respects a number of observations can be made about the nature of change and reform in policing policy, drawing from the discussions presented in previous chapters.

Police Reform and Policing Policy: Incrementalism, Mixed Parentage, and Cycles

The first observation to make is that police reform is in many respects a *cumulative* process; particular pillars of police reform have been built on precedent established by earlier reform agendas and changes in policing policy. Reform is often *incremental* (Lessman, 1989), particularly in sensitive or highly political areas, and develops in a staged framework of innovation and transformation. This was evident in a number of police reforms considered here. For example, policies around the issue of police complaints have been characterized by the incremental and cumulative extension of the role of the 'independent' element in the complaints process (as discussed in Chapters 1, 2, and 5; Smith, 2005). The 'lay element' of police complaints was first introduced in the 1970s in the form of the Police Complaints Board, which involved members independent of the police in *reviewing* police investigations into, and decisions about, complaints against the police. The independent element was later reinforced in the 1980s in the shape of the Police Complaints Authority, which created the independent *supervision* of investigations undertaken by the police into complaints against the police. Later still, through the *Police Reform Act 2002*, the independent elements were strengthened extensively with the establishment of machinery for the fully independent *investigation* of complaints against the police, at least in certain cases. The case for the fully independent investigation of complaints was around well before the model eventually saw the light of day (Reiner, 1992: 234–6), but it was only through a process of incremental development that it did. Before that, compromise and caution appeared to rule the day; to jump the whole distance in one go from fully internal to fully independent investigation of police complaints may not have been politically possible given the balance of circumstances at the time. The system might need 'softening up' with partial reform before going the whole hog. Another example of incrementalism is the 'civilianization' agenda (considered variously in Chapters 2, 3, 4, and 5), the relinquishing of former 'police roles' to civilian staff. This began in a highly cautious way, with the civilianization of roles in areas such as public relations and media management. However, over time and in haltering ways, the process moved further and further into the heart of 'police' functions, until it reached the stage where not only *patrol* (through the PCSO scheme) but also police *investigations* were opened up to non-warranted officers—by means of the Investigative Support Officer role. Given the huge controversies (normally involving the Police Federation) which always surround the relinquishing of police roles to others, even to those within the police organization, it would be difficult to imagine civilianization going this far in one swoop. Incrementalism allowed this to happen by stealth.

A second observation on the nature of police reform follows this: reforms can have *multiple sources of influence*. Although the various 'policy drivers' have been considered in separate discussions, it will be apparent from the frequency with which certain police areas have appeared throughout this study that many policing policies have mixed parentage. They have been spurred on at different times by different sources of influence. There are two excellent examples of this. Returning to the case of PCSOs, it was evident from Chapter 2 that the model had some roots in community policing *overseas*—the 'police patroller' and city warden schemes in the Netherlands. However, as has just been noted, the PCSO scheme also has roots in the wider and longer term *VFM* agenda around, as has just been seen, the civilianization of police roles. Furthermore, an immediate spur for the introduction of PCSOs was the *political* desire to develop 'reassurance policing', a central pillar of New Labour's police reform agenda, by means of more visible patrol of the streets. Another example of mixed parentage might be 'community-based policing'. As was seen in Chapter 1, a major force behind the development of community-based policing and police-community consultation were the '*system failures*' associated with inner-city disorders in the early 1980s. However, and in line with the notion of the cumulative nature of some areas of police reform noted earlier, community-based policing was shaped by a range of other influences. First, as was seen in Chapter 2, an emphasis on close contact between the police and the community came with the package of *problem-oriented policing*, in some ways an American *import*. Secondly, community-based policing was reinforced by the growth of *new public management* (discussed in Chapter 3), with its emphasis on 'consumerism' and the notion of the community as the 'customers' of the police service. Thirdly, community-based policing was driven by the *internal* influence of 'police visionaries' and 'policy entrepreneurs', as seen in Chapter 4. Finally, and once again, community-based policing, in this case in the form of 'community engagement', was seen as a key component of 'reassurance policing' in Labour's *political* strategy for police reform.

A third observation on police reform is that in some respects police reform is *cyclical*; police reform agendas, and the debates and discourses which surround them, seem to have a habit of being reinvented if not repeated at other political junctures. One example of this is the issue of the 'right to silence'. As was made clear in Chapters 1, 4, and 5, the debate over the right to silence was a recurring theme from the late 1970s through to the mid-1990s. It arose in the deliberations surrounding the Royal Commission on Criminal Procedure, the outcome of which was that the 'police case' for amending the right to silence was rejected by the Commission when it reported in 1981. During the mid-1980s, the then Conservative Home Secretary, Douglas Hurd, established a working party to review that right (Greer, 1990), although no decision to amend it that stage was made. The issue was to re-emerge, as was seen in Chapter 4, with the police submissions to the Royal Commission on Criminal Justice, although the Commission, reporting in 1993, did not support amending the right to silence. Despite this, and amidst the political climate of the mid-1990s and with Michael Howard as Home Secretary, the right to silence was indeed to be amended along the lines suggested by ACPO, with the *Criminal Justice and Public Order Act 1994*. Only then it seemed, did the argument over the right to silence abate.

Another example of the cyclical nature of police reform lies with the political discourses surrounding the 'case construction' that policing *needs* reforming in the first place. As was seen in Chapters 3 and 5, there was a strong sense of déjà vu about New Labour's police reform agenda as it emerged in the early years of the new century. The sentiments surrounding the case for reform, stated both formally and informally, were remarkably similar to the political discourses which were articulated by *Conservative* politicians in the late 1980s and early 1990s. Common themes to justify a new regime of police reform were:

- the view that the police sector had been treated 'generously' in the years before relative to some other areas of the public sector;
- the view that despite that generous treatment police performance had been less than satisfactory—'where's the return' for the money spent?
- the view that police leadership lacks the 'quality' necessary for the challenges which now face the service;
- the view that the police remained the 'last un-reformed' public service and that, as a consequence, a comprehensive programme of reform is necessary;
- the view that there are 'too many' individual police forces and that the smallest police forces should be amalgamated to make them into more viable units.

What this cycle may expose more than anything else is the extent to which the police, in Britain at least, have managed to hold on to traditions and established approaches to working which other public services have not. It is difficult to deny that major changes have taken place within British policing over the period reviewed in this study—and the revelations of *difference* on *Life on Mars* provides some testimony to that. Nevertheless, there is also a degree of *resilience* to change which is characteristic of the police relative to other public services. For example, despite the best efforts of governments, the geography of police forces in England and Wales remains almost exactly what it was in the early 1970s; what other public service can point to such *continuity* in organization over such a period of time? To reiterate the case presented in Chapter 5, this relates to the unique status of the public police within the discourse of the politics of crime and law and order. Governments seemed obliged to tread cautiously between demanding better 'results' from the police on the one hand and being seen as 'pro-police'—or at least as not being seen as 'anti-police'—on the other. Ironically, there was another dimension to the cycle of police reform discourses considered above. In the case of both reform agendas, as was seen in Chapter 5, explicitly and extensively with the Conservatives in the mid-1990s, more implicit and partial with Labour midway through the first decade of the new century, there was a degree of *retraction* from the initial reform agenda and the case surrounding it over time. As other political priorities overtook events, in both cases the 'appetite' for police reform was lessened. If that is the case one wonders when the cycle will repeat itself in the future. This raises the issue of the *future of police reform*.

The Future of Police Reform

Reviewing the spectrum of police reform in Britain since the late 1970s provides opportunities to draw out some of the longer term trends in policing which one might assume will be continue to be features of police reform in the future. In many respects these constitute what police scholars have referred to as policing responses to the challenges of maintaining security in 'late modern' or 'postmodern' societies (Johnston, 1998 and 2000: 18–32; McLaughlin, 2007: 87–114; Wright, 2002; Reiner, 2000: 216–7), and, along the lines of what was referred to earlier as 'policy convergence', tend to be features of policing across developed and many developing societies. As outlined in the Introduction, late modern societies are characterized by ongoing social change entailing a number of structural shifts (Johnston, 1998). First, late modernity involves *economic change* around the expansion of 'mass private property', the growth of the service economy, increasing flexibility in the management of enterprises and in the workforce in both the private and public sectors. Secondly, late modernity is characterized by *globalization* which creates contradictory forces of greater economic uniformity and internationalization of communications on the one hand, and economic fragmentation and the reinforcement of cultural identities on the other hand. In Johnston's terms globalization is accompanied by 'an unstable combination of tendencies: centralization and decentralization; internationalization and nationalism; homogeneity and diversity; fragmentation and consolidation' (Johnston, 1998: 194). Thirdly, late modernity entails the fragmentation of the system of *social stratification*, replacing traditional social stratification along the predominance of social class with multiple social divisions, together with class based divisions, around race, religion, ethnicity, gender, and nationality. This creates new forms of problems for social control agencies who are confronted with many and varied forms of potential social conflict, at times when their own machineries are still adapted more to suit the traditional, more homogeneous structures of social division. Fourthly, late modernity is characterized by *reconfigurations of the state*, in particular, the state's role as both controller and deliverer of public services gives way increasingly to one focusing on the former, with the latter the responsibility of a wide range of bodies, public, private, and voluntary; there is a growing division between the 'steering' and 'rowing' functions in the provision of public services, as discussed in Chapter 3.

The challenges of late modernity have a range of consequences for the police sector. For Johnston the major consequences of late modernity for policing are two-fold (see also Reiner, 2000: 216–17): 'sectoral restructuring' and 'spatial restructuring' (Johnston, 1998: 196–205). Sectoral restructuring is characterized by: the *privatization* of police functions; the growth of *hybrid* policing ('grey' policing involving a variety of social control agencies); and *civil* policing, such as the 'city warden' scheme discussed in Chapter 2. Spatial restructuring involves a variety of movements, some of them contradictory: the *centralization* or 'nationalization' of policing, particularly around specialist national units concerned with serious and organized crime, terrorism and so on (as discussed in Chapters 3 and 5); the *internationalization* of policing (in the European context by means of such organisations as Europol); and the *localization* of policing—the strengthening of the local delivery of policing and local accountabilities, as discussed in Chapter 5. The forces of late modernity are pulling and pushing the police organization in a variety of directions, some of them seemingly contradictory (Reiner, 2000: 217).

Considering the range of police reforms discussed in this study, and taking into account some of the features of 'late modern' policing as identified, it is possible to present an inventory of the predominant *tendencies* exhibited within British police reform over the past three decades or so which offer some indication of the likely patterns of police reform in the *future*. These tendencies overlap and interact and seem destined to remain and develop as integral features of British policing over the longer term.

The Decentring of the Public Police

The public police have never enjoyed a true 'monopoly' over the delivery of 'policing' services. As Johnston (1992) made clear (see also Button, 2002), 'private policing' in various forms has always accompanied public policing and the interface between private and public policing has always been a complicated one. However, for long periods of time the public police remained the *core* provider of most policing services and remained very much at the *centre* of the organization, determination and delivery of those services. That situation has most definitely given way to what has been called in post-modern theory a process of *decentring* (Giddens, 1990). The public police, in the form of a body of sworn officers with a mandate to control crime and maintain order, have, through a range of reforms, become increasingly a *part of* the machinery for crime control and order maintenance whereas at one stage they *were* essentially that machinery.

The earliest signs of that process came with the 'civilianization' agenda which emerged in the mid-1980s (Chapter 3—also Chapter 5). Although civilianization did not itself actually involve the *loss* of functions from the police organization—the 'work' involved stayed within the police organization as such and simply moved from being the responsibility of sworn officers to being the responsibility of civilian employees—civilianization was significant in two ways. First, symbolically, it entailed the shift of functions *away* from the regular officer and towards others with very different origins and traditions. Secondly, civilianization began a process of questioning and challenging which was to accelerate over time and which ultimately encouraged a range of other providers to enter the scene and engage in the business of 'policing'. The 'shedding functions' agenda continued with the Posen Review of core and ancillary tasks (Chapters 3, 4, and 5) and the measures which followed in its wake. One consequence of this agenda was that *local authorities* began to take responsibility for areas of work, such as dealing with noise pollution, which up to that point had been part of the police 'mandate'. This was to be the thin end of the wedge, because under New Labour, and with the *Crime and Disorder Act 1998*, local authorities were to be made responsible for 'community safety', an umbrella term which included not just social disorder but *crime reduction* itself (Chapters 2, 3, and 5). Within this framework and under statute the public police were *one part* of the crime reduction machinery—decentring almost by law. The 'thin blue line' was becoming 'one of many'.

However, the decentring process was to take an even more dramatic form with the establishment of the PCSO scheme and its linkage with 'neighbourhood policing teams' (Chapters 2 and 5). This was *plural policing* (Crawford et al, 2005), often seen as a key feature of policing late modernity (McLaughlin, 2007: 128), not by stealth but by design. Not only would PCSOs be responsible for what was formerly very much police territory, patrol (and accentuated further with the arrival of Investigative Support Officers—Chapter 2), but they would also have the power to *punish*, through the fixed penalty scheme. The 'mixed economy of policing', however much 'fragmented' or part of a unity called the 'extended family of policing' (Chapter 2), had well and truly arrived; literally, the public police were not to be the only kids on the block.

The decentring of the public police has also taken another form. With the shift towards 'regulatory governance' and the growing significance of bodies that regulate, audit and inspect the police organization (Chapters 3 and 5), the *discretion* and virtual autonomy over police decision-making formerly enjoyed by chief officers has diminished. Coupled with government-led national policing plans and nationally-determined performance measures, the regulatory machineries were increasingly moving chief officers from the helm of their forces to the status of custodians of decisions made elsewhere. More and more, chief officers would embody *delegated authority* in place of *operational independence*. In part this is linked to the growing emphasis on police *performance* and its interface with the *politicization* of policing.

The Politicization of Policing and the Rise and Rise of the Performance Culture

It is possible to identify three broad phases in the development of the *performance culture* and VFM within and around British policing. In the 1980s it was about a gentle 'steer' from government that the police service pay heed to the virtues of *economy* and *efficiency*, in what for the police service were times of relative plenty. The emphasis was primarily on *inputs*—how resources could be most efficiently utilized. The encouragement by government for police forces to move on civilianization, for example, was driven by the hope that forces would be able to make economies by deploying less well paid staff to undertake functions previously the responsibility of sworn officers. In doing this, governments tended to take a very much 'hands off' approach to police performance and leave it to forces to take initiatives and decide on priorities. At this stage governments did not get involved in the business of priority setting for the police—with the possible exception of the interventionist role taken by the Thatcher government in relation to the NUM strike of the mid-1980s (Chapter 5).

By the mid-1990s the picture hand changed. Governments were becoming much more concerned with police *effectiveness*, the 'Third E'; alongside continuing attempts to make police forces make the most efficient use of their resources, governments were now asking the question 'where's the return?' on money provided for what was still a 'privileged' part of the public sector in terms of levels of expenditure. What had emerged, due in part to the growth of audit and inspection, was an increasing determination by governments to *drive up police performance* in terms of the *outputs* of policing activity. There were two primary mechanisms for driving up police performance at this stage. On the one hand governments had started getting involved in *priority setting* 'on behalf' of the police. The *Police and Magistrates' Courts Act 1994* had established the powers of the Home Secretary to set out national 'objectives' for the police, what it was the police were to concern themselves with; the objectives were to frame policing policies at force level (Chapter 5). The first step in driving up performance was to state what the key 'outputs' of police services should be. One the other hand, through the good offices of the Audit Commission and HMIC, the police were presented with a suite of national *performance indicators* which were to be used to forge *performance league tables*. Pressures to drive up performance would come from the exposure of 'relative performances' by police organizations—'naming and shaming' in the performance context. In this respect there was still an onus on police forces to take the initiative; the role of government was to set out broad priorities and enable the production of information which forces themselves would respond to, or not. 'Best value' under New Labour turned the screws a little tighter by *requiring* forces be more challenging in considering their performance (Chapter 3); the best value 'reviews' however remained the responsibility of the forces themselves.

In due course these approaches gave way to a third phase within the performance culture. 'Driving up performance' would become much more the more direct responsibility of central government. Labour's police reform programme in the early years of the new century created a range of mechanisms oriented to *results* and *delivery* (Chapters 3 and 5). First there would be centrally determined *plans* for policing—more assertive than 'objectives'. Secondly a suite of national *standards agencies* would be established to monitor performance at force level, guide forces on the means of improving their performance and, if necessary, intervene directly to manage 'failing forces' or failing units within forces. Thirdly, linked to this, government would set demanding *targets* for performance in all areas of policing activity. The pressures to drive up performance were becoming relentless. 'Improvement' and 'modernization' were the order of the day. The performance culture was by now almost an oppressive one, and the 'management culture' within the police (Foster, 2003: 212–3) was by now barely distinguishable from the boardroom.

In the policing context, the rise and rise of the performance culture, and the increasing tendency to treat policing services as business operations—including what some have called the 'commodification' of policing (Loader, 1999; Newburn, 2001)—is the effect of more than the general spread of 'new public management' or 'managerialization' (McLaughlin, 2007: 96–7) across the policing world, although that has been a very powerful force (Chapter 3). A key driver of this development has also been the *politicization* of crime and policing (Chapter 5). Police organizations will continue to be pressured to perform better because of the *political imperative* for governments to deliver 'results' on the crime front, or at least to be seen to be demanding results. Crime and insecurity are now mainstream features of political discourse, having become issues of central concern for both major political parties within the trajectory of the politics of law and order (Downes and Morgan, 2007).

Crime and insecurity are not just *a* concern of government, in many respects they have become *the* concern of government. That concern now spans the full range, from low-level 'incivilities' and disorders, through 'volume crime', onwards through serious and organized crime, and upwards to the threat of terrorism—particularly since the events of 9/11 and 7/7 (McLaughlin, 2007:197–212; Downes and Morgan, 2007: 232–3). Tackling crime and generating security are matters no serious political movement can ignore; that is so in part because of the way in which discourses around fear and insecurity have been employed by political parties as they compete for electoral support. As expanding fear and anxiety continue to be core features of the 'crime complex' (Garland, 2001: 163) and as political discourses revolve around 'governing through crime' (Downes, 2001), the political imperative is set for governments to demand *results* from those charged with controlling crime and maintaining security.

It is the unique role of the *police* within the politics of law and order and the politicization of crime which places them very much in the firing line of political ambitions (Chapter 5). Practically and symbolically the police are central players in the political agendas for dealing with crime and insecurity. As has been argued in the previous chapter, this unique role can mean political parties fight to demonstrate their *support* and backing for the police, it can also mean that they are 'too hot to leave alone' as governments endeavour to deliver on the crime and insecurity fronts. This scenario has been a key driver of the rise and rise of the performance culture within and around policing, a trajectory certain to continue in the future. Getting *results* from the police, in terms of crime control, reassuring the public, and containing the threat of terrorism, has increasingly been, and looks set to continue to be, a major goal of governments in the battle over law and order. A public service that was (allowed to be) the slowest to respond to the emergence of the performance culture may now find itself under most long-term pressure to demonstrate its adherence to it. Ironically, however, these very pressures can service to *empower* the police in other ways.

The Reinvention of the Police Constable

The 'decentring' of the public police referred to above may only be part of the story. Alongside processes of decentring, associated with notions of *loss* of power and authority or at least the sharing of power and authority, there lies a very different notion of *empowerment of the officer* (Chapter 5). This was initially articulated in Alderson's conception of community policing, and the notion of the police officer as 'social diagnostician' and mobilizer of community resources (Chapters 1 and 5). According to this notion the officer/constable would be proactive rather than reactive, identifying problems in the making rather than responding to them when they have been realized, and able to work with others in the community, including other service providers, in social problem prevention. In parallel with Alderson's vision there emerged the model of problem-oriented policing, with its sense of the police officer as problem identifier, as problem researcher, and as problem-solver, and then again as evaluator and assessor. These notions were not about loss of power and authority but rather about enhancement of role and empowerment of the front-line officer.

The very processes which have generated the pluralisation and fragmentation of policing have also created space for the *reinvention of the constable*. The diminution of the regular police 'monopoly' over crime control and order maintenance work has forged a vacuum of *leadership* which the regular police, at the lowest levels of the organization, can fill. This parallels the division between 'steering and rowing', which has become a feature both of the role of government in the provision of public services, and the activities of the public services in the delivery of front-line services (Chapter 3). The role of the responsible authority is to steer policy and ensure that delivery of services take place and are of the right quality and price; the actual delivery ('rowing') is done by other agencies, public, private, and voluntary. The model which has emerged and seems likely to bed in even further is of the constable in the position of *steering* crime control and order maintenance work on the one hand, and others within the 'mixed economy of policing' doing the 'rowing'. The steering role is about identifying problems at an early stage, finding out as much as possible about them (causes, possible solutions), identifying the resources available to respond and *leading* the team that does the responding. Plural policing may take the public police out of the core of delivery but that creates the space for the public police to sit at the core of the *leadership* of that delivery.

This model was evident in the notion of *advanced constable* as developed within the 'Workforce Modernization' agenda (Chapter 3). The extent to which this entails the potential *empowerment* and *enrichment* of the role of constable was spelt out in the ACPO Workforce Modernization Programme (ACPO: 2007), which referred to the 'Advanced Constable' as involving:

> a move from the traditional "sole trader", omni-competent model, in which the constable carries out a wide range of functions, many of which require relatively low skills, to one where the Advanced Constable, working within

one specific policing capability, concentrates on performing demanding tasks at a higher level of expertise.

The Programme actually identifies two categories of Advanced Constable: 'technical expert' with high levels of specialist knowledge in key areas, and 'team leader', which has an emphasis on leadership in front-line activity. It also refers to the possibility of new 'Supra Powers' which could be granted to Advanced Constables, such as the power to impose 'interim ASBOs' on individuals as preventative control measures. This is nothing less than the *reinvention* of the role of constable as 'expert', 'leader', and owner of special powers not available to other members of the 'team' to be led. With the fragmentation and pluralization of policing delivery comes the reinvention of the constable as the 'glue' to hold delivery together. That 'glue' is also about furthering *community engagement* with policing.

Citizenship Policing

A common thread tying many of the reforms considered in this study together is *citizen engagement* with policing. What has emerged and looks certain to remain as a central theme of future police reforms is what might be called 'citizenship policing'. Marshall (1965) defined 'citizenship' in terms of three set of 'rights', civil rights (rule of law and liberties), political rights (rights to participate in the democratic process), and social rights (rights to basic standards of welfare). It could be argued that the development of citizen engagement with the police constitutes a form of 'social right' of citizens to be informed on, comment on, advise on, monitor, guide, and even direct public policing. The old local police authorities set up under the *Police Act 1964* had always provided opportunities for citizen participation in policing, but only in terms of forums for 'reporting back' on decisions made and actions taken by the police, and even then to an audience limited to local councillors and magistrates (Reiner, 2000: 188–9). However, police reform since has seen the rise and rise of community engagement with policing in differing forms.

The first significant step along this path was what followed Scarman in the form of police-community consultation machineries, set up to enable the police to 'consult' with local communities and for those communities to be 'informed' about the policing of their communities (Chapter 1). Another form of citizen engagement came at around the same time and from the same agenda in terms of lay visitors to police stations. 'Opening up' the police organization to citizens had begun, even if in small ways. Other forces kept the issue alive. One the one hand policing developments such as community policing, neighbourhood watch, and problem-oriented policing (Chapter 2) were sending out messages that the community, whether it had the 'right' to be engaged in policing or not, was a *resource* for policing, something to be accessed and, if possible, mobilized in the furtherance of crime control, and order maintenance. On the other hand, fuelled in part by New Public Management (Chapter 3), the growth of *consumerism* in policing (Loader, 1999; Reiner, 2000: 208) ensured that the citizen-as-customer/consumer of policing services would never be left out of the equation. Finding out what citizens thought about the quality of the services the police provided was to become part of the police planning cycle.

Citizen engagement over time however has shifted gradually from the model of *passive* engagement of the community—'listening to' the police—to one of the *active* involvement of the community, in terms citizens stating preferences and priorities for policing. This was emerging with the 'Quality of Service' initiatives of the early 1990s (Chapter 4) when police associations began, at least in stated form, to emphasize taking on board the *public's* priorities for policing in policy-making. It was given further impetus with New Labour's commitment to move from the model of 'policing by consent' of the community to 'policing by active cooperation' with the community (Home Office, 2003a; McLaughlin, 2005). The idea of the District Policing Partnership Boards (DPPBs), implemented initially in Northern Ireland and soon finding their way across the water (Chapter 2), was to take this active engagement further. In this case police priority-setting would have a base at Basic Command Unit (BCU) level, as well as at force and national levels. Furthermore, one dimension of neighbourhood policing was to enable policing priority-setting to take place at the 'micro-local' level, the parish or even street levels as well as at the less local levels (Chapter 5).

Citizenship policing was also evident through other channels. In some ways the involvement of 'independent members' on the reconstituted police authorities, created by the *Police and Magistrates' Courts Act 1994* (Chapters 4 and 5), was one (limited) form of citizen engagement because it widened the pool of those serving as police authority members to include local people from backgrounds other than elected members and magistrates. The Labour government talked of various ways of enhancing the direct engagement of communities in policing (Home Office, 2003a). Firstly, was the possibility of establishing 'community advocate schemes' working as the 'voice' of the community and individuals within it (Home Office, 2003a: 17–19). Again, such a scheme would operate at the 'micro-local' and BCU/DPPB levels as ways of holding the police at those levels more directly accountable to the community. Secondly, were 'neighbourhood panels', made up of local volunteers, those involved in neighbourhood watch, wardens, and others, to develop a 'bottom up' approach to community safety issues (Home Office, 2003a: 19–22). Thirdly, the idea of directly elected 'police boards' was floated, whereby citizens could vote for candidates who would stand for election on crime and community safety issues alone, rather than the current arrangement with the police authorities where elected members have been voted in through the normal local elections. These were all possible ways of enhancing active participation of citizens in decisions and actions on crime control and community safety.

A final channel for 'citizenship policing', as discussed earlier, has been the cumulative extension of the 'independent' element in the police complaints process (Chapters 1, 2, and 5). Through the oversight machineries, citizens not only have the right to make complaints against the police, they are aware that other citizens, those working within the complaints bodies, can take an active part in the processes by which those complaints will be dealt with. Furthermore, those oversight bodies have a role in guiding the police service on policing policies and practices as well as being responsible for responding to individual complaints.

Citizenship policing, together with the other developments and dimensions of police reform presented here, look certain to remain part of the landscape of police reform in the foreseeable future—not just in Britain but elsewhere. The *decentring* of the public police, the rise of the *performance culture*, the *reinvention* of the police officer, and *citizenship policing* have been major themes of police reform in the past and will, it is argued, continue to be in the future. There is evidence of this in a document which emerged as work on this study was being completed and which may, subject to events, become a critical statement on the future of British policing and for British police reform in the years ahead. In April 2007 the Conservative Party, in opposition, published a consultation paper, *Policing for the People* (Conservative Party, 2007), an extensive statement on Conservative thinking on policing and, significantly given what was stated earlier about the centrality of crime and policing in contemporary political discourse, the first major detailed statement of policy proposals to emerge from the newly 'modernizing' Conservative Party under David Cameron.

Policing for the People claimed that the British police face five major challenges (Conservative Party, 2007: 16):

- the 'terrorist threat';
- the 'protective services gap'—in particular the problem of tackling serious crime which cuts across police force borders;
- the need to sustain 'community policing';
- the need to increase police *accountability*, particularly at the *local* level;
- delivering value for money.

In responding to these challenges a number of possible proposals were presented (this was not yet a full policy statement) which covered the following areas (Conservative Party, 2007: 17–23):

- *Force structures*: the report points to the case for maintaining the existing 43 forces but with strengthened 'local accountability'—mainly at the BCU level—and also a *national* police force in the form of a 'Serious Crime Force'.
- *Workforce reform*: the report calls for a more *'flexible'* workforce and better police *leadership*; specific ideas include a new rank of 'senior constable', fixed term contracts for BCU commanders, performance-related pay, and the 'senior staff college' modelled along the lines of the Armed Forces.

- *Reducing the burden of bureaucracy*: the report calls for reductions in the 'paper-work' required from officers.
- *Reducing central intervention*: the case is made to reduce centralized *performance* frameworks but to *increase* performance frameworks at local level.
- *'Freeing-up' the police*: the report proposes that the police 'family' be *extended* to include a cadre of part-time 'police reservists' under the PCSO scheme and greater use of *wardens* and volunteers (the latter to help run police stations).
- *More accountable policing*: the report proposes a 'right to policing' for local communities; it also proposes *directly elected police commissioners* in place of police authorities, along the lines of American governance frameworks.

Policing for the People calls for police reforms which in fact would reinforce the core dimensions of police reform outlined earlier. The *decentring* of the pubic police and the *pluralization* of policing would be furthered through the addition of 'reservists' and the expansion of the role of wardens and volunteers. The rise of the *performance culture* would be sustained through further *value for money* measures and enhances *local performance* frameworks. The *reinvention* of the police officer would take the form of a new rank of *special constable*. Finally *citizenship policing* would be reflected in the *directly elected* police commissioners. The framework of 'late modern' policing would, it seemed, be as safe in the hands of the Conservatives as it had been under New Labour.

There is another message coming out from the agenda presented in *Policing for the People*. Coming so hot on the heels of Labour's own 'radical' police reform agenda, it was clear that the march of police reform, rather than stop to rest, was if anything going to pick up pace under the Conservatives. The solutions offered to remedy the 'problems' making the case for reform may have looked different, but the political determination that there *be* reform seemed just as strong as it had been under New Labour. For a service for so long labelled the last 'unreformed' area of the public sector, it seems that reform has become as much a part of the fabric of British police organization as the British 'bobby on the beat'.

References

ACPO (1990) *Setting the Standards for Policing: Meeting Community Expectations* London: Association of Chief Police Officers

ACPO (1995) *In Search of Criminal Justice* London: Association of Chief Police Officers

ACPO (1999) *Action Guide to Identifying and Combating Hate Crime* London: Association of Chief Police Officers

ACPO (2001) *Blue Print for Policing in the 21st Century* London: Association of Chief Police Officers

ACPO (2005) *Hate Crime: Delivering a Quality Service* London: Association of Chief Police Officers

ACPO/Centrex (2005) *Guidance on the National Intelligence Model* London: ACPO/Centrex

ACPO (2007) *ACPO National Workforce Modernisation Programme* retrieved 3 April 2007 from: <http://www.workforce-modernisation.org>

Alderson, J. (1979) *Policing Freedom* Plymouth: Macdonald and Evans

Alderson, J. (1984) *Law and Disorder* London: Hamish Hamilton

Alderson, J. (1998) *Principled Policing* Winchester: Waterside Press

Allen, M. and Cooper, S. (1995) 'Howard's Way: A Farewell to Freedom?' *Modern Law Review* **58**, 3

Anderson, D. and Killingray, D. (eds) *Policing the Empire: Government, Authority and Control, 1830–1940* Manchester: Manchester University Press

Ashby, D. (2005) 'Policing Neighbourhoods: Exploring the Geographies of Crime, Policing and Performance Assessment' *Policing and Society* **15**, 4

Atkinson, R. (1990) 'Government During the Thatcher Years' in Savage, S. and Robins, L. (eds) *Public Policy Under Thatcher* London: Macmillan

Audit Commission (1988a) *Administrative Support for Operational Police Officers* London: HMSO

Audit Commission (1988b) *Improving the Performance of the Fingerprint Service* London: HMSO

Audit Commission (1989) *Improving Vehicle Fleet Management in the Police Service* London: HMSO

Audit Commission (1990) *Calling all Forces: Improving Police Communication Rooms* London: HMSO

Audit Commission (1991) *Reviewing the Organisation of Provincial Police Forces* London: HMSO.

Audit Commission (1993) *Helping With Enquiries: Tackling Crime Effectively* London: HMSO

Audit Commission (1994) *Cheques and Balances: A Framework for Improving Police Accountability* London: HMSO

Audit Commission (1995) *Local Authority Performance Indicators—Vol 3 (Police and Fire Services)* London: HMSO

Audit Commission (1996) *Streetwise: Effective Police Patrol* London: HMSO

Bacharach, P. and Baratz, M. (1969) 'Decisions and Non-Decisions: An Analytical Framework' in Bell, R., Edwards, D. and Wagner, H. (eds) *Political Power: A Reader in Theory and Research* New York: The Free Press

Baker, D. (2002) 'Public Order Policing' in Prenzler, T. and Ransley, J (eds) *Police Reform: Building Integrity* Sydney: Hawkins Press

Baker, K. (1993) *The Turbulent Years: My Life in Politics* London: Faber and Faber

Baldwin, J. (1992) *Video-Taping Police Interviews With Suspects—An Evaluation* London: Home Office, Police Research Group

Barker, A. (1998) 'Political Responsibility for UK Prison Security—Ministers Escape Again' *Public Administration* **76**, 1

Bartlett, W. and Le Grand, J. (1993) 'The Theory of Quasi-Markets' in Le Grand, J. and Bartlett, W. (eds) *Quasi-Markets and Social Policy* London: Macmillan

Bauman, Z. (2001) *Liquid Modernity* Cambridge: Polity Press

Bayley, D. (2001) *Democratizing the Police Abroad: What To Do and How To Do It* Washington: National Institute of Justice

Bayley, D. and Shearing, C. (2001) *The New Structure of Policing* Washington: National Institute of Justice

Bennett, C. (1991) 'What is Policy Convergence and What Causes It? *British Journal of Political Science* **21**, 2

Benyon, J. and Bourn, J. (eds) (1986) *The Police: Powers, Procedures and Proprieties* Oxford: Pergamon Press

Bichard, M. (2004) *The Bichard Inquiry Report* London: HMSO

Blair, I. (1985) *Investigating Rape: A New Approach* London: Croom Helm

Blair, T. (1999) 'Facing the Modern Challenge: The Third Way in Britain and South Africa' Speech given in the Parliament Building, Cape Town, South Africa, 8 January 1999

Boin, A. and t' Hart, P. (2000) 'Institutional Crises and Reforms in the Policy Sectors', in Wagenaar, H. (ed) *Government Institutions: Effects, Changes and Normative Foundations* Boston, MA: Kluwer

Botswana Police Service (2003) *Corporate Development Strategy 2003–9* Gaborone: Botswana Police Service

Bottomley, K. and Pease, K. (1986) *Crime and Punishment: Interpreting the Data* Milton Keynes: Open University Press

Bowling, B. (1999) 'The Rise and Fall of New York Murder' *British Journal of Criminology* **39**, 4

Boyne, (2000) 'External Regulation and Best Value in Local Government' *Public Money and Management* **20**, 3

Braithwaite, J. (1989) *Crime Shame and Reintegration* Cambridge: Cambridge University Press

Braithwaite, J. (2000) 'The New Regulatory State and the Transformation of Criminology' in Garland, D. and Sparks, R. (eds) *Criminology and Social Theory* Oxford: Oxford University Press

Brathwaite, J. (2005) *Hard to Hear Voices: A Comparison of Internal and External Ethnic Minority Pressure Groups Within the Policing Sector* Portsmouth: University of Portsmouth (unpublished Doctoral Thesis)

Bratton, W. (1997) 'Crime is Down in New York: Blame the Police' in Dennis, N. (ed) *Zero Tolerance: Policing a Free Society* London: Institute of Economic Affairs

Briscoe, S. (2001) 'The Problem of Mobile Phone Theft' *Contemporary Issues in Crime and Justice* **56** March

Brogden, M. and Nijhar, P. (2005) *Community Policing: National and International Models and Approaches* Cullompton: Willan

Bromwich, M. and Lapsley, I. (1997: 'Decentralisation and Management Accounting in Central Government: Recycling Old Ideas?' *Financial Accountability and Management* **13**, 2

Brown, A. (2004) 'Anti-Social Behaviour, Crime Control and Social Control' *The Howard Journal* **43**, 2

Brown, J. (1997) 'Equal Opportunities and the Police in England and Wales: Past, Present and Future Possibilities' in Francis, P., Davies, P. and Jupp, V. (eds) *Policing Futures: The Police, Law Enforcement and the Twenty-First Century* Basingstoke: Macmillan

Buckley, J. (2006) 'The Reid Technique of Interviewing and Interrogation' in Williamson, T. (ed) *Investigative Interviewing: Rights, Research and Regulation* Cullompton: Willan

Bull, R. and Horncastle, P. (1988) 'Evaluating Training: the Metropolitan Police's Recruit Training in Human Awareness/Policing Skills' in Southgate, P. (ed) *New Direction in Police Training* London: HMSO

Bunyan, T. (1985) 'From Saltley to Orgreave via Brixton' *Journal of Law and Society* **12** 3

Burrows, J. (1989) 'Achieving "Value for Money" From Police Expenditure: The Contribution of Research' in Weatheritt, M. *Police Research: Some Future Prospects* Aldershot: Avebury

Butler, A. (1994) *Police Management* London: Gower

Butler, D. and Kavanagh, D. (1974) *The British General Election of February 1974* Basingstoke: Macmillan

Button, M. (2002) *Private Policing* Cullompton: Willan

Byford, L. (1982) *The Yorkshire Ripper Case: A Review of the Police Investigation of the Case* London: HMSO

Carrabine, E. (2005) 'Prison Riots, Social Order and the Problem of Legitimacy' *British Journal of Criminology* **45**, 6

Clarke, C. (2005) 'Police Structures Review'—letter to the Association of Police Authorities, 6 December 2005

Clements, P. (2006) *Policing a Diverse Society* Oxford: Oxford University Press

Coffey, S., Brown, J. and Savage, S. (1992) 'Policewomen's Career Aspirations: Some Reflections on the Role and Capabilities of Women in Policing in Britain' *Police Studies* **15**, 1

Coleman, W. (1994) 'Policy Convergence in Banking: A Comparative Study' *Political Studies* XLII

Conservative Party (2007) *Policing for the People: Interim Report of the Police Reform Taskforce* London: Conservative Party

Cope, S. and Goodship, J. (2002) 'The Audit Commission and Public Services: Delivering for Whom?' *Public Money and Management* Oct–Dec 2002

Cortell, A. and Peterson, A. (1999) 'Altered States: Explaining Domestic Institutional Change' *British Journal of Political Science* **29**, 1

Cox, B., Shirley, J. and Short, M. (1977) *The Fall of Scotland Yard* Harmondsworth: Penguin

Crawford, A. (1998) *Crime Prevention and Community Safety: Politics, Policies and Practices* Harlow: Longman

Crawford, A. (1999) *The Local Governance of Crime: Appeals to Community and Partnership* Oxford: Oxford University Press

Crawford, A. (2003) 'The Pattern of Policing in the UK: Policing Beyond the Police' in Newburn, T. (ed) *Handbook of Policing* Cullompton: Willan

Crawford, A. and Lister, S. (2006) 'Additional Security Patrols in Residential Areas: Notes From the Marketplace' *Policing and Society* 16, 2

Crawford, A., Lister, S., Blackburn, S., and Burnett, J. (2005) *Plural Policing: The Mixed Economy of Visible Patrols in England and Wales* Bristol: The Policy Press

Crawshaw, R., Cullen, S. and Williamson, T. (2007) *Human Rights and Policing* (2nd Edition) Leiden: Martinus Nijhoff

Crewe, I. (1994) 'Electoral Behaviour' in Kavanagh, D. and Seldon, A. (eds) *The Major Effect* London: Macmillan

Crompton, G. and Jupe, R. (2002) 'Delivering Better Transport? An Evaluation of the Ten-Year Plan for the Railway Industry' *Public Money and Management* 22, 3

Cullen, W. (1996) *The Public Inquiry into the Shootings at Dunblane Primary School* London: HMSO

Dahrendorf, R. (1995) 'Preserving Prosperity' *New Statesman and Society* 14, 29 December 1995

Daugbjerg, C. and Marsh, D. (1998) 'Explaining Policy Outcomes: Integrating the Policy Network Approach With Macro-Level and Micro-Level Analysis' in Marsh, D. (ed) *Comparing Policy Networks* Buckingham: Open University Press

de Bruijn, J. and ten Heuvelhof, E. (1995) 'Policy networks and governance' in Weimer, D. (ed) *Institutional Design* Boston: Kluwer Academic Publishers

Defence Select Committee (2005) *Written Evidence by the Ministry of Defence* March 2005

Degeling, P. and Colebatch, H. (1993) 'Structure and Action as Constructs in the Practice of Public Administration' in Hill, M. (ed) *The Policy Process: A Reader* Hemel Hempstead: Harvester Wheatsheaf

Denmark, B. (2005) *Ethical Investigation: Practical Guide for Police Officers* London: Foreign and Commonwealth Office

Dennis, N. (ed) *Zero Tolerance: Policing a Free Society* London: Institute of Economic Affairs

Dennis, N. and Mallon, R. (1997) 'Confident Policing in Hartlepool' in Dennis, N. (ed) *Zero Tolerance: Policing a Free Society* London: Institute of Economic Affairs

DETR (1998a) *Modern Local Government: In Touch with the People* London: DETR

DETR (1998b) *Modernising Local Government: Improving Local Services through Best Value* London: DETR

DFID (2004) *Human Rights Review: A Review of how DFID has integrated Human Rights into its Work* London: Department for International Development

DFID (2005) *Understanding and Supporting Security Sector Reform* London: Department for International Development

Dixon, D. (1999) 'Corruption and Reform: An Introduction' in Dixon, D. (ed) *A Culture of Corruption: Changing an Australian Police Service* Sidney: Hawkins Press

Dolowitz, D. and Marsh, D. (1996) 'Who Learns What From Whom? A Review of the Policy Transfer Literature' *Political Studies* 44, 2

Dolowitz, D. and Marsh, D. (2000) 'Learning From Abroad: The Role of Policy Transfer in Contemporary Policy-Making' *Governance: An International Journal of Policy and Administration* **13**, 1

Donovan, P. (1997) 'Tough on Liberty: Has Labour Changed Sides on Law and Order?' *The Independent* 26th February 1997

Downes, D. (2001) 'The Macho Penal Economy: Mass Incarceration in the United States—A European Perspective' *Punishment and Society* **3** (1)

Downes, D. and Morgan, R. (1997) 'Dumping Hostages to Fortune: the Politics of Law and Order' in Maguire, M., Morgan, R. and Reiner, R. (eds) *The Oxford Handbook of Criminology* Oxford: Clarendon Press

Downes, D. and Morgan, R. (2007) 'No Turning Back: The Politics of Law and Order Into the Millennium' in Maguire, M., Morgan, R. and Reiner, R. (eds) *Oxford Handbook of Criminology* Oxford: Oxford University Press

Drucker, P. (1955) *The Practice of Management* London: Heinemann

Dunleavy, P. (1995) 'Policy Disasters: Explaining the UK's Record' *Public Policy and Administration* **10**, 2.

Dunleavy, P. and Hood, C. (1994) 'From Old Public Administration to New Public Management' *Public Money and Management* **14**, 3

Eck, J. and Spelman. W. (1987) 'Who Ya Gonna Call?: The Police as Problem-Busters' *Crime and Delinquency* **33** 1

Elliot, J. (1988) 'Why Put the Case Study at the Heart of Police Training?' in Southgate, P. (ed) *New Directions in Police Training* London: HMSO

Emsley, C. (1992) 'The English Bobby: An Indulgent Tradition' in Porter, R. (ed) *Myths of the English* Cambridge: Polity Press

Evans, M. and Davies, J. (1999) 'Understanding Policy Transfer: A Multi-Level, Multi-Disciplinary Perspective' *Public Administration* **77**, 2

Evans, R. and Webb, M. (1993) 'High Profile—But Not That High Profile: Interviewing of Young Persons' in Mathias, P. (ed) *Aspects of Police Interviewing: Issues in Criminological and Legal Psychology* Leicester: British Psychological Society

Farnham, D. and Horton, S. (1993a) 'The Political Economy of Public Sector Change', in Farnham, D. and Horton, S. (eds) *Managing the New Public Services* London: Macmillan

Farnham, D. and Horton, S. (1993b) 'The New Public Service Managerialism: An Assessment' in Farnham, D. and Horton, S. (eds) *Managing the New Public Services* London: Macmillan

Fahsing, I. (2007) 'Investigative Interviewing in the Nordic Region' in Milne, B., Savage, S. and Williamson, T. (eds) *International Developments in Investigative Interviewing* Cullompton: Willan

Fennell, D. (1988) *Investigation into the King's Cross Fire* London: HMSO

Fielding, N. (2005) *The Police and Social Conflict* (2nd edition) London: Glass House Press

Fielding, N. and Innes, M. (2006) 'Reassurance Policing, Community Policing and Measuring Police Performance' *Policing and Society* **16**, 2

Fisher, H. (1977) *The Confait Case: Report* London: HMSO

Fisher, R., and Geiselman, R. (1992) *Memory-Enhancing Techniques for Investigative Interviewing: the Cognitive Interview* Springfield: Thomas

Fitzgerald, G. (1989) *Report of a Commission of Inquiry Pursuant to Orders in Council* Queensland: Goprint

Forbes, I. (2004) 'Making a Crisis out of a Drama: the Political Analysis of BSE Policy-Making in the UK' *Political Studies* **52**, 2

Forster, A. (2002) *Euroscepticism in Contemporary British Politics* London: Routledge

Foster, C. and Plowden, F. (1996) *The State Under Stress* Buckingham: Open University Press

Foster, J. (2003) 'Police Cultures' in Newburn, T. (ed) *Handbook of Policing* Cullompton: Willan

Frosdick, S. and Marsh, P. (2005) *Football Hooliganism* Cullompton: Willan

Gamble, A. (1981) *Britain in Decline* London: Macmillan

Gamble, A. (1988) *The Free Economy and the Strong State: The Politics of Thatcherism* Basingstoke: Macmillan

Garland, D. (2001) *The Culture of Control* Oxford: Oxford University Press

Giddens, A. (1976) *New Rules of Sociological Method: A Positive Critique of Interpretive Sociologies* London: Hutchinson

Giddens, A. (1979) *Central Problems in Social Theory: Action, Structure, and Contradiction in Social Analysis* Berkeley: University of California Press

Giddens, A. (1990) *The Consequences of Modernity* Cambridge: Polity Press

Giddens, A. (1993) *Sociology* Cambridge: Polity Press

Giddens, A. (1998) *The Third Way: The Renewal of Social Democracy* Cambridge: Polity Press

Gilmour, I. (1992) *Dancing with Dogma: Britain Under Thatcherism* London: Simon and Schuster

Glenndinning, J. and Bullock, R. (1973) *Management by Objectives in Local Government* London: Charles Knight

Goldstein, H. (1979) 'Improving Policing: A Problem-Oriented Approach' *Crime and Delinquency* April 1979

Gough, I. (1979) *The Political Economy of the Welfare State* London: Macmillan

Grant, W. (1989) *Pressure Groups and British Politics.* London: Palgrave Macmillan

Greer, S. (1990) 'The Right to Silence: A Review of the Current Debate' *Modern Law Review* **53**, 6

Gregory, J. and Lees, S. (1999) *Policing Sexual Assault* London: Routledge

Grieve, J. (2007) Personal communication

Grieve, J. and French, J. (2000) 'Does Institutional Racism Exist in the Metropolitan Police Service?' in Green, D. (ed) *Institutional Racism and the Police: Fact or Fiction?* London: Institute for the Study of Civil Society

Griffiths, W. (1997) 'Zero Tolerance: A View From London' in Dennis, N. (ed) *Zero Tolerance: Policing a Free Society* London: Institute of Economic Affairs

Groenewald, H. and Peake, G. (2004) *Police Reform Through Community-Based Policing: Philosophy and Guidelines for Implementation* New York: Saferworld/International Peace Academy

Goldstein, H. (1990) *Problem-Oriented Policing* New York: McGraw-Hill

Goldstein, H. (1996) 'Problem-Oriented Policing: The Rationale, the Concept and Reflections on its Implementation', paper delivered to the Conference on Crime Control in Theory and Practice, Cambridge University (10 July 1995) Police Research Group, London: Home Office

Gudjonson, G. (2006) 'The Psychology of Interrogations and Confessions' in Williamson, T. (ed) *Investigative Interviewing: Rights, Research and Regulation* Cullompton: Willan

Hale, C., Heaton, R. and Uglow, S. (2004) 'Uniform Styles? Aspects of Police Centralization in England and Wales' *Policing and Society* **14**, 4

Hale, C., Uglow, S. and Heaton, R. (2005) 'Uniform Styles II: Police Families and Policing Styles' *Policing and Society* **15**, 1

Hall, N. (2005) *Hate Crime* Cullompton: Willan

Harfield, C. (2006) 'SOCA: A Paradigm Shift in British Policing' *British Journal of Criminology* **46**, 4

Harper, G., Williamson, I., Clarke, G. and See, L. (2002) *Family Origins: Developing Groups of Crime and Disorder Reduction Partnerships and Police Basic Command Units for Comparative Purposes* London: Home Office

Hauber, A., Hofstra, B., Toornvliet, L. and Zandbergen, A. (1996) 'Some New Forms of Functional Social Control in the Netherlands and their Effects' *British Journal of Criminology* **36**, 2

Hay, C. (1996) *Re-Stating Social and Political Change* Buckingham: Open University Press

Hayden, C., Williamson, T. and Webber, R. (2007) 'Schools, Pupil Behaviour and Young Offenders' *British Journal of Criminology* **47**, 2

Hayes, M. (1997) *A Police Ombudsman for Northern Ireland? A Review of the Police Complaints System in Northern Ireland* Belfast: Northern Ireland Office

Heaton, R. (2000) 'The Prospects for Intelligence-Led Policing: Some Historical and Quantitative Considerations' *Policing and Society* **9**

Heidensohn, F. (1996) 'The Impact of Police Culture: Setting the Scene. Women in Policing Focusing on the Mechanical and Political Environment', paper presented to the Australian Institute of Criminology Conference, Sydney, Australia, July 1996

Hillyard, P. (1997) 'Policing Divided Societies: Trends and Prospects in Northern Ireland and Britain' in Francis, P., Davies, P. and Jupp, V. (eds) *Policing Futures* London: Macmillan

HMIC (1997) *Policing with Intelligence* London: HMSO

HMIC (2003) *Diversity Matters* London: HMSO

HMIC (2004) *Modernising the Police Service* London: HMSO

HMIC (2005) *Report of Her Majesty's Inspector of Constabulary 2004–5* London: HMSO

HMIC (2006) *Closing the Gap: A Review of the 'Fitness for Purpose' of the Current Structure of Policing in England and Wales* London: HMSO

HMSO (1999) *Modernising Government* London: HMSO

Holdaway, S. (1996) *The Racialisation of British Policing* Basingstoke: Macmillan Press

Holdaway, S. and O'Neill, M. (2007) 'Black Police Associations and the Lawrence Report' in Rowe, M. (ed) *Policing Since Macpherson* Cullompton: Willan

Home Affairs Select Committee (1989) *Home Office Expenditure: Common Police Services; ACPO Secretariat; Police Recruitment: Prisons Expenditure; Trial Delays and Custodial Remand* London: HMSO

Home Office (1983) *Circular 114/1983* London: Home Office

Home Office (1984) *Criminal Justice: A Working Paper* London: Home Office

Home Office (1986) *Circular 12/1986* London: Home Office

Home Office (1988) *Civilian Staff in the Police Service* London: Home Office

Home Office (1993a) *Inquiry into Police Responsibilities and Rewards* London: Home Office

Home Office (1993b) *Police Reform: A Police Service for the Twenty-First Century* London: Home Office

Home Office (1994) *Review of Police Core and Ancillary Tasks: Interim Report* London: Home Office

Home Office (1995) *Review of Police Core and Ancillary Tasks* London: Home Office

Home Office (2001a) *Criminal Justice: The Way Ahead* London: Home Office

Home Office (2001b) *Policing a New Century: A Blueprint for Reform* London: Home Office

Home Office (2003a) *Policing: Building Safer Communities Together* (Green Paper) London: Home Office

Home Office (2003b) *Respect and Responsibility—Taking a Stand Against Anti-Social Behaviour* London: Home Office

Home Office (2004a) *National Policing Plan 2005–8: Safer, Stronger Communities* London: Home Office

Home Office (2004b) *Building Communities, Beating Crime* London: Home Office

Home Office (2005a) *Police Standards Unit: Annual Report* London: Home Office

Home Office (2005b) *Neighbourhood Policing: Your Police; Your Community; Our Commitment* London: Home Office

Home Office (2005c) *Lawrence Steering Group 6th Annual Report* London: Home Office

Home Office (2006a) *Bichard Inquiry Recommendations: Third Progress Report* London: Home Office

Home Office (2006b) *Police Workforce Modernisation: Impact Assessment of Changes to Workforce Mix* London: Home Office

Hood, C. (1991) 'A Public Management for All Seasons' *Public Administration* 69,1

Hood, C., Scott, C., James, O., Jones, G. and Travers, T. (1999) *Regulation Inside Government: Waste-Watchers, Quality Police and Sleaze-Busters* Oxford: Oxford University Press

Hopkins-Burke, R. (2005) *An Introduction to Criminological Theory* Cullompton: Willan

Horton, S. (1993) 'The Civil Service' in Farnham, D. and Horton, S. (eds) *Managing the New Public Services* London: Macmillan

Husain, S. (1988) *Neighbourhood Watch in England and Wales: A Locational Analysis* London: Home Office Crime Prevention Unit

IPCC (2007) 'The IPCC's Guardianship Role' Retrieved March 24, 2007, from <http://www.ipcc.gov.uk?index/about-ipcc/guardianship.htm>

IPSOS/MORI (2006) Retrieved October 2006 from <http://www.ipsos-mori.com/polls/trends/bpoki-law.shtml>

Irish Council for Civil Liberties (2003) *ICCL Policy Paper on Police Reform* Dublin: Irish Council for Civil Liberties

Jay, P. (1994) 'The Economy 1990–4' in Kavanagh, D. and Seldon, A. (eds) *The Major Effect* London: Macmillan

Jenkins, S. (2006) *Thatcher and Sons: A Revolution in Three Acts* London: Allen Lane

Jenkins-Smith, H. and Sabatier, P. (1994) 'The Dynamics of Policy-Oriented Learning' in Sabatier, P. and Jenkins-Smith, H. (eds) *Policy Change and Learning: An Advocacy Coalition Approach* Boulder, CO: Westview Press

Johnston, L. (1992) *The Rebirth of Private Policing* London; Routledge

Johnston, L. (1998) 'Late Modernity, Governance and Policing' in Brodeur, J. (ed) *How to Recognize Good Policing: Problems and Issues* London: Sage

Johnston, L. (2000) *Policing Britain: Risk, Security and Governance* Harlow: Pearson Education

Johnston, L. (2005) 'From "Community" to "Neighbourhood" Policing: Police Community Support Officers and the "Police Extended Family" in London' *Journal of Community and Applied Social Psychology* **15**, 3

Johnston, L., Donaldson, R. and Jones D. (2004) 'Evaluation of the Deployment of Police Community Support Officers in the Metropolitan Police Service' (Final report, University of Portsmouth, unpublished)

Jones, P. (1981) 'Police Powers and Police Accountability: The Royal Commission on Criminal Procedure' *Politics and Power* **4**

Jones, T. (2003) 'The Governance and Accountability of Policing' in Newburn, T. (ed) *Handbook of Policing* Cullompton: Willan

Jones, T. and Newburn, T. (1997) *Policing After the Act* London: Policy Studies Institute

Jones, T. and Newburn, T. (eds) (2006) *Plural Policing: A Comparative Perspective* London: Routledge

Jones, T. and Newburn, T. (2006) 'The United Kingdom' in Jones, T. and Newburn T. (eds) *Plural Policing: A Comparative Perspective* London: Routledge

Jones, T. and Newburn, T. (2007) *Policy Transfer and Criminal Justice: Exploring US Influence Over British Crime Control Policy* Maidenhead: Open University Press

Jones, T., Newburn, T. and Smith, D. (1994) *Democracy and Policing* London: Policy Studies Institute

Judge, T. (1994) *The Force of Persuasion* Surbiton: The Police Federation

Kavanagh, D. (1994) 'A Major Agenda?' in Kavanagh, D. and Seldon, A. (eds) *The Major Effect* London: Macmillan

Keeler, J. (1993) 'Opening Windows for Reform: Mandates, Crises and Extraordinary Policy-Making' *Comparative Political Studies* **25**, 4

Kelling, G. and Coles, C. (1996) *Fixing Broken Windows: Restoring Order and Reducing Crime in Our Communities* New York: Simon and Schuster

Kempa, M. and Johnston, L. (2005) 'Challenges and Prospects for the Development of Inclusive Plural Policing in Britain: Overcoming Political and Conceptual Obstacles' *The Australian and New Zealand Journal of Criminology* **38**, 2

Knapp, W. (1972) *Report on the Commission to Investigate Alleged Police Corruption* New York: George Braziller

Kumar, K. (1995) *From Post-Industrial to Post-Modern Society* Oxford: Basil Blackwell

Laming, Lord (2003) *Inquiry into the Death of Victoria Climbie* London: HMSO

Lea, J. and Young, J. (1984) *What is to be Done About Law and Order?* Harmondsworth: Penguin

Laugharne, A. and Newman, K. (1985) *The Principles of Policing and the Guidance of Professional Behaviour* London: Metropolitan Police

Laycock, G. and Tilley, N. (1995) *Policing and Neighbourhood Watch: Strategic Issues* London: Home Office Police Research Group

Leigh, A., Read, T. and Tilley, N. (1996) *Problem-Oriented Policing: Brit POP* London: Home Office

Leigh, A., Read, T. and Tilley, N. (1998) *Brit Pop II: Problem-Oriented Policing in Practice* London: Home Office

Leigh, A., Mundy, G. and Tuffin, R. (1999) *Best Value Policing: Making Preparations* London: Home Office

Leishman, F., Cope, S. and Starie, P. (1996) 'Reinventing and Restructuring: Towards a "New Policing Order"' in Leishman, F., Loveday, B. and Savage, S. (eds) *Core Issues in Policing* London: Longman

Leishman, F. and Savage, S. (1993) 'The Police Service' in Farnham, D. and Horton, S. (eds) *Managing the New Public Services* London: Macmillan

Lessman, S. (1989) 'Government, Interest Groups and Incrementalism' *European Journal of Political Research* **17**, 4

Levi, M. (2003) 'Organised and Financial Crime' in Newburn, T. (ed) *Handbook of Policing* Cullompton: Willan

Lindblom, C. (1979) 'Still Muddling, Not Yet Through' *Public Administration Review* 19

Lippert, R. (2002) 'Policing Property and Moral Risks Through Promotions, Anonymization and Rewards: Crime Stoppers Revisited' *Social and Legal Studies* **11**, 4

Lipsky, M. (1980) *Street-Level Bureaucracy: Dilemmas of the Individual in Public Services* New York: Russell Sage Foundation

Loader, I. (1999) 'Consumer Culture and the Commodification of Policing and Security' *Sociology* **33**, 2

Loader, I, Girling, E. and Sparks, R. (1998) 'Narratives of Decline: Youth, Disorder and Community in English "Middletown"' *British Journal of Criminology* **38**, 3

Loader, I. and Mulcahy, A. (2003) *Policing and the Condition of England* Oxford: Oxford University Press

Long, M. (2003) 'Leadership and Performance Management' in Newburn, T. (ed) *Handbook of Policing* Cullompton: Willan

Long, T. (2002) 'Delivering Joined-Up Government in the UK: Dimensions, Issues and Problems' *Public Administration* **80**, 4

Loveday, B. and Reid, A. (2003) *Going Local: Who Should Run Britain's Police?* London: Policy Exchange

Lubans, V. and Edgar, J. (1979) *Policing by Objectives: A Handbook for Improving Police Management* Connecticut: Social Development Corporation

Macpherson, W. (1999) *The Stephen Lawrence Inquiry* London: HMSO

Maguire, M. (1991) 'Complaints Against the Police: the British Experience', in Goldsmith, A. (ed) *Complaints Against the Police: The Trend to External Review* Oxford: Oxford University Press

Maguire, M. (2003) 'Criminal Investigation and Crime Control' in Newburn, T. (ed) *Handbook of Criminal Investigation* Cullompton: Willan

Marinetto, M. (2003) 'Who Wants to be an Active Citizen? The Politics and Practice of Community Involvement' *Sociology* **37**, 1

Marsh, D. (1998) 'The Development of the Policy Networks Approach' in Marsh, D. (ed) *Comparing Policy Networks* Buckingham: Buckingham University Press

Marshall, T. (1965) *Social Policy* London: Hutchinson

Martin, J. and Evans, D. (1984) *Hospitals in Trouble* Oxford: Blackwell

Marwick, A. (1990) *British Society Since 1945* London: Penguin

Matassa, M. and Newburn, T. (2003) 'Policing and Terrorism' in Newburn, T. (ed) *Handbook of Policing* Cullompton: Willan

Matthews, R. and Young, J. (eds) (1986) *Confronting Crime* London: Sage

Matthews, R. and Young, J. (eds) (1992) *Issues in Realist Criminology* London: Sage

Mawby, R. C. (2002). *Policing Images : Policing, Communication and Legitimacy*. Cullompton: Willan.

Mawby, R. C. and Wright, A. (2003) 'The Police Organisation' in Newburn, T. (ed) *The Handbook of Policing* Cullompton: Willan

McArdle, A. and Erzen, T. (eds) (2001 *Zero Tolerance: Quality of Life and New Police Brutality in New York City* New York: New York University Press

McLaughlin, E. (2002) 'The Crisis of the Social and the Political Materialisation of Community Safety' in Hughes, G., McLaughlin, E. and Muncie, J. (eds) *Crime Prevention and Community Safety* London: Sage

McLaughlin, E. (2005) 'Forcing the Issue: New Labour, New Localism and the Democratic Renewal of Police Accountability' *Howard Journal* **44**, 5

McLaughlin. E. (2007) *The New Policing* London:Sage

McLaughlin, E., Muncie, J. and Hughes, J. (2001) 'The Permanent Revolution: New Labour, New Public Management and the Modernization of Criminal Justice' *Criminal Justice* **1**, 3

McLaughlin, E. and Murji, K. (1995) 'The End of Public Policing?' in Noaks, L., Levi, M. and Maguire, M. (eds) *Contemporary Issues in Criminology* Cardiff: Cardiff University Press

McLaughlin, E. and Murji, K. (1998) 'Resistance Through Representation: "Story Lines", Advertising and Police Federation Campaigns' *Policing and Society* **8**, 4

McLaughlin, E. and Murji, K. (2001) 'Lost Connections and New Directions: Neo-Liberalism, New Public Managerialism and the Modernization of the British Police' in Stenson, K. and Sullivan, R. (eds) *Crime, Risk and Justice: The Politics of Crime Control in Liberal Democracies* Cullompton: Willan

McNee, D. (1983) *McNee's Law* London: Collins

McNulty, T. (2007) Presentation on 'Police Modernisation' delivered to the 'Police Reform: 20/20 Vision' Conference, John Grieve Centre, Gresham, Bucks 31 October, 2007

McRobbie, A. (1994) 'Folk Devils Fight Back' *New Left Review* 203 Jan/Feb

Metropolitan Police (1983) *4 Area Strategic Plan* London: Metropolitan Police

Metropolitan Police Service (2001) 'Metropolitan Police Service: Response to the White Paper *Policing a New Century*' London: MPS

Millie, A. and Herrington, V. (2005) 'Bridging the Gap: Understanding Reassurance Policing' *Howard Journal* **44**, 2

Milne. B., Savage, S. and Williamson, T. (eds) (2007) *International Developments in Investigative Interviewing* Cullompton: Willan

Milne, R., and Bull, R. (1999) *Investigative Interviewing: Psychology and Practice.* Chichester: Wiley.

Milne, B., Shaw, G. and Bull, R. (2007) 'Investigative Interviewing: the Role of Research' in Carson, D., Milne, B., Pakes, F., Shalev, K. and Shawyer, A. (eds) *Applying Psychology to Criminal Justice* Chichester: Wiley

Mintrom, M. (1997) 'Policy Entrepreneurs and the Diffusion of Innovation' *American Journal of Political Science* **41**, 3

Mintrom, M. and Vergari, S. (1996) 'Advocacy Coalitions, Policy Entrepreneurs, and Policy Change' *Policy Studies Journal* **24**

Morgan, R. and Maggs, C. (1984) *Following Scarman* Bath: Bath University Social Policy Papers

Morgan, R. and Newburn, T. (1997) *The Future of Policing* Oxford: Oxford University Press

Morris, T. (1994) 'Crime and Penal Policy' in Kavanagh, D. and Seldon, A. (eds) *The Major Effect* London: Macmillan

Mulcahy, A. (2005) 'The "Other" Lessons From Ireland? Policing, Political Violence and Policy Transfer' *European Journal of Criminology* 2, 2

Mulcahy, A. (2006) *Policing Northern Ireland Conflict: Conflict, Legitimacy and Reform* Cullompton: Willan

Mullin, C. (1990) *Error of Judgement: The Truth about the Birmingham Bombings* London: Poolbeg Press.

Nash, M. and Savage, S. (1994) 'A Criminal Record?: Law, Order and Conservative Policy' in Savage, S., Atkinson, R. and Robins, L. (eds) *Public Policy in Britain* London: Macmillan

National Centre for Policing Excellence (2005) *Practice Advice on Core Investigative Doctrine* Wyboston: NCPE

National Crime Faculty (1996) *Investigative Interviewing: A Practical Guide* Bramshill: NCF/National Police Training

NCIS (2000) *The National Intelligence Model* London: National Criminal Intelligence Service

NPIA (2007) *The National Police Improvement Agency* Retrieved March 2007 from <http://www.npia.police.uk>

Newburn, T. (1999) *Understanding and Preventing Police Corruption: Lessons from the Literature* London: Home Office Policing and Reducing Crime Unit

Newburn, T. (2001) 'The Commodification of Policing: Security Networks in the Late Modern City' *Urban Studies* 38, 5–6

Newburn, T. (2002) 'Atlantic Crossings: "Policy Transfer" and Crime Control in the USA and Britain' *Punishment and Society* 4, 2

Newburn, T. (2003) 'Policing Since 1945' in Newburn, T. (ed) *The Handbook of Policing* Cullompton: Willan

Neyroud, P. (2001) *Public Participation in Policing* London: Institute for Public Policy Research

Neyroud, P. (2003) 'Policing and Ethics' in Newburn, T. (ed) *The Handbook of Policing*

Neyroud, P. and Beckley, A. (2001) *Policing, Ethics and Human Rights* Cullompton: Willan

Nicol, C., Innes, M., Gee, D. and Feist, A. (2004) *Reviewing Murder Investigations: An Analysis of Progress from Six Police Forces* London: HMSO

Nobles, R. and Schiff, D. (2000) *Understanding Miscarriages of Justice: Law, the Media and the Inevitability of a Crisis.* Oxford: OUP.

Northern Ireland Affairs Committee (2005) *The Functions of the Office of the Police Ombudsman for Northern Ireland* London: HMSO

O'Connor, J. (1973) *The Fiscal Crisis of the State* New York: St James Press

Orr, J. (1997) 'Strathclyde's Spotlight Initiative' in Dennis, N. (ed) *Zero Tolerance: Policing a Free Society* London: Institute of Economic Affairs

Osborne, D. and Gaebler, T. (1992) *Re-Inventing Government: How the Entrepreneurial Spirit is Transforming the Public Sector* Reading MA: Addison-Wesley

Pakes, F. (2004) *Comparative Criminal Justice* Cullompton: Willan

Patten, C. (1999) *A New Beginning: Policing in Northern Ireland. Report of the Independent Commission on Policing for Northern Ireland* London: HMSO

Patten, C. (2006) *Not Quite the Diplomat* London: Penguin

Pinch, P. and Patterson, A. (2000) 'Public Sector Restructuring and Regional Development: The Impact of Compulsory Competitive Tendering in the UK' *Regional Studies* 34, 3

Piore, M. and Sabel, C. (1984) *The Second Industrial Divide: Possibilities for Prosperity* New York: Basic Books

Pollard, C. (1997) 'Zero Tolerance: Short-Term Fix, Long Term Liability?' In Dennis, N (ed) *Zero Tolerance: Policing a Free Society* London: Institute of Economic Affairs

Pollitt, C. (2002) 'The New Public Management in International Perspective: an Analysis of Impacts and Effects' in McLaughlin, K., Osborne, P. and Ferlie, E. (eds) *New Public Management: Future Trends and Current Prospects* London: Routledge

Poole, L. (1988) 'Police Training: A Skills Approach' in Southgate, P. (ed) *New Directions in Police Training* London: HMSO

Prenzler, T. (2002a) 'Corruption and Reform: Global trends and Theoretical Perspectives' in Prenzler, T. and Ransley, J. (eds) *Police Reform: Building Integrity* Sydney: Hawkins Press

Prenzler, T. (2002b) 'Independent Investigation of Complaints' in Prenzler, T. and Ransley, J. (eds) *Police Reform: Building Integrity* Sydney: Hawkins Press

Prenzler, T. and Ransley, J. (eds) (2002) *Police Reform: Building Integrity* Sydney: Hawkins Press

Price, C. and Caplan, J. (1997) *The Confait Confessions* London: Marion Boyars.

Punch, M. (1985) *Conduct Unbecoming* London: Tavistock

Punch, M. (2000) 'Police Corruption and its Prevention' *European Journal of Criminal Policy and Research* **8**

Punch, M. (2003) 'Rotten Orchards: "Pestilence", Police Misconduct and System Failure' *Policing and Society* **13**, 2

Punch, M., van der Vijver, K. and Zoomer, O. (2002) 'Dutch "COP": Developing Community Policing in the Netherlands' *Policing: An International Journal of Police Strategies and Management* **25**, 1

Quick, B. (2006) Letter to all Chief Constables and Chairs of Police Authorities London: ACPO

Ranson, S. and Stewart, J. (1994) *Managing for the Public Domain: Enabling the Learning Society* London: Macmillan

Reiner, R. (1981) 'The Politics of Police Powers' *Politics and Power* **4**

Reiner, R. (1991) *Chief Constables* Oxford: Oxford University Press

Reiner, R. (1992) *The Politics of the Police* (2nd Edition) Hemel Hempstead: Harvester Wheatsheaf

Reiner, R. (2000) *The Politics of the Police* (3rd Edition) Oxford: Oxford University Press

Riddell, P. (1989) *The Thatcher Decade* Oxford: Blackwell

Rimmer, S. (2007) Presentation on 'Police Modernisation' delivered to 'Police Reform: 20/20 Vision' conference, John Grieve Centre, Gresham, Bucks, 31 October 2007

Rose, D. (1996) *In the Name of the Law: The Collapse of Criminal Justice* London: Jonathan Cape

Rose, N. (2000) 'Government and Control' in Garland, D. and Sparks, R. (eds) *Criminology and Social Theory* Oxford: Oxford University Press

Rose, R. (1991) 'What is Lesson Drawing?' *Journal of Public Policy* **11**

Rowe, M. (2004) *Policing, Race and Racism.* Cullompton: Willan.

Roycroft, R., Brown, J. and Innes, M. (2007) 'Reform by Crisis: The Murder of Stephen Lawrence and a Socio-Historical Analysis of Developments in the Conduct of Major Crime Investigations', in Rowe, (ed) *Policing Beyond Macpherson* Cullompton: Willan

Rozenberg, J. (1994) *The Search for Justice* London: Sceptre

Runciman, Viscount (1993) *Royal Commission on Criminal Justice* London: Home Office

Ryan, M. (2003) *Penal Policy and Political Culture in England and Wales* Winchester: Waterside Press

Sabatier, P. and Jenkins-Smith, H. (eds) (1993) *Policy Change and Learning: An Advocacy Coalition Approach* Boulder CO: Westview Press

Saferworld (2007) 'What we do', retrieved from <http://www.saferworld.org.uk> (26 March 2007)

Sanders, A. and Young, R. (1995) 'The "PACE" Regime for Suspects Detained by the Police' *Political Quarterly* 66

Sanders, A. and Young, R. (2003) 'Police Powers' in Newburn, T. (ed) *Handbook of Policing* Cullompton: Willan

Sato, H. (1999) 'The Advocacy Coalition Framework and the Policy Process Analysis: The Case of Smoking Control in Japan' *Policy Studies Journal* 27, 1

Savage, S. (1984) 'Political Control or Community Liaison? Two Strategies in the Reform of Police Accountability' *Political Quarterly* 55, 1

Savage, S. (1990) 'A War on Crime? Law and Order Policies in the 1980s' in Savage, S. and Robins, L. (eds) *Public Policy Under Thatcher* London: Macmillan

Savage, S. (1998) 'The Geography of Police Governance' *Criminal Justice Matters* June 1998

Savage, S. (2003) 'Tackling Tradition: Reform and Modernisation of the British Police' *Contemporary Politics*. 9, 2

Savage, S., Charman, S. and Cope, S. (2000) *Policing and the Power of Persuasion* London: Blackstone

Savage, S., Cope, S. and Charman, S. (1997) 'Reform Through Regulation: Transformation of the Public Police In Britain' *Review of Policy Issues* 3, 2

Savage, S. and Milne, B. (2007) 'Miscarriages of Justice and the Investigative Process' in Newburn, T., Williamson, T. and Wright, A. (eds) *Handbook of Criminal Investigation* Cullompton: Willan

Savage, S. and Nash, M. (2001) 'Law and Order Under Blair: New Labour or Old Conservatism' in Savage, S. and Atkinson, R. (eds) *Public Policy Under Blair* London: Palgrave

Savage, S., Poyser, S. and Grieve, J. (2007) 'Putting Wrongs to Right: Campaigns Against Miscarriages of Justice' *Criminology and Criminal Justice* 7, 1

Savage, S. and Wilson, C. (1987) 'Ask a Policeman: Community Consultation in Practice' *Social Policy and Administration* 21, 3

Scarman, Lord. (1981) *The Scarman Report: The Brixton Disorders* London: HMSO

Scott, C. (2000) 'Accountability in the Regulatory State' *Journal of Law and Society* 27, 1

Scraton, P. (2004) 'Death on the Terraces: The Contexts and Injustices of the 1989 Hillsborough Disaster' *Soccer and Society* 5, 2

Seldon, A. (1994) 'The Conservative Party', in Kavanagh, D. and Seldon, A. (eds) *The Major Effect* London: Macmillan

Self, P. (2000) *Rolling Back the State: Economic Dogma and Political Choice* New York: St Martins' Press

Seneviratne, M. (2004) 'Policing the Police in the United Kingdom' *Policing and Society* 14, 4

Sewell, W. (1992) 'A Theory of Structure: Duality, Agency and Transformation' *American Journal of Sociology* **98**, 1

Shearing, C. (1993) 'A Constitutive Conception of Regulation' in Grabosky, P. and Braithwaite, J. (eds) *Business Regulation and Australia's Future* Canberra: Australian Institute of Criminology

Shepherd, E. (1988) 'Developing Interview Skills: A Carer Span Perspective' in Southgate, P. (ed) *New Directions in Police Training* London: HMSO

Sherman, L. (1978) *Scandal and Reform: Controlling Police Corruption* Berkeley LA: University of California Press

Smith, G. (2004) 'Rethinking Police Complaints' *British Journal of Criminology* **44**, 1

Smith, G. (2005) 'A Most Enduring Problem: Police Complaints Reform in England and Wales' *Journal of Social Policy* **35**, 1

SOCA (2007) *SOCA Annual Plan, 2006/7* London: Home Office

Stalker, J. (1988) *Stalker* London: Harrap

St-Yves, M. (2007) 'International Developments in Investigative Interviewing: Successfully Effecting Change in Custodial Questioning' in Milne, B., Savage, S. and Williamson, T. (eds) *International Developments in Investigative Interviewing* Cullompton: Willan

Stephens, M. and Becker, S. (eds) (1994) *Police Force, Police Service* London: Macmillan

Stradling, S. and Harper, K. (1988) 'The Tutor Constable Attachment, the Management of Encounters and the Development of Discretionary Judgement' in Southgate, P. (ed) *New Directions in Police Training* London: Home Office

Straw, J. (1995) 'Straw and Order' *New Statesman and Society* 15th September 1995

Taylor, Lord Justice (1989) *The Hillsborough Stadium Disaster: 15th April 1989* London: HMSO

Taylor, R., Wasik, M. and Leng, R. (2004) *The Criminal Justice Act 2003* Oxford: Oxford University Press

Thomas, R. (2001) 'UK Economic Policy: The Conservative Legacy and New Labour's Third Way' in Savage, S. and Atkinson, R. (eds) *Public Policy Under Blair* Basingstoke: Palgrave

Tilley, N. (2003) 'Community Policing, Problem-Oriented Policing and Intelligence-Led Policing' in Newburn, T. (ed) *Handbook of Policing* Cullompton: Willan

Uglow, S. with Telford, V. (1997) *The Police Act 1997* London: Jordans

Waddington, P. (1986) 'Defining Objectives: A Reply to Tony Butler' *Policing* 2 1

Waddington, P. (1999) *Policing Citizens: Authority and Rights* London: UCL Press

Waddington, D., Jones, K., and Critcher C. et al (1989) *Flashpoints: Studies in Public Disorder* London: Routledge

Walker, C. (1999) 'Miscarriages of Justice in Principle and Practice' in Walker, C. and Starmer, K. (eds). *Miscarriages of Justice: A Review of Justice in Error* London: Blackstone.

Walker, C. (2002) 'Miscarriages of justice and the correction of error' in McConville, M. and Wilson, G. (eds) *The Handbook of the Criminal Justice Process* Oxford: OUP.

Walker, N. (2000) *Policing in a Changing Constitutional Order* London: Sweet and Maxwell

Walker, N. (2003) 'The Pattern of Organised Policing' in Newburn, T. (ed) *Handbook of Policing* Cullomptom: Willan

Walkley, J. (1987) *Police Interrogation: Handbook for Investigators* London: Police Review Publishing

Washnis, G. (1976) *Citizen Involvement in Crime Prevention* Massachusetts: Lexington

Wasik, M. and Taylor, R. (1995) *Criminal Justice and Public Order Act 1994* London: Blackstone

Waters, I. (1996) 'Quality of Service: Politics or Paradigm Shift?' in Leishman, F., Loveday, B. and Savage, S. (eds) *Core Issues in Policing* London: Longman

Weatheritt, M. (1986) *Innovations on Policing* London: Croom Helm

Williamson, T. (ed) (2006) *Investigative Interviewing: Rights Research and Regulation* Cullompton: Willan

Wolff Olins (1988) *A Force for Change: A Report on the Corporate Identity of the Metropolitan Police* London: Wolff Olins

Wood, J. (1997) *Royal Commission into the New South Wales Police Service: Final Report* Sydney: Government Printer

Wright, A. (2002) *Policing: An Introduction to Concepts and Practices* Cullompton: Willan

Zahid Mubarek Inquiry (2005) *Report of the Zahid Mubarek Inquiry* London: HMSO

Zander, M. (1986) 'The Act in the Station' in Benyon, J. and Bourn, J. (eds) *The Police: Powers, Procedures and Proprieties* Oxford: Pergamon Press

Zander, M. (1995) *The Police and Criminal Evidence Act 1984* (3rd Edition) London: Sweet and Maxwell

Zander, M. (2005) *The Police and Criminal Evidence Act 1984* (5th Edition) London: Sweet and Maxwell

Index